Your Dream Career For Dummies®

Cheat Sheet

At-a-Glance Plan to Reach Your Dream Care...

Finding your dream career is like searching for a hidden treasure. Your best st... ...lues as you can about what works for you. The following steps are a nuts-and-bolts ... ...ation that I present throughout the book:

- ❏ Take stock of your current situation (Chapter 1).
- ❏ Find your personal style (Chapter 3).
- ❏ Define your ideal lifestyle needs (Chapter 4).
- ❏ Pinpoint your preferred work environment (Chapters 5 and 6).
- ❏ Specify your favorite passions, skills, and interests (Chapters 7 and 8).
- ❏ Brainstorm a list of viable career ideas (Chapter 9).
- ❏ Select your Top Two Career Ideas (Chapter 10).
- ❏ Explore additional career possibilities based on your skills (Chapters 11 through 13).
- ❏ Investigate your Top Two Career Ideas (Chapters 14 and 15).
- ❏ Blend your dream career with your life realities (Chapters 16 and 17).
- ❏ Develop your personal action plan to achieve your dream career (Chapters 18 and 19).

Basic Questions for Your Informational Interviews

Talking with people in your field of interest is one of the best ways to gain a realistic and current picture of your new career. Here's a handy list of questions to help you start planning your informational interviews:

- ✔ What is the outlook for this profession?
- ✔ What is your day like?
- ✔ What are your key responsibilities?
- ✔ What are the pros and cons of working in this industry right now?
- ✔ How does this job impact your life?
- ✔ How did you get into this field?
- ✔ Do you know anyone who entered this field with my background?

Look to Chapter 15 to figure out whom to interview and what questions to ask.

Identifying the Passions That Bring You Alive

Evidence of your passions is in front of you every day. Use the following filters to follow the clues to find your passions and interests:

- ✔ **Listen for a change in your voice:** When your speech quickens, your conversations about a topic are long, or you're insistent about the value of a topic, you are on the trail of a passion.
- ✔ **Notice your excitement level:** When your excitement picks up, pay attention to what you're doing.
- ✔ **Track your curiosity:** When you have a desire to know more, follow the thread.
- ✔ **Visit memory lane:** Consider fascinations you've had since you were a kid.
- ✔ **Notice how you help others:** Think about things you do for others.
- ✔ **Recognize a sense of mission:** Notice when a past experience gives you a vision of what could be different.
- ✔ **Catalog the tools you love to use:** What you enjoy using in your work and play can lead you to your passions.
- ✔ **Spot your natural talents:** Claim the skills you do without thinking.

Chapters 7 and 8 offer additional ways to identify your passions, interests, and natural talents.

For Dummies: Bestselling Book Series for Beginners

Your Dream Career For Dummies®

Cheat Sheet

Using the Web to Jump-Start Your Search for Career Ideas

The following Web sites are good places to start if you want to find out more about your next career:

- **Occupational Outlook Handbook** (www.bls.gov/oco/): Check out potential careers and salary information.
- **Wetfeet.com** (www.wetfeet.com): Explore your favorite careers and industries.
- **Monster.com** (http://jobprofile.monster.com): Read the job profiles.
- **Salary.com** (www.salary.com): Conduct your compensation research.
- **Career Guide to Industries** (www.bls.gov/oco/cg/home.htm): Research your industry of interest.
- **Weddle's** (www.weddles.com/associations/index.cfm): Access professional associations related to your career.

Chapter 14 provides additional resources for your career exploration whether you want to proceed online or offline.

Defining Alternatives to the 9-to-5 Schedule

When changing careers, you may find that one of the following nontraditional work arrangements suits you better than working 9 to 5, five days a week. In case some of these terms may be unfamiliar to you, here's a quick look at what they mean:

- **Compressed workweek:** Work 40 hours in three or four days, instead of the typical five days.
- **Job share:** Partner with someone else to split the workload, and the pay, of one job.
- **Contract work:** Contract with a company through an employment agency to work for the duration of a specific project.
- **Telecommute:** Set yourself up with the equipment you need to perform your job from home.
- **Freelance:** Develop a working relationship with several companies so that you can choose the projects you want to work on.
- **Home-based business owner:** Launch a business that you run from your home.

Chapters 5 and 6 provide more details about these and other work arrangement options.

Keeping an Open Mind

As you explore your options, you're putting one toe into the unknown. Although it can be unnerving not to know The Answer to your career puzzle, the key to success is to keep an open mind as you explore your options:

- Think ideally.
- Listen to your longings.
- Let your procrastination tell you what doesn't work for you.
- Stay focused on the essence of what you want.
- Turn away from things that repel you.
- Pay attention to what attracts you.
- Understand your unique style.
- Brainstorm with an open, expansive mind.
- Focus on possibilities and opportunities.
- Explore your career ideas to understand them.
- Test your potential career before you make the leap.

Chapter 2 gives you pointers on how to keep your spirit of discovery engaged as you pull together the clues to your dream career.

For Dummies: Bestselling Book Series for Beginners

Your Dream Career

FOR DUMMIES®

by Carol L. McClelland, PhD

Foreword by Richard N. Bolles

WILEY

Wiley Publishing, Inc.

Your Dream Career For Dummies®

Published by
Wiley Publishing, Inc.
111 River St.
Hoboken, NJ 07030-5774
www.wiley.com

WILEY

About the Author

As a pioneering career-change consultant, Carol McClelland, PhD, has helped thousands of clients, students, and readers discover more fulfilling careers and lives.

Carol believes a good career is one in which you can be yourself at work, live your life fully, and feel engaged by the work you do. She guides people from all walks of life to create careers based on their unique dreams of how they want to live. With her support, her clients start their own businesses, enter the corporate world, find niches in nonprofits, return to school, or re-create their own position within the same company. To find out more about her perspective and her career-change programs, visit her site, www.careerclarityprogram.com, and her blog, www.findyourdreamcareer.com.

Carol's unique understanding of the emotional aspects of changing careers grew from her professional and personal experiences. She became interested in transitions in 1983 while completing her PhD in industrial/organizational psychology at Purdue University. As an organizational consultant within a major insurance company, Carol facilitated various corporate transitions and mentored new employees while dealing with her grief surrounding her father's death and a period of severe burnout that led to her own career change.

Carol shares her ideas about the emotional side of career changes and other life changes in *The Seasons of Change: Using Nature's Wisdom to Grow through Life's Inevitable Ups and Downs* (Conari Press, 1998). To find out more about *The Seasons of Change* and her retreats and programs on this topic, visit her site, www.seasonsofchange.com, and her blog, www.hopeandinsight.com.

In 2002, Carol began training other Transition Professionals to use her Career Clarity Program and The Seasons of Change Model with their clients in transition. Details about the training programs are described on the sites listed earlier.

In addition to teaching career-related courses at Purdue University and San Jose State University, Carol presents at conferences and meetings and is a guest on radio talk shows nationwide.

Note to readers: I always enjoy hearing from my readers. If you have questions about your career-change journey or if you have a success story to share, please use the contact page on my Web site to send me a note.

Dedication

To my niece, Grace, and my nephews, Sean, Patrick, Danny, and Aidan: May they each find their passion in life and live in a world that supports them in using their talents to the fullest.

Author's Acknowledgments

Revising my original *For Dummies* book, *Changing Careers For Dummies,* has been a true joy. The opportunity to enhance and update the book has been inspiring, exciting, and gratifying. I hope you find your dream career in your journey through this book.

I want to begin by thanking my acquisitions editor, Kathy Cox, for taking the time for lunch in October 2004, where the idea for this revision came to light. I'm grateful to Carol Susan Roth, my agent, for stepping in to finalize the deal. I've thoroughly enjoyed working with my editors, Alissa Schwipps, Tina Sims, and Marilyn Maze, who each provided key thoughts that strengthened this book. Although I haven't worked with them directly, I appreciate the graphics and layout teams who transformed my Word documents into the book you hold in your hand. And finally, I'm grateful to the marketing and publicity teams for the work they do to bring this book to those who need it most — career changers everywhere.

My Career Clarity clients and my Career Clarity Coaches have each contributed to this revision with their questions, requests, suggestions, and experiences. I thank each of them and several specific Career Clarity Coaches, Brenda Davis, Jeremy Castilino, Rebecca Kieler, and Juanita Mast, who reviewed and strengthened several lists in this book. I continue to be indebted to those who contributed so graciously to the first book.

I've been blessed to have a wonderful support team while I divided my time between my writing, my work with clients, and my training classes for professionals. I'm grateful to Jean Hansen, Lynda Nuremberg, Sherry Grantham, and Vilma Guevara for taking on the administrative tasks that lightened my workload. I couldn't have kept my business functioning and growing without their help. Aleta Cooper and Susan Goodwin, with joy in their hearts, helped me keep my physical world functioning smoothly. A special thanks goes to Veronica Conway, Gloria Balcom, Ellen Silva, the eWomen Publishing Network, and Kelley Falk for the work we did between deadlines to enhance my overall business.

My family continues to be one of my greatest sources of support. As always, I find great joy in the connection I have with my Mom; my brother, Tom; his wife, Amy; and the McKids. I've been thrilled this year to reconnect with my grandmother's cousin, Lorraine Phillips, and to meet her nieces. It's been quite an experience to learn about my great-grandfather's career aspirations during the 1920s. I also want to thank Karen and Mark, and Vicky and Tony (welcome to the family!) for welcoming me into the family with open arms.

My favorite memory while writing this book was the last-minute road trip my husband, Kent Fields, and I took to see the once-in-a-lifetime spring bloom in Death Valley. It's an amazingly freeing feeling to know that I can be in the middle of nowhere and open my laptop in a tent to enter the editing changes I've made while waiting for a ranger talk to start. The ultimate flextime/flexplace work experience. Have laptop, will travel!

To my husband, Kent: Your ever-present love, continuous support, creative input, and patience over the last six months have been invaluable. Here's to our next road trip escape! I can't wait!

Publisher's Acknowledgments

We're proud of this book; please send us your comments through our Dummies online registration form located at www.dummies.com/register/.

Some of the people who helped bring this book to market include the following:

Acquisitions, Editorial, and Media Development

Senior Project Editor: Alissa Schwipps

Acquisitions Editor: Kathy Cox

Senior Copy Editor: Tina Sims

Editorial Program Assistant: Courtney Allen

Technical Editor: Marilyn Maze

Senior Editorial Manager: Jennifer Ehrlich

Editorial Assistants: Hanna Scott, Nadine Bell, Melissa Bennett

Cover Photo: © Phil Banko/Getty Images/Stone

Cartoons: Rich Tennant (www.the5thwave.com)

Composition Services

Project Coordinator: Adrienne Martinez

Layout and Graphics: Andrea Dahl, Mary Gillot, Lauren Goddard, Denny Hager, Lynsey Osborn

Proofreaders: Jessica Kramer, Carl Pierce, Shannon Ramsey

Indexer: Anne Leach

Special Help: Jenny Baylor

Publishing and Editorial for Consumer Dummies

> **Diane Graves Steele,** Vice President and Publisher, Consumer Dummies
>
> **Joyce Pepple,** Acquisitions Director, Consumer Dummies
>
> **Kristin A. Cocks,** Product Development Director, Consumer Dummies
>
> **Michael Spring,** Vice President and Publisher, Travel
>
> **Kelly Regan,** Editorial Director, Travel

Publishing for Technology Dummies

> **Andy Cummings,** Vice President and Publisher, Dummies Technology/General User

Composition Services

> **Gerry Fahey,** Vice President of Production Services
>
> **Debbie Stailey,** Director of Composition Services

Contents at a Glance

Table of Contents

Foreword

Most forewords are written to urge you to read the book. But I know you are going to like this book, so you need no urging there.

What I want to urge in this foreword is something else, and that is the importance of career change, and more particularly, the importance of considering a career change in your own life.

Experts tell us that the average person goes through the job hunt eight times. I have observed that each time we go through a job hunt, we face a crossroads: Should we do a mechanical job search, or should we do a life-changing job search?

The mechanical job search is basically a matching process. It is so mechanical, even the Internet can do it for us. Your resume. All the employers' job openings. Is there a match? The site's "robot" will give you the news by morning. That's the mechanical job search.

The life-changing job search is different. If the mechanical job search starts with the labor market as "the given," the life-changing job search starts with you as "the given." The mechanical job search assumes that you're going to go on doing basically what you were doing before, but the life-changing job search assumes that all bets are off. You have certain transferable skills. They can be used anywhere. So, where would you most like to work? What would you most like to do for the rest of your life? Dream, dream, dream. More often than you can imagine, those dreams can be turned into reality!

A life-changing job search is, of course, just another phrase for "career-change." But I call it life-changing, because it involves so much more than just changing your career. In fact, there are four things that inevitably get weighed in a life-changing job search.

The first is the center of your life, which involves a reconsideration of what you want your life to revolve around. If it's currently work, do you want it to be family instead; or if it's currently making money, do you want it to be God instead? That sort of thing.

The second is the constants in your life. What about you has remained constant through all these years? Your skills, your values, your friends, what? Do an inventory, and then put these in their order of importance.

The third is the context of your life. What gives you perspective about your life? How do you measure how well you're doing in life? For many, this context of their life is God. If that's not yours, what is?

The fourth (and final) one is alternatives. You need to ask yourself how many alternative ways you have of describing what you most enjoy doing. How many alternative ways do you have of describing your target organizations or plans? How many alternative ways do you have of searching for that? A life-changing job search is a search for alternatives, so as to have more freedom.

If it's a life-changing job search you're weighing, that is to say, a career-change, plus, you can do no better than to read this book. It's one of the best I've ever read on career change. Carol has really done her homework, and she offers very many helpful ideas to guide you on your way.

— Richard N. Bolles, author of *What Color Is Your Parachute?*
A Practical Manual for Job-Hunters And Career-Changers (2005 Edition)

Introduction

· ·

*W*hether you're changing careers by choice or due to circumstances beyond your control, you stand on the brink of an awesome experience.

Thanks to advances in technology and added flexibility in the workplace, more employment options exist today than in any other time in history. Take advantage of this opportunity to create a new career for yourself that not only taps your favorite talents but also lets you live the life you want to live.

Although it's normal to have some concerns about how your career change will unfold, walk into this opportunity with an open mind. The chapters in this book show you, step by step, how to gain clarity about your next career move. Giving yourself the gift of exploration allows you to discover previously unexplored options and solutions.

If you want, or need, to make a career change, don't let a shaky economy or a personal situation stop you from looking to the future. The first stages of a career change involve imagining, thinking, exploring, and planning. You can embark on these steps now — without disrupting your current employment situation. After you know more about your new direction, you can decide when to make your move.

About This Book

A dream career is more than a career that allows you to use your talents and skills in a satisfying and fulfilling way. A dream career also allows you to express who you are and to live the life you want.

Many career change programs focus on what you want to do in your work — the passions and skills you want to use. As a result, you sometimes end up in a situation where you have a great job that's at cross purposes with who you are and how you want to live. Try as you might, you can't find a way to include your needs and desires in the picture.

Rather than have you squeeze your personal life in around the edges of a great career, *Your Dream Career For Dummies* has you start by understanding who you are and what you want at a personal level. Then, by using that information as a foundation, you build a career that enables you to thrive in all areas of your life — not just at work.

Some sections of this book may be more relevant to you and your situation than others. You can dip in and out wherever you like because, like all *For Dummies* books, each chapter is a stand-alone module. That said, identifying your next career is a process that unfolds one step at a time. As a result, there's a thread that ties all the chapters together, as the worksheets you do in the early chapters help you gain clarity in the later chapters.

In this book, you won't find text that drones on and on. Instead you find short, concise, get-right-to-the-point explanations about worksheets that walk you through the process of understanding your own situation in more depth. During your journey, you may access other resources as well to help you research your career ideas and explore your options.

Whether you want to make a change in the next couple of months or the next few yea[...] information, worksheets, and examples in this book help you do the following:

- ✔ Open your mind to creative exploration
- ✔ Deepen your sense of your personal style and lifestyle needs
- ✔ Define what you need in your work environment
- ✔ Transform your passions and interests into viable career options
- ✔ Explore numerous career ideas
- ✔ Blend your ideal career with the realities of your life
- ✔ Outline your action plan to find a job, start a business, or return to school

Conventions Used in This Book

The following conventions are used throughout the text to make things consistent [...] to understand:

- ✔ All Web addresses appear in `monofont`.
- ✔ New terms appear in *italic* and are closely followed by a clear definition.
- ✔ **Bold** is used to highlight the action parts of numbered steps.

Foolish Assumptions

I assume that some of the following statements apply to you, in which case you'll [...] book especially helpful in your quest to find a new career:

- ✔ You absolutely dread getting up in the morning to go to work, but you keep [...] on because you have no idea how to identify your next career.
- ✔ You have an idea for your next career, but no matter how hard you try, you [...] to get from here to there.
- ✔ You may be facing a layoff and want to plan ahead.
- ✔ You need to make a good living, and you want to spend more time with you[...] enjoying your hobbies.
- ✔ Your job isn't so bad, but you wish it had more meaning or made a contrib[...]
- ✔ You've worked hard for years at a job that wasn't especially satisfying, an[...] want a career you thoroughly enjoy, or you've retired and find that you ar[...] need an infusion of cash.
- ✔ You've graduated recently, and your work isn't what you thought it would[...]

I assume that if you're currently out of work, you may want to focus first on fir[...] interim job. Then, after you have some income coming in, you can come back [...] your dream career options. As you might expect, thinking creatively and expl[...] options freely is difficult when you aren't sure how you're going to pay this m[...] gage or rent. Another benefit of this strategy is that you can use your interim [...] laboratory to clarify what you know you want in your next career.

Foreword

Most forewords are written to urge you to read the book. But I know you are going to like this book, so you need no urging there.

What I want to urge in this foreword is something else, and that is the importance of career change, and more particularly, the importance of considering a career change in your own life.

Experts tell us that the average person goes through the job hunt eight times. I have observed that each time we go through a job hunt, we face a crossroads: Should we do a mechanical job search, or should we do a life-changing job search?

The mechanical job search is basically a matching process. It is so mechanical, even the Internet can do it for us. Your resume. All the employers' job openings. Is there a match? The site's "robot" will give you the news by morning. That's the mechanical job search.

The life-changing job search is different. If the mechanical job search starts with the labor market as "the given," the life-changing job search starts with you as "the given." The mechanical job search assumes that you're going to go on doing basically what you were doing before, but the life-changing job search assumes that all bets are off. You have certain transferable skills. They can be used anywhere. So, where would you most like to work? What would you most like to do for the rest of your life? Dream, dream, dream. More often than you can imagine, those dreams can be turned into reality!

A life-changing job search is, of course, just another phrase for "career-change." But I call it life-changing, because it involves so much more than just changing your career. In fact, there are four things that inevitably get weighed in a life-changing job search.

The first is the center of your life, which involves a reconsideration of what you want your life to revolve around. If it's currently work, do you want it to be family instead; or if it's currently making money, do you want it to be God instead? That sort of thing.

The second is the constants in your life. What about you has remained constant through all these years? Your skills, your values, your friends, what? Do an inventory, and then put these in their order of importance.

The third is the context of your life. What gives you perspective about your life? How do you measure how well you're doing in life? For many, this context of their life is God. If that's not yours, what is?

The fourth (and final) one is alternatives. You need to ask yourself how many alternative ways you have of describing what you most enjoy doing. How many alternative ways do you have of describing your target organizations or plans? How many alternative ways do you have of searching for that? A life-changing job search is a search for alternatives, so as to have more freedom.

If it's a life-changing job search you're weighing, that is to say, a career-change, plus, you can do no better than to read this book. It's one of the best I've ever read on career change. Carol has really done her homework, and she offers very many helpful ideas to guide you on your way.

— Richard N. Bolles, author of *What Color Is Your Parachute?*
A Practical Manual for Job-Hunters And Career-Changers (2005 Edition)

How This Book Is Organized

I divide *Your Dream Career For Dummies* into five parts. A quick review of the Table of Contents and the following description of the parts gives you a solid overview of the entire book. If you want information about a particular topic, the Index can also help you locate it.

Part I: Setting the Stage for Your Career Change

The chapters in Part I help you explore what is and isn't working in your current career and life so that you can determine what you need and want for yourself and your family in your next career.

Part II: Finding Your Passions

Use the extensive checklists, worksheets, and brainstorming techniques in this part to discover your passions and interests and then parlay them into a list of up to 40 viable career ideas. Chapters toward the end of Part II help you trim your ideas down to your two best ideas.

Part III: Exploring Possible Career Directions

The chapters in this part describe career ideas that may intrigue you if you have a certain skill, talent, or interest. For each career area, I provide a description of the career area that spells out what the career entails and what it takes to be in the career, related jobs and specialties that show you professional alternatives, and links that take you to the primary professional association for the career area so that you can further your exploration. Use the diverse information in this part as a springboard to brainstorm ways to weave your talents into careers that satisfy you and fit your life.

Part IV: Bringing Your Dream Career to Life

After you have a career idea or two that you want to pursue, Part IV helps you blend your dream career ideas with what you know you need for your life to run smoothly. Through exploration, conversation, and experimentation, you refine your ideas until you have enough confidence in your direction to take action. Depending on your situation, your next step may focus on getting more training, launching your job search, or starting a business.

Part V: The Part of Tens

Changing careers can be a roller coaster of emotions because, for a time, you're between two lives. You can't go back, and yet you don't know enough to fast-forward to your new life. The chapters in this part guide you through two of the toughest hurdles: convincing yourself, with good reason, that the idea you're contemplating is indeed a good move for you and showing you creative ways to get from where you are now to where you want to be — living the life your dream career enables you to live.

Icons Used in This Book

Throughout the book, icons appear in the margins to alert you to special information.

When you see this icon, you know that the text includes an example to show you how to use a worksheet or a multistep process.

This symbol marks an important truth that's worth repeating. Taking note of these ideas can help you make progress with your career change.

The information next to this icon always includes a helpful hint to keep your career change moving forward as smoothly as possible. Whether the tip is a time saver or a step saver, paying attention to these hints helps you move forward.

Any information next to this icon is something you want to be wary about. Watch your step when you see a Warning.

Where to Go from Here

You don't have to read this book from cover to cover to gain valuable insights about your next career. Each chapter covers some part of the career change puzzle, and some chapters may be more relevant to your situation than others. If you launch into a chapter that builds on something from a previous chapter, the text points you to the precise section or worksheet you need to complete to make the most of the current chapter.

If you are just beginning your quest for a new career and aren't sure where to start, I suggest going through the book chapter by chapter to build your picture of what you want one layer at a time.

If you've already done some thinking about your next career, read the following options to choose your best next step:

- ✔ If you hear a voice inside that questions whether you can change careers, I encourage you to use Chapter 2 as a resource to open your mind to possibilities and discover how to help yourself move forward when you feel stuck.

- ✔ If you know that your personal life is a key factor in defining your dream career, spend some time reading Chapters 3 and 4.

- ✔ When your work environment and work community are a crucial part of your dream career, Chapters 5 and 6 help you articulate what you want out of your work setting.

- ✔ If you're anxious to discover what you'll do in your dream career, the activities in Chapters 7 and 8 are a key to your success. After you have some ideas about what you want to do in your work, use Chapters 9 and 10 to brainstorm a set of viable career ideas for yourself.

- ✔ When you have a career idea or two in mind, use Chapters 14 and 15 to expand what you know about your ideas.

By setting your sights on your dream career, you're embarking on a journey. As with any kind of travel, you won't reach your destination instantaneously or effortlessly, but in a way the travel itself is part of the adventure. Enjoy the paths, discoveries, and even the detours that unfold as you move toward your next career.

Part I
Setting the Stage for Your Career Change

The 5th Wave   By Rich Tennant

CAREER MART

Aspirin

In this part . . .

Finding your dream career is like searching for a hidden treasure. The more clues you have in hand, the more likely you are to track down the prize. This part assists you in identifying the clues to what truly works for you in terms of your personal style, your lifestyle, and your work style.

Chapter 1

Evaluating Your Current Situation

. . . .

In This Chapter

▶ Checking in with yourself and your life

▶ Assessing your current work situation

▶ Evaluating the work you do

▶ Getting a sense of your priorities

. . . .

Did you know that you're sitting on a gold mine? The very same job that frustrates you or bores you to tears holds a number of valuable clues about your future career. In the same vein, the points of stress in your life can, with a little thought, prove to be enlightening, as well.

This chapter helps you assess where you are today. Taking some time to get a sense of yourself and your life at this point in time creates a foundation for building your next career. The more you know about what you want and need in your life, the more you can create a new career that fits you and enhances your life. To make this process as easy for you as possible, a series of worksheets walks you through this discovery process one step at a time.

If you aren't working, use your last job as your frame of reference for this chapter. Or if you've been at home raising your children, recovering from an illness, or caring for a relative, think of your current experiences as your "job" in the following worksheets.

Making the Worksheets Work for You

Each worksheet in this chapter consists of a list of elements in the left-hand column that are relevant to your personal life or your current job. When you rate each element, put an X into the appropriate box:

> ✔ **Good:** This element enhances your life or work.

> ✔ **Okay:** This element could be better or it could be worse. It either fluctuates or is generally mediocre.

> ✔ **Not So Good:** This element in some way diminishes your quality of life or your enjoyment of your work.

After you make your rating, note the reasons why you rated each element the way you did, using the following guidelines:

> ✔ If you marked an element "Good," explain what's working.

> ✔ If you marked an element "Okay" or "Not So Good," indicate what's not working in this area of your work or life.

If you see any elements that aren't listed but are relevant to you, add them in the blanks at the bottom of each table.

In Worksheet 1-8, you have an opportunity to review your responses to Worksheets 1-1 through 1-7 to get an overview of yourself and your life. At that point you identify the elements of your life that are most important to take into account as you create your new career.

As Sarah, a photography studio manager from Connecticut, completed Worksheet 1-1 later in this chapter, she discovered some very important information about how her personal life impacts her career. Review Figure 1-1 to see her responses. As you can see, Sarah is feeling stretched to the limit right now as she juggles her family responsibilities and her work tasks. Her time is so limited that she rarely has time for herself and her needs. What she takes away from this worksheet is that she definitely needs to take her new family situation into account as she envisions her next career.

Elements of Who and How You Are	Good	Okay	Not So Good	Why?
Your state of health	X			I'm healthy and have energy.
Having time for yourself			X	My infant and my work leave me little time for myself.
Exploring your interests and hobbies			X	I spend more time doing activities with my family than doing my own activities.
Reaching for your dreams			X	Who has time! Yet I often find myself thinking of a better future.
Understanding your own personality and style		X		I think I understand my own personality and style pretty well.
Living in alignment with your values		X		Definitely wish I could spend more time with my children. Yet at the same time I feel it's important to fulfill my responsibilities at work.
Balancing your needs and those of others			X	I'm not handling this very well due to the points I've made above.
Improving my appearance			X	I know I'd feel better about myself if I could update my image and lose the weight from my last pregnancy.

Figure 1-1:
Sarah's view of herself.

Looking at Your Personal Life

Because you're reading this book to create a new career, you may question why I start out by asking about your personal life. The way I've always looked at it, a career works best when it fits with your life. The more you know about yourself and how you want to live, the more you know about your new career.

If you've been working too hard or totally focusing on how frustrated you are with work, you may have lost track of yourself in the process. To make clear decisions about your future career, you must reach in to find the true you again. Looking at your life through different lenses can help you see yourself more clearly.

✔ Take a moment to think about the last time you really let go of work. Perhaps you took a long weekend or an extended vacation. How did it feel to relax and enjoy life?

✔ Now, think about how you feel at the end of the day or after a week at work. Do you feel like yourself or does it take you a while each night to re-find yourself?

Rate the elements of how and who you are in Worksheet 1-1 to take stock of how you are these days. Evaluating this information helps you clarify what's working and not working in your current situation. Later you use this information to verify that your new career idea is a good fit for you.

Elements of Who and How You Are	Good	Okay	Not So Good	Why?
Your state of health				
Having time for yourself				
Exploring your interests and hobbies				
Reaching for your dreams				
Understanding your own personality and style				
Living in alignment with your values				
Balancing your needs and those of others				

Worksheet 1-1: Evaluating various facets of yourself and your life.

Before you can focus clearly on the future, you must also take a close look at your current lifestyle. If some aspects of your life work well, you want to keep those aspects intact. If certain areas of your life are not satisfying, you can find ways to alleviate the problems by making different decisions about your future.

Put your career and time at work on the back burner for a moment and think about your personal life. As you scan your life, answer these questions for yourself:

✔ How do you live your life? What do you like about it? What could be better?

✔ How do you socialize with others?

✔ What do you do for fun?

✔ How do you and your family spend time together?

✔ How is your financial situation?

✔ How happy are you with where you live?

Assess how you're living by rating the elements listed in Worksheet 1-2. Later, this information helps you know that your new career not only supports you but also enhances the life you want to live.

Elements of How You Live	Good	Okay	Not So Good	Why?
Your social life				
Your leisure time and activities				
Your relationship with your children				
Your relationship with your partner				
Your interactions with your family				
Your financial situation				
Your home				
Your city and neighborhood				

Worksheet 1-2: Assessing how you live.

Sizing Up Your Current Work Arrangement

It's Sunday night. In ten hours, you have to get up and go to work. On a scale from 1 to 10, how would you rate the intensity of your Sunday Night Blues? Are you looking forward to returning to your office, seeing your colleagues, and using your creative skills? Or do you once again dread the thought of another five days stuck at work doing tasks that bore you, interacting with people who bug you, and dealing with office politics?

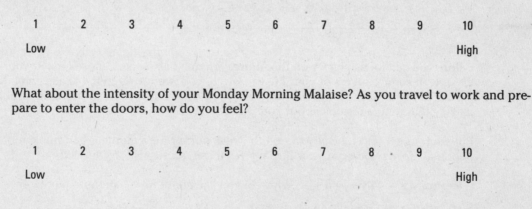

| 1 | 2 | 3 | 4 | 5 | 6 | 7 | 8 | 9 | 10 |
| Low | | | | | | | | | High |

What about the intensity of your Monday Morning Malaise? As you travel to work and prepare to enter the doors, how do you feel?

| 1 | 2 | 3 | 4 | 5 | 6 | 7 | 8 | 9 | 10 |
| Low | | | | | | | | | High |

Although these two questions serve as a quick barometer of how you feel about your work, looking at the pros and cons of each element of your work arrangement gives you insights about what you eventually need from your job to live the life you want.

Think about your work and your life over the last month and ask yourself the following questions:

- ✔ Does your current work arrangement allow you to live the life you want?
- ✔ Have you missed any opportunities due to the demands of your job?
- ✔ How has your schedule worked for you?
- ✔ How does your workload impact your life?
- ✔ What do you like or dislike about the way your work is structured, whether you work full-time or part-time?

Worksheet 1-3 lets you clarify how you feel about how you work. Evaluating your current work situation helps you pinpoint ways your new career can improve your satisfaction at work.

Elements of Your Time at Work	Good	Okay	Not So Good	Why?
Your work schedule				
Your contract				
Your vacation time				
Your sick time				
Your ability to handle personal appointments during work time				

Worksheet 1-3: Thinking about how you work.

Your income and benefits also impact how you live your life. Think about the past year, both the high points and the low points. Ask yourself the following questions:

- ✔ What have you been able to do as a result of having the income you do?
- ✔ Did you use any of your benefits this year? How did they work for you?
- ✔ Did your pay schedule meet your needs?
- ✔ Did the form of income you received (salary, commission, overtime pay, or stock options) have any effect on your lifestyle?
- ✔ What haven't you been able to do as a result of your income or benefits?

Worksheet 1-4 gives you a space to jot down your thoughts about important issues regarding your pay and benefits. Being clear about your needs helps you set your sights on a career that's a good fit.

Elements of Your Pay and Benefits	Good	Okay	Not So Good	Why?
Your income				
Your benefits				
How you are paid				

Worksheet 1-4: Evaluating your pay and benefits.

For some people, the environment in which they work is more important than what they do on the job. By looking at what does and doesn't work for you in your work environment, you gain valuable clues that help you evaluate the fit of future work environments.

In your mind's eye, think about your day at work — from the moment you leave your home to the time you return. Ask yourself the following questions:

- What is your commute like?
- How do you feel arriving at work?
- How does your body respond when you enter the building?
- How do you feel while you are at work?
- What is your return commute like?
- How do you feel when you get home from work?

The sensations and impressions you feel as you answer these questions give you insights about how specific elements of your work environment affect you on a daily basis.

Use Worksheet 1-5 to rate how happy you are with specific aspects of your current work environment. In addition to noticing what doesn't work in your current job, remember to take note of elements of your work that you enjoy and want to re-create in your new work setting.

Elements of Your Work Environment	Good	Okay	Not So Good	Why?
The kind of company				
The size of your company				
The industry you are in				
The company culture				
Your commute				
Your company's surroundings				
The interior of your building				
Your personal work space				
How you have to dress				

Worksheet 1-5: Judging your state of mind about your work surroundings.

At first glance, you may feel as though you have little choice about whom you work with. You can, however, choose a career that allows you to interact with the kinds of people you enjoy most, whether they're colleagues who share your interests or clients who receive your services.

To discover more about what does and doesn't work for you in your current work community, take an imaginary walk through the halls of your office. Think about the people you work with on a regular basis:

- ✔ Envision stopping at each office or cubicle to get a sense of your interactions with each person.
- ✔ Revisit the meetings you've attended this week.
- ✔ Take a mental look at your e-mail inbox. Whose names show up there?
- ✔ Who comes to mind when you scan your telephone log or messages?

With your impressions fresh in your mind, rate the following categories of people you interact with at work in Worksheet 1-6. Your response to the question "Why?" may, in this case, be a person's name.

Worksheet 1-6: Rating your satisfaction with the people in your work world.

Elements of Who You Work With	Good	Okay	Not So Good	Why?
Your co-workers				
Your employees or support staff				
Your manager				
The management				
Your customers or clients				
Your vendors				

What's Working and Not Working about the Work You Do

Obviously what you do on your job impacts how you feel about your career. Think about the tasks and projects you've worked on this year and ask yourself the following questions:

- ✔ How do you feel when you do your work?
- ✔ What bores you?
- ✔ What excites and motivates you?
- ✔ When do you feel engaged by your work?

Take some time to write down your thoughts in Worksheet 1-7 regarding the elements that make up your work tasks. Although you may be fed up with your current job, you may find, upon reflection, that you actually enjoy some pieces of what you do. Understanding your current situation in detail gives you insights about what elements of your current work may be worth carrying forward into a new career.

Elements of the Work You Do	Good	Okay	Not So Good	Why?
The tasks you do				
The skills you use				
The topics you address				
The process you follow				
The meaning you find in your work				

Worksheet 1-7: Assessing your work.

Recording Your Key Needs

Look over the worksheets in this chapter to get an overview of what's going on in your work and life. Then take it deeper. Identify five factors that, if resolved, would allow you to love your life and your work more than you do now. By identifying these issues now, you know what issues you'd like to resolve with your next career. In fact, in Chapter 16 you return to this list to find the right fit between your personal needs and desires and your potential career ideas.

Use Worksheet 1-8 to write down your key needs. If you can, state your needs in terms of what you want rather than what's lacking in your life right now. For instance, write down "I need more flexibility" rather than "I don't have enough flexibility." If you recognize that something isn't working for you but you don't know exactly how you want to fix the situation, don't sweat it. Just record your observation the best you can. As you explore the upcoming chapters, you may discover a new perspective that allows you to articulate your needs more clearly.

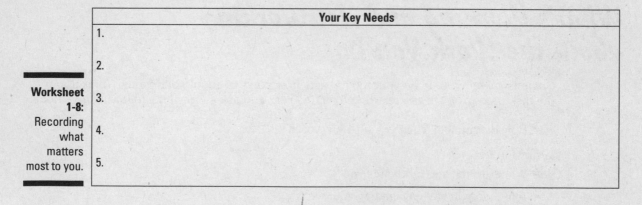

Your Key Needs
1.
2.
3.
4.
5.

Worksheet 1-8: Recording what matters most to you.

Although you picked up this book to identify your next career, the worksheets in this chapter may show you that another part of your life isn't working very well. If you feel desperate to leave your current job, living situation, or relationship, you may be in a toxic situation. If you're so worn out by the end of the day that you can't think straight, you may find it hard to make progress on your career change. The fact is that just making it through the day takes all you've got. You have two possible strategies: Minimize your exposure to the person, setting, or situation that feels toxic or just get out in whatever way you can create. Reach out for support from a friend or a professional if you don't see an immediate way out. After you feel safer, you can focus on your goal to change your career and make much more progress.

Chapter 2

Opening Yourself to Discovery

· ·

In This Chapter

▶ Thinking big

▶ Knowing what appeals to you — and what doesn't

▶ Looking for signs that you're on the right track

▶ Transforming procrastination into action

· ·

*1*dentifying a new career is a journey of discovery. Along the way you experience the twists and turns of new dreams, unexpected dead ends, and discoveries full of potential.

As with any journey, it helps to prepare yourself with skills you may need along the way. Throughout this chapter, you experiment with the perspectives, skills, and processes that help you make the most of your journey.

Appreciating the Benefits of Thinking Ideally

In Chapters 2 through 14, I ask you to think in ideal terms about various elements of your personal life and your professional life. Your goal, in each chapter, is to describe the best possible solution or situation for you and your family.

At first these requests may seem like pie-in-the-sky ways to address your practical need for a new career. After all, you need results sooner rather than later. In the end, however, exploring your ideal vision leads you to more successful outcomes than focusing on the practicalities of your situation. Here's why this approach works:

✔ The journey you're embarking on helps you create a career that fulfills you professionally, while allowing you to express yourself completely and live your life fully. If you focus only on resolving the current frustrations you have about your career, you're likely to miss key pieces of the puzzle. For instance, you might not lift your vision high enough to see that there are ways to improve both your career and your life substantially without much extra effort.

✔ You're also more likely to be creative when you think from an ideal perspective. From this elevated vantage point, you think more expansively, take more risks, and see more possibilities than when you focus on what's realistic and feasible. Although finding your most realistic path to your new career is an important part of Chapters 14 through 19, you can't embark on that process until you have a clear vision of your dream career.

✔ When you focus on your ideal situation, you're likely to fulfill more of your needs and desires than if you focus your attention only on reasonable next steps. A plan based on reason, and reason alone, is likely to leave you wanting more. Incorporating your ideal picture into your plans infuses your vision with life and excitement.

If you're like most people, you may not spend much time in your daily life thinking of best-case scenarios. In fact, this new perspective may take some getting used to. Take a moment to practice thinking ideally in Worksheet 2-1.

If you had all the time, resources, and support you need, what three things would you do with your time? Remember to think as ideally as possible here. Be expansive. Tap into your wildest dreams and dearest hopes — even if you've never dared to express them before. Your dream may be to work with animals, work part time, live in a warmer climate during the winter months, or use your creative skills. Although your dream may feel impossible at the moment, continue to keep your focus on your ideal.

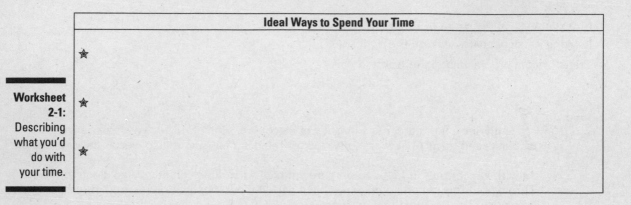

Worksheet 2-1: Describing what you'd do with your time.

Ideal Ways to Spend Your Time
★
★
★

Identifying What Attracts and What Repels You

Another key to discovering your next career rests on your ability to know what attracts you, what draws you in, and what intrigues you. Throughout this book, you look at lists, recall former jobs, and imagine yourself in various situations. In each case, I ask you to select the elements that are most attractive to you.

By knowing what attracts you about a setting, a person, a profession, or a topic, you can begin to develop an ideal picture of how you want to work and what you want to do on the job. Furthermore, with this knowledge, you can begin to bring more of what you like into your life on a daily basis.

Take a moment to record, in Worksheet 2-2, six things in your home or neighborhood that attract you. There's really no wrong answer here. Pay attention to what your eye is drawn to whether it's a certain architectural detail, a beautifully designed landscape, a particular paint color, or an artistic object. Later you apply this same skill to elements of your career, but it's often easier to practice using this skill while observing physical aspects of your environment.

Now look back at what you wrote and focus for a minute on how you feel when you notice you are attracted to something in your life. Do you feel a warmth within you, an excitement, or a sense of freedom? Whatever you feel is fine. Try, if you can, to put your feelings into words in the second section of Worksheet 2-2. Knowing how you feel when you're attracted or drawn to something is a wonderful asset when you're trying to find a career you enjoy. Whenever you feel this feeling in the future, you know to pay attention because you've just run across something that intrigues you.

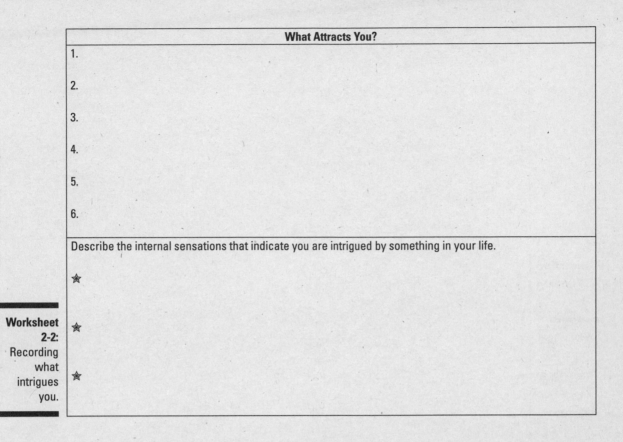

What Attracts You?
1.
2.
3.
4.
5.
6.
Describe the internal sensations that indicate you are intrigued by something in your life.
☆
☆
☆

Worksheet 2-2: Recording what intrigues you.

Knowing what repels you is just as important as knowing what appeals to you. When you know something repels you, you do your best to avoid that thing or situation. If you aren't consciously aware of what repels you, you don't turn away fast enough — you try to make it work or you try to talk yourself into settling or making do. Force-fitting yourself into an unsavory situation is time consuming, distracting, and draining. The key is to know, as soon as possible, that you're repelled by a work environment, a job task, or a person — before you get so involved in the situation or relationship that you'll find it hard to get out gracefully.

Take a moment to identify the things around you that repel you. Start with your physical surroundings. Are you repelled by a spot on the carpet, clutter in a neighbor's yard, a piece of furniture that needs to be replaced, or a decorative style that's too sterile or gaudy for your tastes? In Worksheet 2-3, record the six things in your house or neighborhood that repel you. Later, the ability to identify what repels you helps you make good decisions about the work environments and job tasks that are best for you to avoid.

Just as you did with things that attract you, review what repels you and note how you feel when you notice that something in your life repels you. If you can, put words to this feeling as well in the second section of Worksheet 2-3.

As you progress through the book, pay attention to how you feel about various ideas and options. When you feel the emotion associated with things that attract and intrigue you, pay attention. That clue is as good as gold!

If you feel repelled by something in a list or from a previous experience, take note! Investing in options that inherently annoy you is a big waste of time and energy. This fact is true even if the solution makes logical sense, loved ones think it's your best move, or you have considerable training in the area in question. If just the idea of something turns you off, imagine the misery you'd feel if you built your next career around this element.

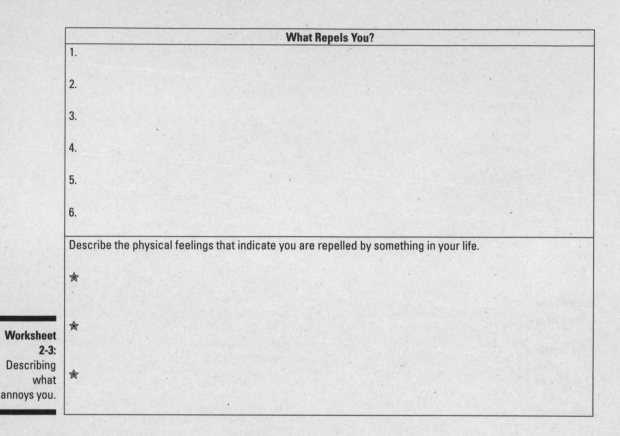

What Repels You?
1.
2.
3.
4.
5.
6.
Describe the physical feelings that indicate you are repelled by something in your life.
☆
☆
☆

Worksheet 2-3: Describing what annoys you.

Spotting Clues to Your Future

Although you're no doubt anxious to discover "The Answer" to your current career dilemma, that answer isn't going to appear in a dream or announce itself in a flashing neon sign. Instead it's going to unfold one layer at a time.

By being observant as you move through each chapter, you can see signs and clues that you're on the right track. Start training your senses to see the following signs that something is taking shape:

Repetition of words and ideas: If you notice that a certain word or idea shows up in a variety of worksheets, you know it's important to you.

Grace, who up until now has been a stay-at-home mom, is looking at her options as she contemplates going back to work. In her descriptions of her ideal lifestyle (Chapter 4) and her preferred work environment (Chapters 5 and 6), she noticed that some phrases appeared repeatedly: "flexibility," "time with my kids," and "able to take care of family needs when necessary." She rather expected to see that trend. What surprised her was the number of times the word "engaged" appeared. She realized that she's ready to plug into a career that engages her mind and challenges her to apply herself.

New insights: If you experience an Aha! moment while doing a worksheet, write down that thought. New insights give you a new way to perceive your situation. Your new perspective may open up new horizons to explore, or the new idea may narrow your focus by clarifying your needs in a new way. Either way, follow through on your insights to see where they take you and what else they reveal. Do an Internet search, talk to a friend, or read a relevant book to learn more about your new discovery. When you know more, reflect on how this information changes or enhances your opportunities.

Sean, a marketing communications director from New York, decided to focus his job search on a skill he'd used in his past jobs: producing. As he scanned various job postings, he discovered that a number of interesting positions were freelance opportunities. Although they're consistent with his ultimate career dream, the unreliable nature inherent in that kind of work runs counter to his current financial goals and family responsibilities. As a result of this discovery, he narrowed his current job search to full-time producing positions. Simultaneously, he decided to set his long-term sights on the freelance world. With this information, he can use his next job(s) to prepare himself to be a candidate for a great project when his responsibilities shift in a couple years.

Increased excitement: If you get excited about anything as you complete the worksheets or you explore an idea, pay attention. Your excitement is a clue to your passions. Follow the thread to see where it leads you. Making a life-changing decision based on just one clue is risky, but it is a great piece of information about what intrigues you.

Jeannette, a pet food manufacturer from Maryland, already knew she was interested in foods, the history of food, and finding creative ways to use food, but the confirmation of her interests, as she worked through the exercises in this book, helped her stay committed to her passion. Every time she moved away from the idea of working with food, she didn't like how she felt. Every time she refocused on food, she felt excited again. To find her niche in the food world, she networked, went to food-related trade shows, attended classes, hooked up with a professor doing research on using food as medicine, and explored the work of various food companies. In the end, she realized she wanted to use her knowledge and passion to find ways to use food to help people heal and be well.

Internal drive to investigate: If you have a question about what a term means or how it might apply to you, take some time to quench your curiosity. If you wonder what a career consists of, explore it in Chapters 14 and 15 to find out more. Your desire to know more is another important clue. Even if the idea you explore doesn't pan out, you become clearer about your needs as a result of your exploration.

As Mary, a human resource representative from Los Angeles, California, contemplated possible careers, she was drawn to learn more about being a physical therapist. In the process of reading about the job, talking to contacts, and exploring possible training programs, she discovered a career she hadn't known existed: occupational therapist. As a result of her discovery, she switched gears and applied to schools with a master's degree in occupational therapy. Last time I talked with her she was completing her first term in school.

Making the Most of Being Stuck

Discovering a new career that suits you and your life is a process. As I mentioned, you will not get "The Answer" you're looking for instantaneously. You can, however, expect to gain new insights, ideas, and clarity at each step of the way.

One essential part of your journey involves feeling stuck. Yes, that's right. I'm here to tell you that you're likely to feel stuck at some point or another during the process. Although you may be tempted to get frustrated and back away from your goal, I encourage you to stick with it. In the moment you feel stuck, you're actually the closest you've been to a breakthrough. Hang in there and use the following sections to find your way through.

After a breakthrough comes and you shift your perspective of your circumstances, you may find a new way to combine your ideas, you may get a new piece of information that opens up new opportunities, or you may meet someone who has the perfect contact for you. You never know upfront what key moves you forward, so stay alert and follow through on any clues that present themselves.

Whenever you feel stuck during the journey, come back to this section for ideas on how to make sense of your situation.

Recognize warning signs

One key to making the most of the times when you feel stuck is to find out how to recognize what you do when you feel stymied. Do you avoid opening this book? Do you complain you aren't getting anything from the process? Do you hear a voice telling you to "give it up — you'll never figure this out"? Do you feel so overwhelmed or frustrated that you can't make any progress?

Most people tend to behave a certain way when they feel stuck. Take a moment to think of other times you've gotten stuck while working on a personal project or a job assignment. Then make a list of your behaviors that can serve as a warning that you're feeling stuck. Record your thoughts in Worksheet 2-4.

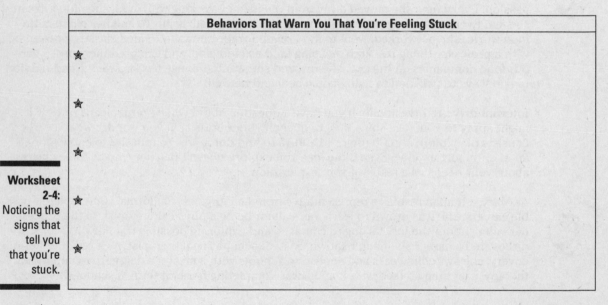

Behaviors That Warn You That You're Feeling Stuck
☆
☆
☆
☆
☆

Worksheet 2-4: Noticing the signs that tell you that you're stuck.

If you notice that you're stepping into your usual stuck pattern, pay attention. Being stuck isn't a sign of failure; it's a sign that you're close to a breakthrough!

Claim your interests

One reason you may feel stuck is that you aren't getting any new answers. You keep coming up with the same needs or career interests no matter what worksheet you fill out. If you were expecting or hoping to come up with a completely new idea and your answers just repeat what you already knew, you most likely feel frustrated.

When this happens, there's a good chance that your answers are confirming something that's true for you! Rather than fight it, claim what you know to be true for yourself, and move to the next step.

If you aren't able to come up with any answers or conclusions at all, keep reading. The process of filling out these worksheets may emphasize a different truth for you — that you aren't interested in much of anything these days or that you don't enjoy things anymore.

If you're feeling this disengaged and you continue working through the book, you're likely to end up feeling very frustrated. You simply can't create a career you love when you aren't interested in or attracted to activities, things, or people.

This news doesn't mean that you must give up; it just means that you need to take a slight detour to wake up your sense of interest. Sometimes, due to life situations, you may get into such a rut that the range of topics and activities you consider shrinks to the point that you get bored. After that happens, your excitement meter quits working. This doesn't have to be a lifelong sentence, however.

Here are some ideas you can act on to expand your horizons again. As you explore each of the tactics, don't worry about how your discoveries apply to your career. Just open your mind to focus on exploring anything that excites you. After you're awake again, you can turn your attention back to your career.

- For the next couple weeks, keep an eye out for any flicker of interest that occurs as you live your life. If you feel even the slightest bit of interest, notice what triggered your attention. Then follow that thread, do an Internet search, read an article, or talk to others who share your interest. Keep going as long as your interest is piqued. If you lose interest, drop that topic and shift your focus to something else.

- Prime the pump a bit by scanning the list of classes at a nearby community college or adult education program. You don't have to take all the classes that appeal to you, but by familiarizing yourself with the class list, you may discover something that interests you.

- Take a look at the events pages in your local paper. See if a book signing, performance, or lecture catches your attention. Attend the event to find out more about the subject or to experience something new.

- Read newspapers and magazines with the sole purpose of finding topics that interest you. Clip any articles you find and put them in a file for later reference in Chapter 8.

- Glance through magazines and pull out anything — images, articles, or simply words — that strikes your fancy. Start a file of such things for your collection. Later, when your file is full, return and sort your items to see what themes show up. After you identify a theme that particularly interests you, explore it to the fullest.

After you reconnect with things and activities you enjoy, begin taking steps to bring more of these activities into your life. Continue exploring topics of interest, participate in things you enjoy, and join a club or organization of people who enjoy what you like.

If you're still not connecting with any interests, you may need to reach out for support. Sometimes stress, depression, and medications can mute your interest level. Get support from a professional if any of these things describe your situation.

Get creative

After you come up with an idea for your future, you may experience feeling stuck because you don't see any way to get where you want to go. No matter how you look at your dream career idea or your dream work situation, you don't see a way to pull it off.

First, don't give up yet! Second, don't invest too much time looking for a logical answer to your dilemma. You've most likely tried the logical route, and that's not giving you a workable answer. Going down that path again is just going to lead to more frustration. Instead put on your creative thinking cap and try this brainstorming process.

1. **Ask yourself where you're feeling stuck in your life/career journey.**

   Do your best to articulate what the problem is. It may be something you crave, a dilemma about how to get two parts of your life to work together, or a situation you're tired of putting up with.

2. **Figure out the essence of what you want.**

   Step back from the specifics of your problem or situation and get to the true essence of your desire. When you resolve this issue, what feeling do you want to have? What's your bottom-line need when all is said and done? In the statement of your problem in Step 1 you most likely focused on the elements of your situation and the circumstances surrounding that situation that aren't working. The key to finding the essence of what you want in the situation is to shift your focus to how you want to feel. Do you want to feel calm, powerful, confident, engaged, or some other emotion? Peel away all the circumstantial facts of the situation to discover your bottom-line need when all is said and done. See Step 2 in Figure 2-1 to see some specific examples of essence statements.

3. **List as many creative, outrageous, funny, or unexpected solutions as you can.**

   Boost your creative juices by putting any perceived or real constraints on your time, money, and resources out of your mind for a time. You get the best results when you step into your ideal mind-set as you do your brainstorming.

4. **Create a list of possible solutions that might work.**

   Use the fun and ideal solutions you came up with in Step 3 as a springboard for identifying possible solutions you can work with. As you review your ideas in Step 3 do you see a theme? Do you see pieces or parts of solutions that might work well together? Do you see a solution you hadn't noticed before? If so, write that one down.

5. **Identify one thing you can do to move closer to getting the essence of what you want.**

   Start thinking of something — an action, a perspective, a contact, or a research task — that gets you one step closer to resolving the situation.

 Do everything within your power to stay focused on creating the essence of what you want as you described it in Step 2. The minute you step back into trying to solve the problem you stated in Step 1, you start running into the specifics of the situation that keep you locked into certain perspectives. By focusing on the essence of what you want, you keep a broader, more ideal perspective that encourages creative thinking and uncovers new solutions you hadn't see before.

 Patrick, a financial planner from Illinois, used this method to brainstorm solutions to two dilemmas in his life: First, he's been craving a Hawaiian vacation for a couple years, but he can't seem to make it happen. Second, he has a three-hour round trip commute that's wearing him down. The commute has gotten so draining that it's affected his relationship with his family. Read through each step he took in Figure 2-1 to see the brainstorming method in action. In both cases, he found that focusing on the essence of what he wanted helped him open up to possibilities he hadn't considered before.

Finding Creative Solutions		
	Vacation Dilemma	**Commute Dilemma**
Step 1: Where are you feeling stuck or frustrated in your life? What are you craving?	I need a vacation! I've been wanting to go to Hawaii for two or three years.	My commute is wearing me out. Three hours of driving a day is too much. I can't stand it for very much longer. By the time I get home, I'm exhausted and can't really enjoy my family.
Step 2: If you take away the specifics of what you want, what's the essence that is left?	I want to get away to relax with my wife. We'd like to spend time in/around water.	I want to be calm when I walk in the door after work. I want energy to play with my kids when I get home.
Step 3: List as many creative, outrageous, funny, or unexpected solutions as you can.	Head to Mexico, take a tropical cruise, visit a retreat center that has a pool and a wide selection of spa services, win a trip to Hawaii, use my frequent flyer miles to take a trip, charter a yacht in the Caribbean, rent a beachfront house for a week, housesit for someone in a great location	Telecommute, work at a satellite office, carpool, take the train, relocate closer to work, find a job closer to home, hire a driver, quit, commute during off hours, commute by plane, find a way to start a home-based business
Step 4: Look at the solutions you listed. What elements draw your attention? Can you combine any elements to create a new solution?	Take a cruise to Mexico, go to resort with spa services, rent a beachfront house down south, spend a week at a retreat center that has a pool or hot tub, swap homes with someone in Florida	Telecommute two days a week and carpool the others, work at a satellite office three days a week and take a train the other two days, investigate career options closer to home to eliminate the commute entirely, talk to friends about creating a vanpool
Step 5: Identify actions you can do to move closer to getting the essence of what you want. If it makes sense, look at both short-term and long-term options.	Research the local retreat centers to see what programs or opportunities are available, explore resorts in Mexico, ask friends for recommendations, look at house rentals in warm, beachfront areas	<u>Short-term solutions:</u> Investigate the vanpool idea for the short term, explore the telecommute options at my current job <u>Long-term solutions:</u> Start looking at career options closer to home

Figure 2-1: Patrick gets creative to resolve two frustrating situations in his life.

Before you try this brainstorming method to resolve a career-related dilemma, I encourage you to use Worksheet 2-5 to get a new perspective on a dilemma from your life outside of your job. Don't start with an area of your life that you've been struggling with for years. Try something a bit more approachable, such as how to create more quiet time in your life, entertain more often, or have more fun on the weekends. After you get familiar with the process, you can use it for any situation, including dilemmas in your career situation.

Finding Creative Solutions	
Step 1: Where are you feeling stuck or frustrated in your life? What are you craving?	
Step 2: If you take away the specifics of what you want, what's the essence that is left?	
Step 3: List as many creative, outrageous, funny, or unexpected solutions as you can.	☆ ☆ ☆ ☆ ☆ ☆
Step 4: Look at the solutions you listed. What elements draw your attention? Can you combine any elements to create a new solution?	
Step 5: Identify actions you can do to move closer to getting the essence of what you want. If it makes sense, look at both short-term and long-term options.	

Worksheet 2-5:
Finding new ways to resolve a problem.

Chapter 3

Uncovering the Real You

In This Chapter

▶ Understanding your personality, values, and idea of success

▶ Considering your dreams and longings

▶ Looking at how your health impacts your career choices

▶ Discovering why you work

*I*s there anything about who you are and your personal style that's absolutely non-negotiable? Anything you refuse to give up or sacrifice for your job or your career?

As you think about your new career, it's a given that you bring yourself to the party. In my opinion, who you are is non-negotiable. For example, if you thrive on being outside and using your artistic talents, you probably aren't going to feel very happy sitting in a cubicle in front of a computer all day. On the flip side, if you love thinking about and working with computers, the free-form life of an artist might drive you crazy. A career that forces or requires you to be someone you aren't is not the career for you. Although you may need to disregard this advice temporarily if you need to take an interim, short-term position to make ends meet, in the long run, that kind of job just drains the life right out of you.

In this chapter, you identify elements of yourself that are important to incorporate into your future career decisions. In Worksheet 3-11 you combine the insights you gained in Worksheets 3-1 to 3-10 so that all your information is at your fingertips. With this summary picture of yourself and your needs, you can immediately identify and side-step job opportunities that may force you to give up being who you truly are.

Discovering Traits That Best Describe You

Who you are is comprised of any number of characteristics, traits, and qualities. Some are likely to be more important to you than others. In fact, some of these qualities may be so important that they define you.

Review the list of keywords in Worksheet 3-1 and put an arrow in front of any words that describe aspects of who you are. This exercise helps you identify the traits that best describe your personality, which, in turn, helps you solidify your view of yourself. The more you know about yourself, the more likely you are to identify a career that allows, and even encourages, you to be yourself at work. If you think of a trait that's not on the list, be sure to add it to your list in Worksheet 3-1.

If you feel stumped, ask your friends and family members for their opinions about your integral traits. Because they don't live in your skin and may be less biased, they may have a better perspective on your personality than you do. But unless you have a really thick skin, be sure to ask others only for your positive qualities!

Possible Personality Traits		
Abstract thinker	Expressive	Perfectionist
Active	Fair	Persuasive
Adaptable	Friendly	Precise
Analytical	Humorous	Punctual
Communicative	Imaginative	Quick
Concrete thinker	Intuitive	Reflective
Consistent	Inventive	Reserved
Deep thinker	Investigative	Resourceful
Detail-oriented	Mediator	Sensitive
Diplomatic	Methodical	Spontaneous
Disciplined	Motivator	Supportive
Efficient	Observant	Versatile
Empathetic	Open-minded	
Enthusiastic	Organized	

Worksheet 3-1: Exploring your personality.

After you've marked all the words that describe you, narrow the field by identifying the six traits that are essential for you to incorporate into a potential career. The best way to focus your list is to think about the traits that best describe who you are or are most important for you to express in your work. If you find a couple of traits that seem similar to you, you can combine them under one trait or come up with a new phrase that combines them. Write down your choices in Worksheet 3-2 and record any thoughts you have about how you want to express each trait in your work.

Your Key Traits	Ways to Express Each Trait in Your Work
1.	
2.	
3.	
4.	
5.	
6.	

Worksheet 3-2: Listing your key personality traits.

If you want to understand more about how you tick by exploring your personality and personal style, check out one or both of the following Web sites. The insights you gain can enhance your list of personality traits in Worksheet 3-2.

✔ **Kiersey Temperament Sorter II (www.advisorteam.com/user/kcs.asp):** The questionnaire at this site helps you discover which of four temperaments you have: Artisans (SF), Guardians (ST), Idealists (NF), Rationals (NT). This two-letter code is half the story. By purchasing one of the reports for $14.95, you receive your full four-letter code (similar to those measured in the Myers-Briggs Typology) that identifies where you stand on four personality dimensions. With this code, you can find out more about your personal style and the work styles, work environment needs, and management styles of those who share your four-letter code. After you know your code, visit www.kiersey.com to read more about your temperament or enter the code into your favorite search engine to find in-depth profiles and discussion groups for those with the same style.

✔ **Enneagram** (www.9types.com/): At this site you find two free tests to help you determine your personality type based on the Enneagram system, an ancient system built on psychological research of high-functioning individuals. By understanding your type, you gain an appreciation of your personal style, your blind spots, and how you can interact more effectively with others.

Finding the Values That Mean the Most to You

Values are those beliefs, ideas, and elements of your life that are most important to you. Depending on who you are, you may find that your relationships with family and friends are crucial to your happiness, or you may find competition and adventure are the elements of life that define who you are. The more aware you are of your values, the better your chances of creating a career that truly fits you.

Using the list in Worksheet 3-3, which was developed by Terry Karp, MA, and Mark Guterman, MA, identify the values that describe the core of who you are. As you read the list, take a moment to think about how each value does or doesn't play out in your life. Some values are likely to be more important to you than others. Put an arrow in front of the values that help define who you are.

Worksheet 3-3: Investigating your values.

Possible Values		
Accomplishment	Family	Nature
Adventure	Friendship	Obligation
Affiliation	Fun	Pleasure
Artistic expression	Harmony	Predictability
Authority	Health	Recognition
Autonomy	Helpful	Respect
Balance	High earnings	Responsibility
Beauty	Honesty	Risk-taking
Challenge	Humility	Self-discipline
Community	Independence	Self-restraint
Competence	Influence	Service
Competition	Integrity	Spirituality
Contribution	Justice	Stability
Control	Knowledge	Status
Cooperation	Leadership	Structure
Creativity	Learning	Teamwork
Curiosity	Love	Time freedom
Diversity	Loyalty	Trust
Duty	Meaning	Variety
Faith	Moderation	Wisdom

Review the values you've marked and then record your top six values in Worksheet 3-4. Then next to each value, write a few words or phrases to explain why this value is important for you to uphold in your career and life. If you have a value that isn't part of the original list, add it to this list.

Clarifying your values is an important step in creating a career that's a good fit for you. Imagine the discomfort of finding a great career only to discover that one of your key values is consistently violated in that industry. For example, if you love animals and your life revolves around helping animals, you may find it difficult to use your biological training in companies that test products on animals. Be aware of your own values so you don't set yourself up for that type of disappointment!

Your Key Values	Why This Value Is Important to You
1.	
2.	
3.	
4.	
5.	
6.	

Worksheet 3-4: Isolating your key values.

Deciding What Success Means to You

While growing up, you probably relied on your family experience, media messages, and your peers' views to define success for yourself. But now you need to come up with your own definition of success. Uncovering how you see success today provides important clues about the best career for you.

Use the following questions to update and explore your personal definition of success and record your thoughts about success in Worksheet 3-5.

- ✔ **When you first started working, how did you define success?** What were you striving to achieve? What made you feel successful?

- ✔ **What makes you feel successful now?** How has your definition of success changed since you first started working? What are you trying to create in your life now?

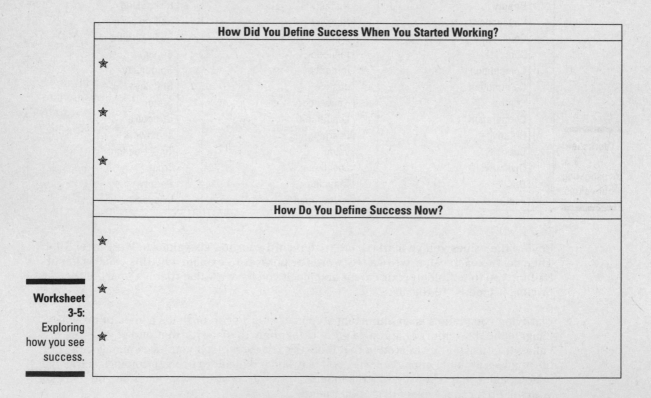

How Did You Define Success When You Started Working?
☆
☆
☆

How Do You Define Success Now?
☆
☆
☆

Worksheet 3-5: Exploring how you see success.

Read the answers you just wrote down. Is your definition of success primarily career-related, or are you looking at life success — how successful you are as a person? If you value your home life but base your sense of success solely on your career achievements, the mixed messages you carry within yourself may create conflict, frustration, and feelings of failure over time.

Bringing your definition of success into alignment with your true values and current goals helps you move forward and create what you want in your life and career.

Tapping into Your Dreams and Longings

Another way to access your unique needs is to pay attention to your dreams, longings, and cravings. Many people think that dreams are desires that never really materialize and that cravings are a need for something they can't or shouldn't have — like chocolate, for instance. But dreams and cravings are more than that. They are also a window to your desires and longings, a gateway to understanding your true needs. Knowing your desires and needs comes in handy when you're building a dream career.

Whether you dream of traveling, long for a private place to think about your life, or crave a less stressful schedule, your desires tell you something important about who you are and what's important to you. If you combine all three of these wishes together, you may realize you would love to travel by yourself to a retreat center for a time. Or you might conclude you want to create a career that allows you time to travel and time for your personal quests.

Although it's not important to know how to interpret your dreams and desires right now, it is important to record them as clues to understanding your personal needs. You can tap into your longings in two ways:

- Pay attention to any craving or wish you have to improve your situation. For example, you might see that a slight change in how your job works (such as the ability to work at home one day a week) would make your life easier in some way.

- Notice when you complain or feel frustrated by a situation at work. A complaint provides a wonderful opportunity to shift your focus from what you don't want to what you do want.

    The tricky part about describing what you do want is that it often triggers a bit of worry. You may wonder why you should bother thinking of what you want if you can't, at the same time, also figure out how to get it. Do your best to stay out of this trap by keeping your focus on what you want, not how you're going to get there. Worry only stifles your creativity, buries your desires, and keeps you feeling stuck.

Take a look at Figure 3-1 to see the list that Sally, a computer programmer from California, created when she described her dreams, longings, and desires. Notice that each of her entries begins with the phrase "I want," which helps her stay focused on the positive.

As you move forward in your quest for a new career, you want to make sure that you create a career that enables you to fulfill your professional dreams as well as your personal longings.

Jot down your longings, cravings, and dreams in Worksheet 3-6 after you've truly listened to yourself. If you find it hard to tap into your dreams and desires on the spot, be more aware of your thoughts, complaints, and wishes over the next week or so to see what surfaces as you go about your daily life.

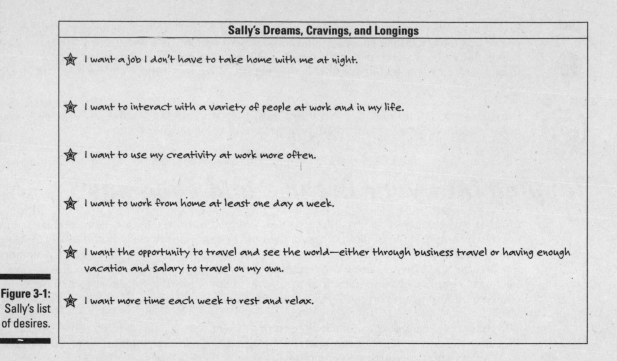

Figure 3-1:
Sally's list of desires.

One more point: Don't be concerned if one of your longings or dreams contradicts another one in your list in Worksheet 3-6. Right now you're recording a variety of things you long for, which awakens you to what you want. Coming up with ways to create what you want in your life ultimately evolves out of the thinking and planning you do in the remaining chapters of this book.

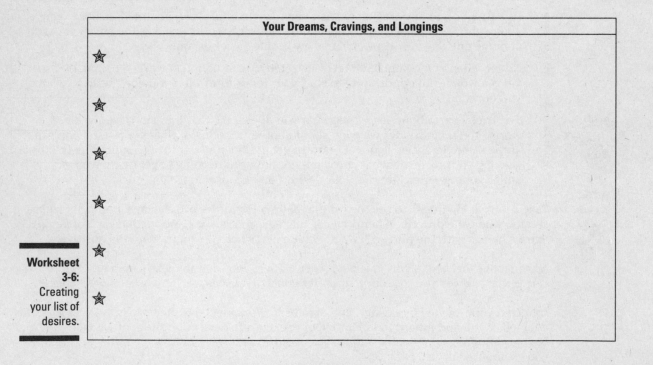

Worksheet 3-6:
Creating your list of desires.

Assessing Whether Your Health Impacts Your Career Choices

Working requires a certain degree of physical and mental well-being. If your health is compromised in any way, you need to make careful choices about your next career so that you can be productive in your career and comfortable in your decision.

Does anything about your state of health impact your choice of career? For example:

✔ A prior illness or physical condition that limits your work activities in some way

✔ Work-related activities that cause you discomfort or that you must force yourself to do

✔ Sensitivities or allergies that impact the kinds of environments in which you can safely work

Use Worksheet 3-7 to stimulate your thinking. Check off the elements that are relevant to you and then describe how your health may impact your options at work. Being clear about your body's working parameters helps you identify the kinds of careers you can explore.

Your Health	How Your Health Impacts Your Career Options
❏ Endurance	
❏ Ability to sit or move	
❏ Strength	
❏ Range of motion	
❏ Chronic pain	
❏ Past injuries	
❏ Energy level	
❏ Mental health factors	
❏ Sleep issues	
❏ Sensitivities or allergies	
❏ Vision or hearing	
❏ Other	

Worksheet 3-7: Examining your health.

Determining What Makes Work Meaningful to You

One way to discover meaning in your work is to ask yourself the question "Why do I work?" At first glance, you may say that you work for the money, and unless you're independently wealthy, your response is an absolutely viable answer.

If you take a second look, however, you may discover that you work for several other important reasons as well. Incorporating these elements into your next career increases the likelihood that your job will be fulfilling and meaningful to you. To begin this exploration, think about four jobs you have held during your years of employment. In Worksheet 3-8, jot down what you received from these jobs besides money.

If you're relatively new to the work world, think of what you've gained by doing volunteer projects, personal projects, or school projects.

Fred, who most recently worked as a realtor in Chicago, found great value in this exercise. Take a look at Fred's answers in Figure 3-2 before you begin your own exploration. If you see something you also gain from your work, feel free to borrow Fred's phrases. I'm sure he'd be delighted to help you out.

Figure 3-2:
Fred's view of what he received from previous jobs.

What Fred Gained from His Previous Jobs		
Job 1: Bishop Pine Realty	Job 2: Executive Director of Not-for-Profit	Job 3: Mortgage Broker
Job satisfaction	Making a difference in the world	High levels of achievement
Social contact	Fulfillment and joy	Prestige
Personally significant work	Opportunities for learning	Personal power
Variety of tasks	Visibility	Challenge
A feeling of independence	Responsibility	Feeling energized

As you review your notes about various jobs, identify your top six reasons for working — besides money — and record them in Worksheet 3-9. Take a moment to write why you value each reason for working.

People who want a meaningful career often want to accomplish something through their work. Take a look at the phrases in Worksheet 3-10 to spark your creative juices. Put an arrow next to the statements in the list, or come up with your own phrase, that best completes the following sentence for you: "Through my work and life I want to. . . ."

Having a clear picture of what gives you meaning in your work allows you, in Chapter 16, to assess whether a potential career will successfully fulfill your desire for meaning. If, for example, you want to improve the environment on a global scale, you may not be satisfied working in a job that has a local impact. Knowing your needs allows you to evaluate whether a particular field or profession will be meaningful enough for you.

If you marked more than three phrases in Worksheet 3-10, see if you can come up with a phrase that best summarizes the kind of meaning you're looking for.

What You Gained from Previous Jobs	
Job 1: _____	Job 2: _____
Job 3: _____	Job 4: _____

Worksheet 3-8: Exploring what you received from previous jobs.

Your Key Reasons for Working	Why You Value Each Reason for Working
1.	
2.	
3.	
4.	
5.	
6.	

Worksheet 3-9: Narrowing down why you work.

Through my work and my life I want to . . .		
Make a difference	Promote a cause	Help people see possibilities
Be of service	Give back to the community	
Leave a legacy	Heal others	
Solve a problem	Give others hope	
Create beauty	Improve others' lives	
Educate others	Help animals	
Invent something of use	Express myself	

Worksheet 3-10: Finding meaning in your work.

Recording What's Uniquely You

In this chapter, you explore your personality, values, dreams, health, and reasons for working. To create a career that is a good match for who you are, you need to have a clear picture of yourself. Review all the worksheets in this chapter and pull the words and phrases that best describe you into Worksheet 3-11. You'll be happy you have them all in one place when you reach Chapter 16 and want to evaluate how well your potential dream careers match your personal needs and values.

	Your Best Profile of You
Your personality traits	
Your values	
Your definition of success	
Your longings	
Your health	
Your reasons for working	
Your meaning in work	

Worksheet 3-11: Defining what's true about you.

Chapter 4

Envisioning Your Dream Lifestyle

....

In This Chapter
▶ Considering the important relationships in your life
▶ Detailing your ideal lifestyle
▶ Determining where you want to live
▶ Making a list of your top desires

....

As you begin building your new career, you want to make sure that the work you create for yourself supports you in living the life you want. This chapter guides you in detailing how you and your family want to spend time together, what you want to do with your time when you aren't working, and where you want to live.

To identify what you value most in life, you complete Worksheets 4-1 through 4-3 and then summarize the key points in Worksheet 4-4. Having all your lifestyle desires in one place helps you in Chapter 16 as you fine-tune your priorities, search for work arrangements that truly work for you, and evaluate possible dream career ideas as you discover them.

Don't just think of your current life as you ask yourself the questions in this chapter. Think instead of the life you'd create for yourself and your family if you could. The more you know about your desired lifestyle, the more proactively you can work to create it.

Looking at How Important Relationships Impact Your Work

As you consider the various relationships in your life, you most likely notice that in each relationship you play a particular role that comes with certain responsibilities. As your relationships change or the individuals in the relationships change, your responsibilities shift in response. You'll probably also realize that when you look at the most important relationships in your life, you also want to spend time enjoying those you love. In some cases this desire may be enough to inspire you to transform your career.

In this section, take a look at your relationships with the important people (and animals!) in your life. Identify the kinds of support they need from you and the kind of time you'd like to spend with them. Thinking this through helps you define what is non-negotiable for you when it comes to finding a career that blends with your personal life.

Bill, a contractor from Indiana, realized that some recent changes in his family situation have put new demands on his time at work. As part of the sandwich generation, his roles as father and son are requiring him to rethink his schedule. In Figure 4-1, an excerpt of his worksheet, you can see that he's responsible for picking his first grader up from after-school care at a certain time each day. This responsibility means that he needs to arrange for someone to cover for him at the work site at the end of each day. In addition, his father's recent heart attack means Bill is spending more time at his parents' house, helping out his mother and making sure the home health staff is providing adequate care for his father. Although this situation is likely to improve over time, his parents are aging, so he realizes his involvement is likely to increase over the next few years.

How Your Relationships Impact Your Work			
Your Loved Ones	Your Role and Responsibility in This Relationship	Your Ideal Time with This Relationship	How This Relationship Impacts Your Career Decisions
Your Children Danny—6	Support my wife with Danny's care on a day-to-day basis. NEW: Pick Danny up each day at 4 pm.	Spend time in evenings and weekends playing and working together on projects he enjoys.	Need to make sure I can leave work each day by 3:30. No exceptions. On each project I must arrange to have someone available to cover late afternoon issues onsite.
Your parents/grandparents Mom and Dad	Dad's heart attack means more time at the house and more frequent visits. Mom needs my moral support and I want to make sure the nursing staff is providing Dad with what he needs.	Sunday dinner is still important family time. Want to keep that up.	Must leave on occasion for emergencies. I'd like to start driving out to the house on my lunch break a couple of days a week.

Figure 4-1: Bill's assessment of his key relationships.

As you read each of the following sections, think about the key relationships in your life. Then write down your thoughts in the Worksheet 4-1. If you don't have a partner, a child, a strong support network of friends, or a pet now but you want to in the future, be sure to account for your desires in Worksheet 4-1. Spell out what is non-negotiable about each relationship when it comes to your future career. Be as specific as you can about how each relationship influences how your career is structured.

You don't have to have all the answers at this point. Your primary goal is to identify how you'd ideally like to spend time with those you love.

Your partner

Whether you're married or dating, your relationship requires a certain amount of time and attention to flourish. Does your work allow you to nurture your relationship? Ask yourself these questions to find out:

- ✔ Do you spend enough uninterrupted private time with your partner?
- ✔ Do you have enough energy after work to enjoy each other's company?
- ✔ Do you get away together often enough?
- ✔ Do you get to have fun together?
- ✔ Does your partner have any special needs that require your attention?

How Your Relationships Impact Your Work			
Your Loved Ones	Your Role and Responsibility in This Relationship	Your Ideal Time with This Relationship	How This Relationship Impacts Your Career Decisions
Your partner			
Your children			
Your parents/ grandparents			
Your friends			
Your pets			

Worksheet 4-1: Describing your most treasured relationships.

Your children

If you have children, you no doubt already know how much their needs and your desire to support them affect your work and life. If you could write your own ticket, what part would you play in your children's lives? Consider your answers to the following questions:

✔ Do you spend the amount of time you'd like with them?

✔ How is your energy level when you see them?

✔ Do you take vacations together?

✔ Are you happy with the activities you share?

✔ Do your children require any special attention from you?

Time is fleeting. If you want to spend time with your kids, now is the time. Don't worry about how you can pull it off. Just use the questions in this section to start thinking about your true desires regarding your children. The clearer you are about your desires, the easier it is to find a way to create what you want.

Your parents and grandparents

Elder care is more and more of an issue as baby boomers age and their parents and grandparents live longer and longer lives.

Look down the road on this one. If you don't support these members of your family right now, count your blessings and enjoy the time you have with your parents or grandparents while they're thriving, knowing that you may be a caretaker at some point in the hopefully far distant future. Think about the following questions:

- How do you keep in contact? Is it as frequent as you'd like?
- How frequently do you want or need to visit?
- Do you or might you have any caregiver responsibilities?
- Do you or might you need to move any family members at some point in the future?
- Who else can share in these responsibilities?

Your friends

Having a solid network of friends adds richness to life. Even when built on a good foundation, all friendships need care and feeding to survive. If your friends have moved away or moved on in different directions, you may need to set aside time to meet new people and develop bonds with them. When thinking about your support network, consider the following questions:

- Do you have a network of friends you can count on?
- Do you spend time with them on a fairly regular basis?
- Do you keep in touch?
- Do you enjoy your friends?
- Are you making new friends?
- Are you accepting social invitations?

Your pets

Pets are great companions, and if you share your life with animals, you know that they require your time and attention. Think about how your pets affect your work life:

- How long can you be away from home at any one time?
- Does having a pet impact your business travel?
- Does your pet have any health needs that impact your work?
- What kind of exercise does your pet need?
- Do you spend the time you'd like with your pet?

Describing Your Desired Lifestyle

Although your relationships have a role in defining your life, other factors may influence your career choices and decisions as well. Each of the personal life factors in the first column of Worksheet 4-2 may impact your career in terms of the amount of time and money you want to devote to these endeavors. In some cases, you may be able to fit these activities around a full-time, 8-to-5 job and be perfectly satisfied. In other cases, you may wish you had more time, more flexibility, or more funds to enjoy the activity to the extent you dream of.

Now's your chance! By figuring out what you truly value, you can factor that activity into your decisions about your next career and how it's structured. Use the second column in Worksheet 4-2 to describe your personal activities. Then in the third and fourth columns, indicate how each activity is likely to impact your time commitments at work and your need for cash!

Think about your ideal here. Don't get dragged down by what you think is feasible in your current situation. Articulate your needs as clearly as possible. You return to them again in Chapter 16 as you blend your ideal career with your ideal lifestyle.

✔ **Your home:** One source of pride and joy in life is often a place called home. How much time do you want to devote to caring for and enhancing your home? Is it important for you to take care of your home all by yourself or would you really like to bring someone in to help you out on a weekly basis or on a project-by-project basis? If you don't enjoy where you live, is purchasing a new home or moving to a different place part of your ideal picture? Remember that this exercise isn't about what works now, but about how you'd like it to be in the future.

✔ **Your faith:** Your devotion to your faith also defines your lifestyle. Depending on your commitment to your beliefs, your activities may extend beyond your time of worship in the form of volunteering, committee work, and outreach. Consider how your commitments might impact how your future career is structured.

✔ **Your volunteer work:** For some people, the time they spend helping others defines them. Do you have a cause you feel strongly about? Are you able to devote the time, money, and energy to helping others in the way you'd like? If you had more time, would you contribute to a cause that's meaningful to you? Would you volunteer through a nonprofit, a church project, or your child's school?

✔ **Your hobbies and interests:** Do you have a personal passion that is important to you? Think about how you might structure your work so that you have more time and energy to devote to your interests. Begin by thinking about whether your current career allows you to pursue your interests to the degree you'd like. For example:

  • If you're a nature photographer, do you have the flexibility in your schedule to travel?

  • If you love to water ski, can you get to the lake frequently enough to do what you love?

  • If you like to quilt, do you have enough time after work to devote to your craft?

If you want to explore ways to transform your hobby or interest into a career, check out Chapter 7, which is all about identifying your passions.

✔ **Your fun time:** No matter what you do for fun, you want to make sure you factor in enough time for activities that relax and entertain you. Think going to the movies, taking a vacation, entertaining, going out to eat, strolling through a park, or curling up with a good book. Whether your needs for enjoyment are simple or extravagant, think about the impact they have on your career.

Factors That Define Your Personal Life			
Personal Life Factors	How Do You Want to Spend Your Non-Work Hours?	How Does This Factor Impact Your Time at Work?	Does Your Desire Impact Your Income Needs?
Your home			
Your faith			
Your volunteer work			
Your hobbies/ interests			
Your fun time			

Worksheet 4-2: Thinking about your hobbies and interests.

Considering Where You Live

Sometimes the place you live has a huge impact on your career options. Although becoming more conscious about how your location influences or limits your career choices may be scary, in the end you have more power because you know the realities you face. For example, if you realize that the career options in your current location are dismal, you may choose to relocate or to create a multifaceted career that allows you to take advantage of what's possible in your area.

Several factors may influence the economy in your area and your career options. Start by thinking about the following issues:

✔ **Weather:** Do any cyclical weather patterns impact your work options? For example, your area may experience dramatic highs and lows in weather, such as extremely cold winters or fry-an-egg-on-the-sidewalk summers, that influence the economy of your community during those times. Or you may live in a temperate climate that encourages a well-balanced economy throughout the year.

✔ **Economy:** Does your local economy have any unique features that define or limit your career options? For example, do any of the following characteristics seem to describe your area?

- Limited variety of industries in the local area
- Slow economy
- Recreation or tourist economic base
- Rural area
- Small town
- Seasonal economy

✔ **Cost of living:** Does the cost of living in your area change your career choices at all? For example, does your mortgage or the cost of fuel require that you make such a large income that your career choices are limited?

✔ **Travel:** Does your commute or access to transportation influence your career choices? For example, would you accept a tempting job offer even if it increased your commute beyond reason? Are you far enough away from a decent airport that extensive business travel is out of the question?

✔ **Communications:** Does your local phone system or Internet access have an impact on your career choices? For example, if you live in a rural area, does the cost for high-speed Internet connections and some voice communication options impact your choice of career?

You may think of other local factors that limit or enhance your career options. Use the space in Worksheet 4-3 to jot down the characteristics of your location that have an influence on your career options.

Location Factors that Influence Your Career	
Local Factors	How Does Your Location Factor Impact Your Career Options?

After you consider the various characteristics that define the area where you live, take a step back to look at the big picture for a moment. Think about why you live where you do. For example, are you living there for one of the following reasons?

- ✔ **By default:** Because you grew up or went to school there and ended up staying

- ✔ **By circumstances:** Because your spouse relocated to the area, your elderly parent lives there, or your child needs to attend a school in the area

- ✔ **By choice:** Because you absolutely love living where you do

Would you rather live in more than one place? Have you always dreamed of having two homes, living in a RV and moving whenever you desire, traveling frequently, accompanying your partner whenever and wherever he or she travels, or seeing your long-distance partner more frequently and for longer periods of time? If you need this kind of flexibility to make the most of your desired lifestyle, consider a portable career, one that allows you to bring in an income from wherever you are. You may want to explore being a writer or editor, running an e-commerce site, or becoming a Web site or graphic designer. Another option may be to create a career that capitalizes on the locations you visit. Perhaps you travel to an area with a unique craft or product that you can import to your area.

If you aren't happy with where you live, finding your dream career right now isn't going to help much. No matter how good that job is, you won't enjoy it because you aren't content with your living situation. Your best bet is to shift gears for the moment to focus your attention on gaining clarity about where you want to live. Make a list of what isn't working about your current living location and another list of what you'd like to have. Do you have any ideas about where you'd like to live? Talk with the other members of your family to determine their needs and desires. Start investigating your target geographic areas by visiting the Quintessential Careers Web site (www.quintcareers.com/researching_companies.html) and scrolling down to the Key Tools for Conducting Country Research. After you have an idea where you'd like to live, become familiar with the local economy and job market to understand what opportunities exist there. Although it's not time to make any sudden moves, you're ready to reconnect with the question of your next career. With your ideal living location in mind, you have a much better chance of creating a career/life picture that meets your needs.

Recording What's Most Important to You at Home

Take a couple of minutes to review what you've written in the worksheets in this chapter:

- ✔ Worksheet 4-1: How Your Relationships Impact Your Work
- ✔ Worksheet 4-2: Factors That Define Your Personal Life
- ✔ Worksheet 4-3: Location Factors That Influence Your Career

Then write down five factors in your personal life that, if resolved, would allow you to love your life and your work more than you do now. These five factors, which you should enter into the relevant section in Worksheet 4-4, can help you evaluate potential career opportunities to see whether they're a good fit or whether they would produce too much conflict to consider.

Be as upfront as you possibly can be about what you want and need to feel fulfilled. Even if you don't or can't get all that you want, acknowledging and voicing what you truly want are the best ways to move your life and career in the direction you desire. Chapters 16 and 17 help you integrate your ideal career ideas with your ideal lifestyle.

Your Personal Life Wish List	
Your relationships	
Your home	
Your faith	
Your volunteer work	
Your hobbies/ interests	
Your fun time	
Your location	

Worksheet 4-4: Recording what you want in your personal life.

Chapter 5

Figuring Out How to Structure Your Work

More work arrangements exist now than in any other time in history. You can work as a full-time employee, a contract employee, or a sole proprietor. As an employee, you may find your employer offers flextime or telecommuting options. As an entrepreneur, you create your own schedule and workplace. Over time, you can create a blend of employment and self-employment or switch back and forth between those options as opportunities knock.

In recent years, companies have come up with a variety of innovative, cost-effective work arrangements to attract and retain talented employees, handle explosive growth, and weather unpredictable downturns. Understanding and remaining open to the options allow you to move into this fluid economy with more confidence and less fear.

The structure of your workweek and how you are paid impact how well your life and work blend together. Understanding what's now possible in the work world and gaining clarity about what works best for you puts you in a good position to make informed decisions about your future and to negotiate whatever you need to make your life work.

Making the Worksheets Work for You

Each worksheet in this chapter helps you explore and define what you want your work arrangement to look like. I encourage you to approach each worksheet with a sense of discovery. Explore what's possible in the world of work in general while paying close attention to what works best for you. As you work through each worksheet, check off the items that seem to fit your needs or that intrigue you in some way.

In some worksheets you may find it easy to say, "Yes, that one works best for me." Other topics, however, may leave you saying, "Ho-hum" because they don't appear, on the surface, to matter that much to you. Even if you don't seem to care one way or the other about a topic, think it through the best you can and take a stand. You never know what clarity and insight some additional thinking on the subject may bring you.

As you complete the worksheets in this chapter, if you hear yourself saying, "I guess I could do that," stop yourself on the spot. The second those words form in your mind, you're getting ready to settle, trying to force-fit yourself into something that *could* work but is not the best option for you. At this stage of the game, keep your focus on your ideal. Allow your mind to explore as many new options, new combinations, and new avenues as you can. Exploration brings to mind new solutions you haven't yet dreamed of.

If you feel drawn to work for yourself, answer the questions in this chapter as thoroughly as you can. Although the way you implement these ideas as a self-employed person may be a little different than what happens in corporate or governmental settings, the concepts themselves are still relevant to you and may stimulate new ways of thinking about your business structure. For additional thoughts on starting a business, see Chapter 19.

If you haven't already done so, I recommend that you take a few minutes to fill out the worksheets in Chapters 3 and 4 to help focus your thinking about the life you want your job to support. If you've already worked through these chapters, take a quick look at Worksheets 3-11 and 4-4 to bring your personal needs to mind.

Determining Your Ideal Work Schedule

If you think a 40-hour workweek is your only option, think again! Companies now offer a variety of work arrangements that give employees the opportunity to take on more flexible work schedules. Flexible schedules help employees reduce the stress and strain of balancing work and home, which in the long run is good business for the company. By offering flexible work arrangements, companies are better able to recruit and retain good employees, reduce absenteeism, and increase shareholder returns through increased employee productivity, creativity, and satisfaction.

Before you attempt to pin down which schedule options appeal to you, use the questions in Worksheet 5-1 to help you define your ideal work schedule. Without calculating anything or trying to figure out the right label for what you want, answer the questions in the worksheet according to what works best for you and your body.

After you've taken one pass through Worksheet 5-1, take another look with a different filter. Ask yourself how you may need to modify your ideal schedule to incorporate what works best for your family, pets, and social life. (Not to mention that you'd like to be home in time to watch *Oprah* every afternoon.) Note any conflicts or inconsistencies that arise as you compare what you need for yourself and what your family needs from you and your schedule. Don't worry about resolving these conflicts at this point; you don't yet have all the information you need to do so. Chapter 16 helps you sort out these conflicts and create workable solutions.

Based on what you discover about your needs and desires regarding time at work in Worksheet 5-1, explore your scheduling options. As you review the options in Worksheet 5-2, put a checkmark next to any scheduling options that help you meet your needs and those of your family.

Even if it doesn't feel like the various options in Worksheet 5-2 are possible, don't strike them from your mind just yet. With some proper prior planning and a well-written proposal, you can forge new trails in your company and community. If you want some assistance, visit the WorkOptions.com Web site (www.workoptions.com), which can take you through the step-by-step process of preparing your case.

Your Scheduling Needs	
Your best starting time?	
Your best quitting time?	
Number of breaks?	
Lunchtime?	
Maximum hours per week?	
Maximum hours per day?	
Which days do you want to work?	
What shift is best for you?	
Number of days per week?	
Any overtime?	
Preferred work pace?	
Need for flexibility to take care of personal appointments and emergencies?	
Ideal amount of paid time off for sick days and personal days?	
Ideal amount of vacation?	

Worksheet 5-1: Discovering what you need in terms of time at work.

In addition to a wider variety of work schedules to choose from, the new world of work also offers a number of contract formats.

Read each option in Worksheet 5-3 and put a checkmark next to any that appeal to you. Consider each of the possibilities, even if they seem out of reach to you at the moment.

The work world is far more fluid than you may have expected when you started working. Although you may be most comfortable with the stability of a full-time job, the realities of the current economy may require you to step beyond your comfort zone to take on a short-term contract or part-time job on occasion. Taking such opportunities allows you to get your foot in the door — and you never know when the company's budget or strategic plan may open up to create a full-time opening. Even if a new position doesn't open up, you've had money coming in the door and you've acquired a new set of skills and experience to strengthen your resume and keep it current.

Worksheet 5-2: Taking charge of your work schedule.

Your Scheduling Options	
❏ Flextime	Working the standard number of hours but starting work, with the manager's permission, at a specific time either earlier or later than the company's standard. Your quitting time shifts to account for your start time.
❏ Gliding schedule	Arriving at work at any time during a flexible band of time without your manager's permission as long as you're at work during the required core hours.
❏ Variable day	Working any number of hours per day as long as you work a total of 40 hours by week's end.
❏ Completely flexible work schedule	Choosing when you work on a daily basis. As long as you get your work done, neither the company nor your manager care how many hours you work.
❏ Shortened workday	Reducing the hours you work each day to five, six, or seven hours.
❏ Shortened workweek	Working the same number of hours each day for four days a week instead of five.
❏ Compressed workweek	Working your 40 hours in less than the typical five days. Several schedules are used. For example: • Four 10-hour workdays each week • Three 12-hour workdays each week • Nine 9-hour workdays over two weeks with the tenth day off
❏ Variable week	Working any days you please as long as you put in 80 hours over a two-week period.
❏ Ad-hoc time off	Having the understanding with your company or manager that you can take off a prearranged amount of time to address family emergencies, medical appointments, children's events, or other issues that must be handled during regular business hours.

Worksheet 5-3: Considering your contract options.

Your Contract Possibilities	
❏ Full-time	Work 40 or more hours per week as a full-fledged employee of the company receiving full pay and benefits.
❏ Part-time	Work less than 40 hours a week by shortening your days or your workweek. Expect your pay to be commensurate with the hours you work and verify your workload is cut to match your reduced hours. Depending on the company's policies, you may or may not receive benefits.
❏ Job-share	Share a full-time job with another employee by splitting up the time worked each week, the pay, and the vacation time. You may act interchangeably and share the duties equally or split the duties according to each person's expertise.
❏ Gradual retirement	Work a reduced number of hours as soon as you become eligible for retirement. Depending on the arrangement, your reduced hours may be for a limited time or for an extended period of time.
❏ Temporary employee/ contractor	Work through a staffing firm or temporary agency, which places you in companies to work as long as they need you, whether it's for a couple days or several months. You can expect the staffing firm to take care of your taxes and to offer you benefits of some sort. At the end of your stint, you may have the option to convert to a permanent status depending on the company's needs and your interest. This option allows you to check out a company and find out whether you want to work there on a long-term basis.
❏ Consultant	Contract with a company to work for a specified length of time or on a specific project. You may be asked to sign up for another round if they like your work or the project is not yet completed. As an independent, you're required to handle your own taxes and provide your own benefits.
❏ Freelancer	Work independently doing projects for one company or several companies at once. You may work very hard for several months and then have a few lighter months; it all depends on the jobs and clients you find and take on, over which you have total control.
❏ Self-employed	You have no contract at all — except to yourself! Run your own business to provide a product or service directly to your customers. Your tasks expand to include marketing, sales, accounting, fulfillment, and shipping, which means you wear and juggle many hats every day.

Getting Paid on Your Terms

Obviously, one of the key reasons you work is to make an income and have access to benefits that make your life easier and less stressful. As you consider changing careers, being aware of your income and benefit requirements puts you in a strong position to negotiate or create what you need in your next career.

One crucial number to know as you enter into your career change is the income you need to live the way you want to live. This number isn't necessarily the amount you live on now, but includes the money you need to do the things you've always wanted to do — whether it's putting a fish pond in your backyard, taking an annual fly-fishing trip to Montana, or starting the savings account you've been talking about for the last decade or so.

Use Worksheet 5-4 to make a ballpark estimate of what it takes for you to live comfortably. As you develop various career options in Part IV, return to this calculation to assess whether your target career provides you with an annual income that meets your needs.

After you figure out what your annual income needs to be, divide your estimated annual income by 12 to determine your monthly income requirement. You'll also probably want to talk with your accountant to understand your tax situation and how that impacts your take-home pay. If you're interested in looking to the future, complete Worksheet 5-4 for each of the next three years. This result shows you how your income needs are likely to change over the years.

If you're thinking of relocating, you may need to adjust your calculations for the cost of living in the new area. To get an idea of these costs, visit the Salary.com Web site at www.salary.com and look for the Cost-of-Living Wizard to determine the power of your salary in your new area.

Your Annual Income Needs	Your Estimate
1. What do you expect to spend to live your life next year? Base your calculations on what it cost you to live last year. If you use a bookkeeping program, this number should be easy to find. If not, scan your check register and credit card statements to see how much you spent. You can also look at your total income last year and add in credit card charges that you made but couldn't pay off during the last year.	$ _____
2. What amount of money do you need to save this year for large purchases you expect to make in the next few years? For example, think about any pending major purchases, like a car or a house, or other large cash outlays, like college tuition for yourself or your children.	$ _____
3. How much debt would you like to pay off next year? Consider outstanding credit card balances, loans from family members, car loans, and equity lines of credit.	$ _____
4. How much would you like to be able to put away into a savings account or investment account each year? Think about establishing an emergency fund, vacation account, college funds for your children, investment account, and retirement plans.	$ _____
5. How much additional income do you need to enhance your life and fulfill your dreams next year? For example, if you want a different day care situation, factor in the added cost. If you want to travel more frequently, include a travel budget. If you plan to have a child, estimate the additional costs for at least the first year or two.	$ _____
Your Estimated Annual Income:	$ _____

Worksheet 5-4: Estimating your income requirements.

Another useful number to have in your back pocket is the least amount of money you could live on for one year. I'm not suggesting that this number is helpful for everyone. However, sometimes paring back your lifestyle and decreasing your need for income can open up interesting options that give you the freedom to step into a new, more fulfilling life. For example, knowing your minimal income gives you added decision-making power if you ever decide you want to start a business (see Chapter 19), cut back your hours, return to school (see Chapter 19), or take a sabbatical to travel. To determine your minimal income needs, carefully evaluate all of your monthly expenses and socializing costs to see what you could do without while making a transition to a new career or lifestyle.

In addition to considering how much money you need to make, consider how often and in what form you need to get paid. Receiving pay for the work you do is no longer always as simple as earning an hourly wage or an annual salary. Companies use a variety of methods to pay employees, temporary or contract workers, independent consultants, expert consultants, and freelancers. Some methods of payment are more consistent and predictable than others in terms of the dollar amount and the expected pay period. For example, you could get paid by the project, by how much you sell, or based on the company's profits.

As you read each description in Worksheet 5-5, put a check mark next to any form of payment you would consider in your next career.

Worksheet 5-5: Deciding how you want to receive your income.

Your Payment Options	
❏ Hourly	Get a check for the hours you worked during the pay period.
❏ Salary	Get a check on a regular, dependable basis for a consistent amount each pay period.
❏ By project	Receive payment for work done on a project. May be paid at predetermined milestones as progress is made.
❏ Commission	Earn a percentage of everything you sell. Sometimes combined with a base salary.
❏ Royalties	Earn a percentage on the sale of something you wrote or created.
❏ Bonus	Receive an extra check as a reward after the completion of a big project, at the end of the year, after cost-savings goals are met, when statistical improvements are made in a project's quality, or for signing on with a new company.
❏ Stock options	Have the option to buy company stocks at a fixed price. Your eligibility for this may be influenced by your tenure in the company, your level, and the rules that govern the company's stock program. Do your research to understand how this complex payment option works in the company.
❏ Profit sharing	Share in the profits of the company. The amount you receive depends on how well the company did during the year.

For more information about payment options, visit www.salary.com and click on Salary Advice on the home page to check out the base salary and stock options sections.

Matching Benefits to Your Needs

Although at this point you can't know for sure what benefits any future employer may offer, you can determine the benefits that are most important to you and your family. If you're considering self-employment or you plan to work for short-term stints at various companies, this exercise proves extremely important, because you won't have a company providing your benefits. Instead, you must understand your needs thoroughly enough to search out ways to provide for the benefits that you and your family need.

If you currently get your benefits through your spouse's employment, you may be tempted to skip this worksheet. Think again. In the current economic landscape, you have no guarantee that you'll always have access to these benefits. Your spouse could be laid off, or the company could be sold to another company that changes the mix of benefits. You need to know exactly what benefits are required to cover your family's needs so that, if required, you can cover these benefits yourself.

In Worksheet 5-6, put a check mark next to any benefits you feel are relevant to you and your family. Don't concern yourself with where the benefits will come from. By having a clear picture of the benefits you need, whether they come through a company or by purchasing them directly, you can assess whether your target careers are a good fit for you and your family.

Your Benefits	
❏ Medical insurance	Covers visits to your doctor and catastrophic health problems.
❏ Dental insurance	Covers visits to your dentist.
❏ Eye care insurance	Covers visits to your eye doctor.
❏ Long-term and short-term disability	Provides replacement income if you should become incapacitated due to illness or accident. This benefit is most important if you have children or a mortgage.
❏ Severance package	Provides money that allows you to transition into your next job. Finding out whether you have the benefit during the hiring process might seem awkward, but it's better to know how the system works before any sparks fly.
❏ Life insurance	Protects the financial well-being of your family in case of your death.
❏ Child care	Provides assistance to employees with children. Options vary by company, from an on-site or near-site child care center that is run or supported by the company to financial subsidies, resources and referral system, options for sick-child care, summer programs, and back-up care.
❏ Elder care	Includes a combination of resources, referrals, seminars, support groups, and long-term insurance for family members to help employees who must care for elderly or ill parents or grandparents. This benefit is gaining popularity as employees take on more and more caregiver responsibilities.
❏ Employee assistance program	Refers you to a counselor if you're wrestling with personal issues that are distracting you from your work. After a few appointments, you may be referred to a counselor who is covered through your medical insurance.
❏ Retirement	Establishes a retirement fund, such as a 401(k), that allows you to contribute pre-tax dollars to your next egg. The company may match your contribution dollar for dollar. If you're close to retirement age and expect to be with the company when you retire, ask about other benefits, such as health insurance, that come to you upon retirement. Make sure to ask how long before you qualify to receive retirement benefits.
❏ Parking/commuting	Provides on-site parking, subsidized off-site parking, or tokens for commuters.
❏ Convenience or concierge services	Eliminates tasks from your to-do list and frees up your time and your mind to work more productively. Independent contractors hired by your company provide a variety of services that may include dry cleaning, housecleaning, take-home meals, pet care, on-site chair massage, legal services, financial consulting, and social outings. Although you generally pay for the services you use, the peace of mind and simplification of your life may make them worthwhile.
❏ Expense account	Gives you a per diem amount or charge card you use to handle expenses while you're away from the office. Depending on your work, you may be assigned a company car, as well.
❏ Community service opportunities	Allows you to take off work hours to volunteer through corporate volunteer programs or more informal arrangements.
❏ Health club	Gives you access to an on-site gym or a full or discounted membership to a nearby gym.

Worksheet 5-6: Thinking through your benefits.

Visit www.salary.com and click on the Salary Advice link to read more about various benefits.

Recording Your Ideal Work Arrangement

Now that you're aware of the wide range of possibilities that exist when it comes to how time and money can work in your career, start creating your ideal picture in Worksheet 5-7. Take a look back at each worksheet in this chapter and pull forward the key features of your ideal work arrangement. Factor in your needs and priorities and those of your family as you describe each feature laid out in Worksheet 5-7.

If your ideal profile looks like a stable, 8-to-5 job with a guaranteed two-week vacation, I encourage you to take another look at this chapter to see how you might expand your options a bit. The days of the secure, career for life are numbered. Even if you had a stable career up until now, don't expect the next ten years to look like the past. In the future, you may have periods of time when you work as an independent consultant, a contract employee, or in a virtual work situation where the majority of your contact with colleagues is long distance. To thrive in the new economy, you must build some flexibility into your picture. If you don't, the current economic realities and trends may do it for you.

Expect to have some loose ends at this stage of the process. You don't yet know enough to tie up all the details. It's okay. In fact, this is a good opportunity to practice sitting with your confusion and allowing the pieces of your puzzle to fall into place as they come to you. If you see obvious inconsistencies or conflicts, hang tight and sort them out in Chapter 16.

Your Ideal Work Arrangement	
Your work schedule	
Your contract	
Amount of pay	
Pay options	
Benefits	

Worksheet 5-7:
How you hope your work is structured.

Chapter 6

Defining Your Preferred Workplace

· ·

In This Chapter

▶ Determining the company type, size, and culture you prefer

▶ Looking at the purpose, reach, and location of your company

▶ Defining your ideal workspace and dress code

▶ Identifying the kinds of people you enjoy working with

▶ Creating a profile of your ideal workplace

· ·

You spend anywhere from 40 to 60 percent of your waking hours at work. With all the time you spend working, you need to work in a place that aligns with who you are — at least you do if you want to be happy with your career. Each worksheet in this chapter helps you discern the kind of company, work area, and work community that best fit your professional and personal needs and wants.

In Worksheet 6-13 at the end of the chapter, you review everything you've checked off in Worksheets 6-1 through 6-12 to create a profile that best describes your ideal workplace.

 Even if a question in one of the worksheets doesn't seem to matter to you one way or the other, force yourself to take a stand on the question anyway. Doing so ensures that you fully consider all of the issues that play a part in selecting a fulfilling career. At the same time, mark only those choices that truly excite and intrigue you. "I could do that" is not a valid response; thinking this way leads you off the path of finding out how you really want to work.

The Kind of Company

When you think of working for a company, you probably think of large, publicly held companies, without realizing all the other options that exist.

As you read about the culture inherent in each kind of company listed in Worksheet 6-1, check off the types of companies that appeal to you.

Type of Company	
❑ Not-for-profit	Fulfills its mission by supporting a cause in a way that makes the company exempt from paying taxes. Because funding usually comes from grants and fundraising efforts, employees may need to be creative to accomplish the company's goals.
❑ Education	Educates people of any age. Schools and academia have a culture that values learning and teaching above all else. The schedule matches the school year, which often means long interim breaks.
❑ Government	Provides services to citizens through government agencies based on programs established by legislation. The culture is fairly stable, although changes may occur when leadership changes.
❑ Public company	Strives to satisfy the stockholders and customers by providing successful services and products. All records are open to the public, which gives you a clearer understanding of how the company is doing before and after you start working there. Public companies tend to be mature and larger in size than other kinds of companies.
❑ Start up, pre-IPO (Initial Public Offering)	Pushes to create a viable product, capture market share, and eventually go public. Start-ups by their very nature (being in the initial stages of building a business) tend to be very fast-paced with a fair amount of scrambling to stay ahead of the wave. Some have funding or venture capital support, which creates additional stability.
❑ Virtual company	Run by a number of people in various geographic locations. Although they may meet in person occasionally, the bulk of their interactions with each other and with customers are done virtually through various forms of technology.
❑ Privately-held company	Owned by an individual or a small group of private investors and has no intention of going public. The company's culture and product lines are likely to be fairly stable. The degrees of flexibility, employee participation, and experimentation depend on the owners and their relationships with the staff.
❑ Family-owned	Owned and operated by one family that may have founded the business. Family dynamics and traditions are usually a part of the in-house politics.
❑ Partner-owned	Run by two people. Assessing the stability and sanity of their relationship gives you an idea of the culture of the company.
❑ Home-based	Run out of someone's home. It's likely to be comfortable and casual, though may be somewhat cramped and prone to family-related interruptions and crises.

Worksheet 6-1: Forming ideas about the kind of company you'd like to work for.

The Company Size

The size of a company also impacts its inherent culture. Typically, the larger the company, the more layers of management and bureaucratic structure you must contend with to get results. In this kind of setting, you probably work in a formal, more impersonal environment than someone who works in a smaller company. Smaller companies often have a more casual feel to them, allowing more access to the top brass and more flexibility to try new strategies.

As you read Worksheet 6-2, imagine yourself in each setting and check off the company sizes that seem to fit your needs. Use your prior experiences and what you know about yourself from Chapter 3 to make these decisions.

Company Size	
❑ Sole proprietor	One person runs the show — you. You play the roles of Chief Executive Officer and Chief Bottle Washer and everything in between. Graphic designers, career counselors, and travel agents who work solo are examples.
❑ Partnership	Two individuals come together to form and run a business such as a restaurant, a retail store, or a consulting company.
❑ Micro business	Four or fewer employees run the business together. Typical examples are a gardening service, a cart-vending business, a booth at a farmers market, and an online business venture.
❑ Small company	Fewer than 1,000 employees. Scitor, Fenwick & West, and David Weekley Homes are examples.
❑ Mid-size company	Between 1,000 and 10,000 employees. Examples are Genentech, Adobe Systems, and Pella.
❑ Large company	Between 10,000 and 100,000 employees. Hewlett Packard, Southwest Airlines, Deloitte and Touche, Merck, Four Seasons Hotels, and Wegmans Food Markets are examples.
❑ Gigantic company	Over 100,000 employees. Examples are Wal-Mart, FedEx, and McDonald's.

Worksheet 6-2: Considering the size of the company you want to work for.

For more examples of companies of various sizes, consult the 100 Best Companies to Work for in America and the Best Small and Medium Companies to Work for in America on the Great Place to Work Web site (www.greatplacetowork.com). The site also has lists of the best companies to work for in Europe, Latin America, and Asia.

Although a big company used to mean that your job was secure, shifts in the economic reality mean that your job could be lifted out from under you regardless of the company's size. Keep your skills up-to-date, your network in place, and a clear picture of where your career is headed. Sometimes a surprise departure from one company brings unexpected opportunities from other corners.

Small businesses have an unbelievably large impact on the economy. Twenty-four million small businesses in the United States make up 99.7 percent of the employers. These businesses employ over 50 percent of the people in the private work force and have generated three-quarters of all new positions over the last decade. In addition to contributing the majority of innovations created in the United States, they also are a great source of employment for first-time employees, older workers, and women. When you start looking at potential employers, don't count small businesses out.

The Company Culture

Although the company size has a hand in how your experience of work plays out, don't underestimate the impact that the overall company culture has on your life. Becoming aware of the variables that make up a company's culture allows you to ask your interviewers crucial questions to verify that their culture matches your career goals and personal needs.

If you're considering a future as a sole proprietor, you create your company culture from scratch. Allow the characteristics in the following list to give you insights about how you want to position your company culture for yourself, your clients, and your customers.

In Worksheet 6-3, place an arrow next to each characteristic you'd use to describe your ideal company culture. This is not the time to restrain yourself. Be as idealistic and optimistic as possible as you use this worksheet to identify the culture you want in your next career.

Company Culture Concepts		

Is ethical
Is honest
Gives back to the community
Is prestigious and well-known
Encourages the participation
  of family members at
  social events
Promotes cultural diversity
Focuses on quality
Is customer driven
Values creativity
Is fiscally responsible
Has sound business practices
Focuses on the bottom line
Is profit driven
Is based on cutting-edge
  technology
	Focuses on wellness
	Is respectful of employees
	Encourages employees to
	  keep reasonable work hours
	Demonstrates flexibility
	Is environmentally aware
	Is socially responsible
	Values the contribution of
	  women and minorities
	Allows me to be myself
	  (clothing, lifestyle, values,
	  and so on)
	Is casual
	Is highly professional
	Is formal
	Has a hierarchical structure
	Is down-to-earth
		Is informal
		Promotes open
		  communication
		Is friendly
		Emphasizes teamwork
		Has a cooperative
		  environment
		Has high professional
		  standards
		Thrives on pressure
		Competes aggressively
		Challenges me
		Is a fun place to work
		Focuses on results
		Is forward thinking
		Is innovative
		Stresses excellence

Worksheet 6-3: Exploring ways to describe your ideal company culture.

Record your top six company culture characteristics in Worksheet 6-4. Next to each characteristic explain why this characteristic is important to you. Exploring your thoughts about each characteristic helps you be as specific as possible about the character of the company you want to work for. If you want a company culture characteristic that you don't see on the preceding list, add it to this one.

Your Desired Cultural Characteristics	Reason This Characteristic Is Important to You
1.	
2.	
3.	
4.	
5.	
6.	

Worksheet 6-4: Picturing the best company culture for you.

The Purpose of the Company

A company that manufactures products differs significantly from one that conducts research. A company's purpose influences its culture, the kinds of jobs it offers, its organizational structure, and its language. As you think about your options, you may realize that you feel at home in one company and like a fish out of water in another.

As you read Worksheet 6-5, notice how you may feel when you think about providing these products and services to customers. Use check marks to indicate any company purposes that match your interests. Even if you don't know the specifics of each kind of environment, pay attention to your initial response to each description. Those that seem interesting may be worth exploring further (see Chapter 14 for more information). Feel free to mark as many as work for you.

Company Purpose	
❏ Provides professional services	Client companies are helped in an intangible way through legal assistance, accounting, consulting services, photographic services, architectural services, advertising services, and management services.
❏ Manufactures a product	Consumers can touch or hold in their hands what the company produces — for example, cars, computers, clothing, or furniture.
❏ Produces, transmits, or processes information	A variety of companies work with information from broadcasting companies, Internet companies, and publishing houses to software producers, telecommunications providers, and motion picture houses.
❏ Does research	Work done in research institutes, think tanks, and institutes of higher education creates new information and inventions.
❏ Entertains	People laugh and enjoy themselves as a result of the company's work.
❏ Sells trade	Goods reach consumers because they've been sold through wholesale and retail channels.
❏ Constructs and builds	Buildings and engineering projects take shape as a result of the company's efforts.
❏ Educates others	People of all ages and walks of life learn skills, knowledge, and new perspectives from the company's efforts.
❏ Provides health care	Using medical care and social assistance, the company provides support to those in need.
❏ Engages in financial or real estate activities	Whether it's financial transactions, insurance, or real estate, your company works with money in a number of ways.
❏ Manages natural resources	Working with natural resources involves raising and tending crops, animals, timber, and fish as well as extracting minerals from the earth.
❏ Supports operations of other companies	The company supports other companies in handling day-to-day operations including staffing, clerical services, security, and collections.
❏ Provides transportation	The company uses a particular mode of transportation to get passengers or cargo to the final destination.
❏ Deals with utilities	Utility services include electrical power, natural gas, water supply, and sewage removal.

Worksheet 6-5: Looking at the purpose of different types of companies.

The Company's Reach

Each company reaches out to its customers, whether they're local clients who come into the shop or global customers whose main contact is over the Web. Think about the kinds of contact you wish to have with your customers or clients. Do you want face-to-face conversations? Would you prefer phone contact? Even if you don't work directly with customers, this question is important because the way the business reaches its customers may impact the work pace, the hours of operations, the technology used, and the extent to which you travel.

Look at the options in Worksheet 6-6 to get a sense of which kind of experience works for you. Mark as many as you like.

Worksheet 6-6:
Scoping out the reach of potential companies.

Company Reach	
❑ Local	Business focuses on local clients and their needs, which means someone working in this business is likely to have face-to-face interactions with clients.
❑ Statewide	Business and operations are located in one state.
❑ Regional	Company serves a particular geographic region.
❑ National	Company focuses attention on one country. A company this large may have branches or departments across the country, which means you may have co-workers you work with only online, by phone, or during brief visits.
❑ Global	Company has a presence throughout the world with its products and services as well as its operations. Note: Any Web-based company has a global scope. Most if not all interactions with clients are likely to be via e-mail, fax, instant message, phone, and videoconferencing.

The Location

The location of your company definitely impacts you, your commute, your ability to get things done on your lunch hour, and your general comfort level. Next to each factor in Worksheet 6-7, spell out your ideal picture for each element.

If you want to run your own business, the decisions you make about your location depend on a number of additional factors, including zoning, foot traffic, availability, and rents. If you think you want to work from home, your answers to the questions in Worksheet 6-7 can help you verify your desire. For more information on starting your own business, see Chapter 19.

Traveling for business, whether occasionally or constantly, can be exciting, disruptive, exhilarating, and exhausting all at once. If you want travel to be part of your career, take some time to think about how far and how often you want to travel. Clearly visualizing your ideal travel schedule helps you make good decisions, when the time comes, about the fit between you and a prospective job. Consider your personal and family priorities as you set your intentions.

Your Work Location	
Acceptable commute distance?	
Any safety requirements?	
Ideal parking situation?	
Preference for surrounding neighborhood or area?	
Required amenities close to work?	
Best place to find the food you want?	
Ideal exterior surroundings?	
Preferred feel of interior?	
Work from home at all?	
Travel for work?	
Have a mobile office?	
Work outside?	

Worksheet 6-7: Thinking about your work location.

The Work Area

Productivity is the name of the game when it comes to work. Do you know what characteristics you need in your personal work space to be efficient, productive, and fulfilled? Although you may not always get *exactly* what you want, knowing your ideal work area requirements may help you steer away from a job with an office space that is definitely counterproductive for you. For example, if the thought of sitting in a cubicle five days a week makes your skin crawl, you may need to look beyond the traditional work space to find happiness.

Worksheet 6-8 lists elements of your personal work space that can enhance or detract from your productivity and satisfaction. Check the ones that strike a chord in you and add any notes to clarify and specify your needs in more detail.

Your Personal Work Space	
❏ Cubicle or office?	
❏ Door you can close?	
❏ Shared office space?	
❏ Privacy requirements?	
❏ Lighting preferences?	
❏ Noise factor?	
❏ Animals in your office?	
❏ Foot traffic?	
❏ Windows?	
❏ View from your window?	
❏ Office colors?	
❏ Feel of office?	
❏ Furniture needs?	
❏ Equipment required?	
❏ Supplies needed?	
❏ Storage space needs?	
❏ Work space needs?	
❏ Meeting space preferences?	

Worksheet 6-8: Laying out your ideal work area.

If you notice as you fill out Worksheets 6-7 and 6-8 that working in a closed building of any variety stresses you out, this section may offer valuable clues about your next career. Would you prefer to work outside? Do you need to move around at will? Would traveling to several locations throughout the week help? Whatever you do, pay attention to your body's response to help you make the right decisions.

The Dress Code

If your comfort or ability to express yourself are tantamount to your happiness, how you dress for work each day may prove to be very important to you. If not, you may consider skipping Worksheet 6-9. Before you settle into thinking that you must wear what you've always worn to work, think about what really makes you happy.

Place a check mark in Worksheet 6-9 next to the dress code that makes you most comfortable. If several options appeal to you depending on your tasks for the day, choose the three that "suit" you best.

Worksheet 6-9: Getting dressed for work.

Your Dress Preferences	
❑ Uniform	Company-specified outfit.
❑ Professional	Formal attire, which may consist of a suit and tie for men and a suit and heels for women.
❑ Professional casual	Coordinated outfits, such as a pair of slacks and a matching shirt or pullover sweater.
❑ Self-expressive	Wardrobe that uses accessories, colors, and designs to add personal flair is encouraged.
❑ Comfortable	Jeans and T-shirt, for example.
❑ Ultra-comfortable	Work clothes, sweats, PJs, your favorite plaid flannel robe and slippers, or perhaps even nothing at all.

Working with the Right People

The people you interact with at work influence how much you enjoy your job, whether they're your co-workers, those who come in-house to perform tasks, or your manager.

Although you can't always choose your colleagues, you can determine the kinds of relationships that work best for you. After you know what you're looking for, if you spot a problem right off the bat in an interview, you know that job isn't for you. For example if you find the hiring manager is overbearing when talking with his assistant or your potential co-workers are a bit snobbish when interacting with you, you may want to think twice about joining this work team. If they're behaving this way when they should be on their best behavior, just imagine what it might be like to work with them on a full-time basis!

If you want to work solo, the term *co-worker* may seem a little off base. In your situation, your co-workers are your colleagues, professionals in your trade association, or people you team up with to work on a particular project.

Think about two of your favorite co-workers over the years. What elements of your working relationship made it work so well? Next, think about two of your least favorite co-workers. What was it about these relationships that made it so hard? To get the full picture in both cases, think of their personalities, style of communication, work style and pace, strengths and weaknesses, and how you socialized with them during and after work hours. Make notes about these four relationships in Worksheet 6-10.

Pull the six most important characteristics from Worksheet 6-10 and record them in the first column of Worksheet 6-11. In the second column, describe why you included each characteristic in your list.

Learning from Your Co-workers	
Favorite Co-worker #1: _____	Favorite Co-worker #2: _____
Least Favorite Co-worker #1: _____	Least Favorite Co-worker #2: _____

Worksheet 6-10: Reminiscing about former co-workers.

Key Co-worker Characteristics	Why Is This Characteristic Important to You?
1.	
2.	
3.	
4.	
5.	
6.	

Worksheet 6-11: Picturing your ideal co-worker.

In an interviewing situation, evaluating your potential co-workers may be hard to do. You may not meet all of them, and if you do, the interaction may be so superficial that you can't make a true assessment of the fit. If you're switching jobs or careers within the same company, your prospective co-workers may play a bigger role in your decision-making process because you may have had an opportunity to interact with them on prior occasions. In either case, trust your intuitive gut sense of your prospective co-workers. Chapter 19 gives you pointers on how to evaluate a position based on the information you gain during an interview.

In this day and age, the people who make up your work team may not be employed by the same company you are. Understanding the various roles people have as they contribute to a company helps you understand the interactions within the company.

The following roles are relevant whether you work in a large company or on your own:

- **Expert consultants:** Hired to use their expertise to resolve specific problems or situations. Often their role and the work they do is dictated by the proposal they themselves create to land the job. Whether they're self-employed or employed by a consulting firm, they may work on other projects for other companies while working on a project for your company.

- **Freelancers:** Complete their piece of the project independently and may submit their work electronically, although they may interact with others to discover what they need to know to get the job done. They typically work on a number of projects for different customers simultaneously.

- **Independent consultants:** Come into the company for the duration of a project as needed to provide a key skill or piece of knowledge that no one within the company has.

- **Temporary employees/contract employees:** Fill in on a short-term basis when a regular employee is out or there's a project crunch and no one within the organization can handle it.

- **Vendors:** Provide your company with key materials for projects and may offer support for the piece they supply.

- **Virtual assistants:** Work from their own offices to provide you with the support you need to get your work done. Great for entrepreneurs and small business owners who don't have the space or financial resources to employ a full-time assistant. For more information about virtual assistants, visit www.assistu.com.

You may talk with your prospective manager during your interview. By knowing the management style that allows you to be most productive, you can ask direct, carefully worded questions to discern whether each prospective manager is someone you can work with productively.

If you're your own boss or planning to be, Worksheet 6-12 requires you to create a split personality for a moment. Answer the questions as accurately as you can as an employee, thinking all the while about how you can better manage yourself.

Use Worksheet 6-12 to record what your manager can do to make you more productive and fulfilled. Begin by putting a check mark next to all of the qualities and traits that your perfect manager would have and then go back and circle the six that are most important to you.

My Best Manager . . .
❏ Tells me what's truly important about a project
❏ Appreciates me and my work
❏ Shares credit for a job well done
❏ Emphasizes results over methods
❏ Communicates expectations clearly
❏ Gives clear instructions
❏ Sets realistic deadlines
❏ Communicates openly about upcoming problems or changes in projects, the staff, or the company structure
❏ Pitches in when the staff is in a bind
❏ Reflects my strengths back to me so I can see them too
❏ Recognizes my contribution
❏ Tells me how I'm doing
❏ Gives me constructive feedback
❏ Treats me with respect
❏ Hires competent co-workers and deals with incompetent ones
❏ Shows compassion and patience if I'm going through a rough time
❏ Trusts me enough to let me do the job the way I believe it needs to be done
❏ Lets me learn and grow from my mistakes
❏ Considers my ideas and those of others
❏ Answers my questions
❏ Speaks truthfully
❏ Laughs with me and sees the lighter side of things
❏ Models what I need to know to do my job well
❏ Keeps promises
❏ Shares the information I need to be effective
❏ Gives me training, resources, and space to do my job
❏ Mentors me
❏ Helps me grow in my career
❏ Helps me see the big picture
❏ Makes fair decisions

Worksheet 6-12: Visualizing the perfect manager for you.

Recording Aspects of Your Preferred Workplace

Use what you discovered throughout this chapter to build a profile of your ideal work situation. Record your ideas in Worksheet 6-13. Be as explicit as possible about what you want and need in your workplace. As you select each element to include in your profile, factor in your priorities and those of your family. Don't worry if you see obvious inconsistencies or conflicts. You can sort those out in Chapter 16.

Your Ideal Workplace	
Kind of company	
Company size	
Company purpose	
Company reach	
Company location	
Your work area	
The dress code	
Your co-workers	
Other players	
Your manager	

Worksheet 6-13: What you wish you had at work.

When you finish your profile, read it over. If your first response is "I want to work at a place like that!" you're on the right track.

 After you read your profile, you may feel a bit discouraged or doubtful. You may worry that such a place doesn't exist and that you're wasting your time to even think about it. Don't let yourself drop into this downward spiral for too long. Instead keep your focus on what works for you. It's true that you may have to make trade-offs in the future, but in the long run you're still going to come out ahead if you're clear about your needs and desires.

Part II
Finding Your Passions

The 5th Wave   By Rich Tennant

"I know he'd be happier in a job he didn't have to take home with him at night."

In this part . . .

Are you still searching for the answer to the age-old question: What am I going to do when I grow up? This part guides you through a brainstorming process to identify your passions and interests. With those clues in hand, you brainstorm several dozen viable career ideas. By the end, you narrow your focus to your top two career ideas.

Chapter 7

Uncovering Skills That Make Time Fly

Surely you have experienced a time when you were so intrigued and involved with what you were doing that you completely lost track of the time. Time flew by, stood still, or seemed to warp in some unusual way. The skills and activities that create that feeling provide valuable clues to discovering a career that you love.

Unfortunately, it can sometimes prove difficult after such an experience to retrace your steps and say for sure what was so intriguing. Use the worksheets in this chapter as triggers to help you uncover or rediscover the skills and activities that bring you this pleasure and satisfaction. By the end of the chapter, you have a list of your Top 20 Favorite Skills to use in Chapter 9 as you brainstorm new career ideas for yourself.

If you get a career idea right off the bat that you want to run with, stop. I encourage you to stick with the process to create as detailed a list as you can. The depth and richness of your entire skill list make the worksheets in Chapter 9 as effective as possible.

Determining Your Innate Areas of Intelligence

Each person possesses natural talents or intelligence in one or more areas. The trick is to figure out in what ways you're naturally gifted and to let your talents guide you to your future career.

During your school years, you most likely thought that good verbal and mathematical skills indicated intelligence, while other talents did not. Thanks to research by Howard Gardner, author of *Frames of Mind: The Theory of Multiple Intelligences,* published by Basic Books, we now know that intelligence encompasses a variety of talents from traditional signs of intelligence to more creative demonstrations of intelligence such as interpersonal skills, musical skills, athletic skills, and artistic skills. In addition, the fact that someone has limited abilities in one area doesn't mean that a person has limited abilities in other areas. In fact, most people tend to excel in two or three areas of the intelligence.

To discover where your talents fall, complete Worksheet 7-1, which is based on seven of the most common intelligences. As you read each section, place a check mark next to any skills you know you have or enjoy. The items in the worksheet are grouped so that similar skills are close together. If you find that a skill you have isn't listed, add it to the list in the extra spaces provided.

Before you get started, take a look at a real-life example. Linda, a meeting planner from Florida, has some skills using words, but she doesn't consider this area to be one of her best strengths. See Figure 7-1 for the first section of Linda's Multiple Intelligence Profile, the place to start when determining your own multiple intelligences.

As Linda completed this section of the checklist, she found skills she uses in her current work (using proper grammar, editing, impromptu speaking, and using basic writing skills, which she wrote in) and some skills she uses in her volunteer work at the library (dramatic reading and storytelling). She also realized that within her stories she always includes vivid descriptions of characters and locations. Before she read this list, she hadn't realized she had that skill.

As you complete Worksheet 7-1, you may find that you check more items or fewer items than Linda did. Your goal is not to check a specific number of items, but to know that each item you select is a skill you have or enjoy in your work or your personal activities. You'll naturally have more skills in some areas than others.

Linda's Multiple Intelligence Profile			
Do you think in words?			
	Using a rich vocabulary		Writing complex documents
✓	Using proper grammar	✓	Editing
	Incorporating figures of speech		Reading with great comprehension
	Using mnemonics		Appreciating poetry
	Creating words	✓	Dramatic reading
	Knowing the meaning of words		Making presentations
	Deciphering the derivation of words		Debating
	Solving word puzzles	✓	Impromptu speaking
	Keeping a journal	✓	Storytelling
	Taking notes		Using humor
	Writing creatively		Memorizing names, dates, and details
✓	Creating vivid descriptions	✓	Using basic writing skills
	Writing poetry		

Figure 7-1:
Linda identifies her favorite skills.

Your Multiple Intelligence Profile	
Do you think in words?	
Using a rich vocabulary	Writing complex documents
Using proper grammar	Editing
Incorporating figures of speech	Reading with great comprehension
Using mnemonics	Appreciating poetry
Creating words	Dramatic reading
Knowing the meaning of words	Making presentations
Deciphering the derivation of words	Debating
Solving word puzzles	Impromptu speaking
Keeping a journal	Storytelling
Taking notes	Using humor
Writing creatively	Memorizing names, dates, and details
Creating vivid descriptions	
Using a rich vocabulary	
Writing poetry	
Do you think in a logical, organized fashion?	
Outlining	Organizing
Using flow charts and diagrams	Scheduling
Counting	Processing logic questions rapidly
Estimating	Seeing cause and effect
Quantifying	Planning events
Doing straight-forward calculations	Planning projects
Doing complex calculations	Prioritizing
Doing calculations in your head	Dividing up tasks
Using abstract symbols	Conducting research

Worksheet 7-1: Identifying your favorite skills.

Using formulas	Making decisions
Programming	Investigating
Identifying numeric patterns	Strategizing
Deciphering codes	Analyzing
Discerning relationships and connections	Comparing
Recognizing patterns	Categorizing
Solving problems	Creating spreadsheets
Reasoning	
Critical thinking	
Processing logic questions rapidly	
Seeing cause and effect	

Do you connect well with others?

Giving feedback	Finding common ground
Receiving feedback	Creating and maintaining synergy
Coaching	Building consensus
Speaking	Understanding group process
Communicating nonverbally	Facilitating group discussion
Empathizing	Recognizing cultural values and norms
Sensing others' motives	Setting goals
Discerning perspectives of others	Helping others brainstorm
Sensing others' moods	Helping others see possibility
Determining who is the best one to do the job	Giving advice
Cooperating	Building others' self-esteem
Collaborating	Motivating others
Getting along well with others	Comforting others
Building relationships	Acknowledging others

Networking	Being a trusted confidante
Putting people at ease	Managing
Extracting information from others	Leading
Interviewing	
Providing customer service	
Clarifying vision	

Do you have a good eye?

Visualizing	Finding the best route
Imagining	Navigating
Forming mental images	Creating charts and diagrams
Recreating experience in mind	Working with charts and diagrams
Creating color schemes	Perceiving from different angles
Having a sense of aesthetics, beauty, or balance	Reasoning through spatial problems
Arranging objects (such as furniture)	Thinking in 3-D
Creating patterns and designs	Recognizing spatial depth and dimension
Painting	Discerning spatial implications
Drawing	Visualizing abstract spatial imagery
Sculpting	Building
Photographing	Assembling
Cartooning	Making models
Designing graphic representations	Taking things apart and putting them back together
Manipulating images	
Having a good sense of direction	
Reading maps	
Mapmaking	

Worksheet 7-1: Page 3.

Do you have a good sense of your body?

Moving to music	Using eye-hand coordination
Dancing to folk music	Using eye-foot coordination
Dancing expressively	Doing martial arts
Choreographing	Using your connection between mind and body
Using your body to express yourself	Knowing your internal body map
Using expressive gestures	Sensing how your body moves
Understanding body language	Sensing bodily feedback
Acting	Having a quick response time
Miming	Having a good sense of timing
Mimicking	Moving with flexibility
Creating with your hands on a large scale	Having agility
Creating with your hands on a medium scale	Having endurance
Doing precision work with your hands	Having a good sense of balance
Handling objects skillfully	
Signing to communicate	
Having finger dexterity	
Exercising	
Playing sports and games	
Using your body in a complicated way	

Do you have an ear for music?

Having a good singing voice	Sensing qualities of a tone
Singing a melody	Recognizing tonal patterns
Remembering a melody	Using tonal intervals
Remembering lyrics	Composing
Harmonizing	Arranging
Blending	Improvising

Keeping time	Listening to music
Picking up the beat	
Making vocal sounds or tones	
Listening for perfect pitch	
Listening for relative pitch	

Do you appreciate nature and its creatures?		
Picking up nuances between large numbers of objects		Organizing collections
Discriminating among living things		Labeling collections
Discerning patterns of life		Understanding animal behavior
Examining things in nature		Sensing animal needs
Sensing formations in nature		Understanding characteristics of animals
Observing natural phenomena		Interacting with living creatures
Recognizing patterns in nature		Caring for plants
Recording detailed observations		Identifying plants
Making sense of natural hierarchies		
Classifying things into hierarchies		
Using scientific equipment to observe nature		
Collecting		

Worksheet 7-1:
Page 5.

If you want to gain more clarity about your Multiple Intelligence Profile, order the Midas (Multiple Intelligences Developmental Assessment Scales) Profile available on the Web at www.miresearch.org/products.php for $15.

While your Multiple Intelligence Profile is fresh in your mind, use the following three steps to refine your list of skills even more:

1. **Begin by eliminating skills you are good at but don't enjoy.**

   Although you may be tempted to think that you should do whatever you're good at, doing something you don't enjoy is a drain whether you excel at the skill or not. Do yourself a favor and cross out any skills in Worksheet 7-1, whether they are checked or not, that you don't enjoy. For example, if you are a skilled editor but now find the process extremely tedious and no longer enjoyable, cross the skill off your list.

The skills you'd rather not pursue in the long run may, in the short run, help you move into a new field or industry. For example, you know you want to move out of bookkeeping and accounting, but your ability to work the numbers may be just what you need to get your foot in the door of a new field or provide you with a reliable income while you start your own company. Don't toss your long held skills away; put them on the back burner for now until you begin plotting how to transition into your new field or position.

2. **Remove the skills you want to use only in your personal life.**

   In certain cases, you may have a skill you thoroughly enjoy but know you want to use only in your hobby or volunteer work. For instance, you may love to cook or build steam engines, but you know that you don't want to incorporate these skills into your work. If you have no interest in or intention of using a talent professionally (you enjoy cooking but not enough to slave over a hot stove for eight or more hours a day!), cross the skill off your list in Worksheet 7-1.

   Don't talk yourself into crossing out something you really would love to incorporate into your work. Although you may not know how or where it will fit in, keep it on your list so it can become part of the brainstorming you do in Chapter 9.

3. **After you have fine-tuned your list in Worksheet 7-1, count the number of items in each section and record the totals in the middle column of Worksheet 7-2.**

Your Multiple Intelligence Profile Summary		
Skill Area from Worksheet 7-1	**# of ✓s**	**Area of Multiple Intelligence**
Thinking in words		Verbal/linguistic intelligence
Thinking in a logical, organized fashion		Mathematical/logical intelligence
Connecting well with others		Interpersonal intelligence
Having a good eye		Visual intelligence
Having a good sense of your body		Body/kinesthetic intelligence
Having an ear for music		Musical intelligence
Appreciating nature and its creatures		Naturalist intelligence

Worksheet 7-2: Tallying up your favorite skills.

Where do you have the highest concentration of check marks? Recognizing your top two or three areas of multiple intelligence gives you a broad sense of the kinds of careers that are likely to match your skills. Later, when you review the careers listed in Chapters 11 through 13, focus your attention on the careers that mirror your areas of multiple intelligence.

Expanding Your List of Favorite Skills

Sometimes looking at how you live your life and do your work can illuminate skills you may not have included in the Multiple Intelligence Profile in Worksheet 7-1. Use this section to enhance your list of talents.

A skill you may overlook is one that is as natural for you as breathing. In fact, it's such a part of you that you assume all people can and do use it in their work.

If you're a whiz at editing, speaking, playing an instrument, facilitating groups, or working with animals and you have a tendency to discount your natural abilities, take a closer look. You may find a clue to your future in a skill that you always assumed everyone brought to the party. (Doesn't the fact that you're the only person willing to give the toast at weddings let you know that most people *don't* enjoy public speaking?)

Begin by thinking about the situations listed in Worksheet 7-3. As you read each description, focus on the skills and actions that come easily to you. In many respects, these talents are second nature to you and are such a part of who you are that you may need to do some detective work to tease them out.

In doing this worksheet, Sam, a community liaison officer from Texas, discovered two skills he'd never given himself credit for. He realized that his ability for impromptu speaking meant he was often the person who put others at ease in uncomfortable social settings and work-related events. Because this is something he does naturally, he never considered this to be a special skill until he did this activity. In addition, he discovered that this same skill helps him defuse difficult exchanges between co-workers, clients, volunteers, and even friends. On many occasions, Sam has been the one to turn a potentially explosive situation into a workable opportunity for clear communication. Sam was somewhat aware of this skill, but until he took the time to do this activity, he hadn't seen how pervasive this particular skill has been in his life at work and at home.

As you complete this section, take a moment to circle any new skills that surface. Do these skills follow the pattern of your Multiple Intelligence Profile or do they bring another element of your skills to light?

If you have difficulty deciding how this exercise applies to you, ask a few trusted friends and family members for skills that they see as a natural part of you that you often take for granted. Write down any additional skills you come up with in the space provided.

The ways in which you help others can also give you additional clues to your passions and talents.

When individuals from each of the groups listed in Worksheet 7-4 call upon you for help, which of your skills and talents do you use? Another way to think about this question is, what do you enjoy doing for others?

If you notice any new skills in this worksheet, circle them so they're easy to see later. Once again, compare these skills to your overall Multiple Intelligence Profile to discover whether they confirm the pattern you've already seen or add to your knowledge about your skills.

If you just find more confirmation of a multiple intelligence you've seen before, don't despair. Seeing similarities in your answers is a wonderful sign that you are on track and beginning to see a strong pattern. If you find a new skill, rejoice in your discovery. At this point, don't spend time worrying about how to make sense of your diverse skills. It's far too early in the process to be making firm decisions about your next career.

What's as Easy as Breathing?
At work: Think about projects, tasks, and interactions you engage in at work.
1.
2.
3.
4.
5.
At home: Consider actions you take around the house and with your family.
1.
2.
3.
4.
5.
In your social life: Review various social situations you encounter with friends, social groups, and strangers.
1.
2.
3.
4.
5.
In your community activities: Search your memory for tasks you handle in your volunteer activities for your church, a nonprofit, or your child's school.
1.
2.
3.
4.
5.
In your hobbies: Think through skills you use in your hobbies.
1.
2.
3.
4.
5.

Worksheet 7-3: Discovering the skills that are a natural part of who you are.

Skills You Use Helping Others	
Co-workers	Manager
1.	1.
2.	2.
3.	3.
4.	4.
5.	5.
Friends	Family members
1.	1.
2.	2.
3.	3.
4.	4.
5.	5.
Organizations you volunteer for	Pets
1.	1.
2.	2.
3.	3.
4.	4.
5.	5.

Worksheet 7-4: How do you help people in your life?

Considering the Processes You Enjoy Most

Another source for understanding your talents is to look at the processes you enjoy in your work. A *process* is a sequence of tasks that remains the same even when the specific nature of the project changes. For example:

✔ Whether you build a tree house or a house, the process of building is similar.

✔ Whether you write an article or a book, the basic process of writing is similar.

✔ Whether you're organizing a drawer of office supplies or a garage, the process of organizing is similar.

Take a look at the following list of processes:

- ✔ Creating
- ✔ Designing
- ✔ Inventing
- ✔ Forecasting
- ✔ Managing a project
- ✔ Composing

- ✔ Planning an event
- ✔ Researching
- ✔ Producing
- ✔ Starting up a project
- ✔ Turning something around
- ✔ Cooking

Do you see what they all have in common? Each and every process ends in "–ing" which means they refer to an action. If you're familiar with what it takes to fulfill one of these actions, you know that several often complex tasks and skills are required to achieve results. If one of these processes is calling your name, you probably enjoy the entire sequence of tasks and want to be in the middle of this action whenever possible.

To uncover your key processes, use this five-step process:

1. **List projects you have enjoyed throughout your life.**
2. **Identify the projects that currently excite you.**
3. **Categorize similar projects into project groups.**
4. **Discover the best theme for each project group.**
5. **Select the processes you enjoy most.**

As you work through this process, pay attention to the real-life example woven into the activity.

1. **List projects you have enjoyed throughout your life.**

   Mike, a salesperson for construction supplies from Colorado, began this activity by taking a tour of his home and taking a walk down memory lane to remember projects he enjoyed over the years. Take a look at part of his initial list of projects in Figure 7-2.

   To prepare yourself for this process, take time to walk around your home for visual cues of your favorite projects. Here are some ideas to get you started:

   • Peer into your closets, attic, and basement for signs of your hobbies.

   • Take a tour of your garage to uncover projects you enjoyed in the past.

   • Look for half-finished projects you wish you had time to complete.

   Your memories may hold clues as well:

   • Think about past and present work projects to identify the parts you enjoy most.

   • Review your volunteer projects.

   • Reminisce about projects you enjoyed as a child.

   In Worksheet 7-5, start listing the projects you've enjoyed at some point in your life. They can be work related, school related, or part of your personal life. What matters is that, when you participated in these projects, you felt excited, fed, and magnetized by the process.

Mike's Favorite Projects			
✳	Writing for my school paper	✳	Building a fort as a kid
✳	Playing with my first camera		Waterskiing
	Reenacting historical battles	✳	Preparing reports at work
✳	Walking through houses being built	✳	Taking landscape photographs
✳	Investigating and researching information for people	✳	Looking at blueprints
✳	Camping		Bird watching
✳	Organizing my slides		Working on cars
	Reading historical biographies		Doing crossword puzzles

Figure 7-2: Mike's list of favorite projects.

Your Favorite Projects			

Worksheet 7-5: Listing the projects you enjoy most.

2. **Identify the projects that currently excite you.**

Return to Worksheet 7-5 and use an asterisk to mark the projects that continue to intrigue and excite you to this day.

Take a look at the projects that still hold Mike's attention by looking at the asterisks in Figure 7-2.

3. Categorize similar projects into project groups.

Review Figure 7-3 to see what project groups Mike created. Note that Mike included one project in two different project groups. What he noticed is that "Taking landscape photographs" tapped into two different ideas: being in nature and photographing.

Now, sort your projects into project groups. As you look at your projects, do you see any projects that are similar? Remember that there are no right answers here. Your projects may in fact fall into several groups, as Mike's did. Your job is to record each grouping you discover in Worksheet 7-6.

TIP

If you have a hard time spotting the themes, write each of your projects on a separate slip of paper. Then move the slips of paper around until you see similarities. You may also find it helpful to do this task with someone who is not as close to the projects as you are.

Mike's Favorite Processes	
Project Group 1:	Project Group 2:
Projects: Writing for my school paper Preparing reports at work Investigating and researching information for people	Projects: Playing with my first camera Taking landscape photographs Organizing my slides
Themes: Writing Researching	Themes: Photographing
Project Group 3:	Project Group 4:
Projects: Walking through houses being built Looking at blueprints Building a fort as a kid	Projects: Taking landscape photographs Camping
Themes: Building Constructing	Themes: Being in nature

Figure 7-3: Mike's project groups and themes.

Your Favorite Processes	
Project Group 1:	Project Group 2:
Projects:	Projects:
Themes:	Themes:
Project Group 3:	Project Group 4:
Projects:	Projects:
Themes:	Themes:

Worksheet 7-6: Finding the themes in your list of projects. Page 1.

Project Group 5:	Project Group 6:
Projects:	Projects:
Themes:	Themes:

4. **Discover the best theme for each project group.**

   Think of a theme as a common thread or process that ties the projects together. You may even find that your group of projects illustrates more than one theme.

   Refer back to Mike's themes in Figure 7-3. Notice that Mike thought two themes were relevant in his first project group: writing and researching.

   Notice also how all of Mike's themes end in "–ing." Search for a word or phrase with an embedded "–ing" and you're on the right track.

5. **Select the processes you enjoy most.**

   Review all your themes to discover the processes you want to incorporate into your next career. Circle the ones you like most.

   As you think about your favorite processes, notice what they add to your knowledge of your Multiple Intelligence Profile.

Recording Your Favorite Skills and Intelligences

Throughout this chapter, you identify a variety of skills you enjoy. Review your list by going back through each section. As you do this, circle the 20 items you most want to incorporate into your next career. Be sure to include the following sections in your review:

- ✔ Worksheet 7-1: Your Multiple Intelligence Profile
- ✔ Worksheet 7-3: What's as Easy as Breathing
- ✔ Worksheet 7-4: Skills You Use Helping Others
- ✔ Worksheet 7-6: Your Favorite Processes

After you feel comfortable with your list, record your Top 20 Favorite Skills in Worksheet 7-7.

Your Top 20 Favorite Skills	
1.	11.
2.	12.
3.	13.
4.	14.
5.	15.
6.	16.
7.	17.
8.	18.
9.	19.
10.	20.

Worksheet 7-7: Creating a list of your favorite skills.

After you complete your Top 20 Favorite Skills list, read it over to confirm that everything on the list feels like you. This list must not only be complete but also be a good representation of who you are because it becomes one of the main building blocks for the brainstorming activity in Chapter 9.

If you find yourself resisting an item, consider leaving it off the list. If you included an item that you think "should" be on this list because it's the family business (embalming has never been your cup of tea) or because you have a great deal of education in the area, please reconsider. If you don't enjoy the skill or if including the skill pressures you to be something you aren't, this skill is more likely to sabotage your happiness than help you achieve it. Do yourself a favor and delete that skill before you start creating your future.

Chapter 8

Discovering Topics That Make You Sizzle with Excitement

- -

In This Chapter

▶ Recognizing topics that intrigue you

▶ Nailing down tools and equipment you like to use

▶ Figuring out which industries appeal to you

▶ Narrowing down your list of interests

- -

Your expertise and interest in a certain area bring with it a particular language, focus, and sense of humor that define your work.

Because you may be looking to take an entirely new professional direction, the questions and worksheets in this chapter help you explore a wide range of interests in your professional life and your personal life. I include a variety of questions in Worksheets 8-1 through 8-4 because I want to trigger your imagination from as many angles as possible to help you create a thorough list of your interests in Worksheet 8-5.

In Chapter 9 you combine the interests you discover in this chapter with the skills and talents you identify in Chapter 7 to brainstorm new career ideas.

Don't be concerned if a particular worksheet doesn't produce any ideas for you. Think about the question a bit and then move on.

Finding the Topics That Always Draw Your Attention

When you read the paper, listen to the news, visit a bookstore, or talk with people, what topics grab your attention? These topics provide valuable clues about your passions, which may ultimately point you in the direction of a particular career. Don't be concerned with how it's going to happen. Just know that identifying your interests opens the door to career ideas that fascinate and delight you.

In Worksheet 8-1, I include a list of topics to get you started, but please don't limit yourself to just this list. Place a check mark next to any and all topics that intrigue, interest, or fascinate you. If additional topics or subtopics come to mind as you read the list, catch them! Don't let them escape or fade away — write them down in the extra space provided at the end of the list.

Your Favorite Topics of Interest

Acting	Ethnicity	Nursing
Adolescents	Etymology	Nutrition
Aerospace	Family	Outdoors
Agriculture	Fashion	Paranormal
Animals	Film	Parenting
Animation	Finance	Peace
Anthropology	Fine arts	Performing arts
Antiques	Fitness	Personal finance
Archaeology	Flowers	Personal growth
Architecture	Food	Pets
Art history	Forensics	Philanthropy
Arts	Furniture	Philosophy
Astrology	Future	Photography
Astronomy	Games	Physics
Automotive	Gardening	Plants
Aviation	Genealogy	Politics
Beauty	Geography	Pop culture
Biology	Geology	Psychology
Bio-tech	Geriatrics	Radio
Bird watching	Government	Real estate
Boating	Health	Recreation
Books	History	Recycling
Business	Home decorating	Relationships
Cars	Home improvement	Religion
Celebrities	Home remodeling	Rescue
Chemistry	Homeopathy	Science
Children	Human rights	Sexuality
Clothing	Humor	Singing
Collectibles	Information	Small business
Comics	technology	Social issues
Community service	Insurance	Sociology
Compensation	Intelligence	Software
Computers	International relations	Space
Cooking	Internet	Spirituality
Crafts	Investing	Sports
Criminology	Jewelry	Storytelling
Cultures	Journalism	Systems
Dance	Justice	Taxes
Death and grief	Languages	Technology
Disabilities	Law	Television
Diversity	Leadership	Theater
Earth sciences	Linguistics	Toys
Ecology	Literature	Transportation
Economics	Magazines	Travel
Education	Mathematics	Trivia
Electronics	Medicine	Volunteerism
Employment issues	Men's issues	Weather
Energy	Mental health	Women's issues
Engineering	Military	
Entertainment	Music	
Entrepreneurs	Myths	
Environment	Nature	
Ethics	Navigation	

Worksheet 8-1: Identifying subjects that intrigue you.

WARNING!

If you don't feel inspired or interested in much of anything these days, the "muscle" that helps you know you're interested in a conversation, drawn to a flavor of ice cream, or pulled to read a book may have atrophied. Using it again reawakens that internal quickening that happens when you enjoy something. Expand your horizons by experimenting — for example, take a class, go to a museum, visit the library, or do things you used to love. Keep your senses open for signs that you're enjoying yourself. Chapter 2 includes some additional strategies for you as well.

Now, take a moment to investigate additional topics you enjoy thinking about and exploring. Use the questions on the left hand side of Worksheet 8-2 to expand your list of favorite topics even further.

Uncovering More Topics of Interest	
Does your bookcase reveal any additional topics? List whatever subjects you discover as you scan your book titles.	
What subjects are you curious about? Perhaps you want to pick up a book on a topic, surf the Web, or talk to an expert to learn as much as you can.	
What interests come to mind as you review the articles you clipped in Chapter 2 as you explored topics you are drawn to?	
What topics do you help others understand?	
What subjects fascinated you as a child?	
What life-changing events have sparked a sense of mission within you?	
Does your voice tell you that you are excited about a particular topic? Pay close attention to the speed of your words, the insistent tone in your voice, and the duration of your monologues. Each sign is a clue to your passion.	

Worksheet 8-2: Discovering other topics of interest to you.

Listing Tools, Equipment, and Raw Materials That Make Your Work Play

If you love the tactile experience of working with your hands, tools, equipment, and raw materials may define the work you love.

The number of tools, equipment, and raw materials is infinite, so use the following lists as a starting point. Then personalize your list by looking around your home and office for other tangible things you enjoy using in your hobbies, projects around the house, your volunteer work, and at work.

Place a check mark in front of any tools, equipment, or raw materials listed in Worksheet 8-3 that you would like to use in your next career. (If tangible things don't float your boat, don't worry about it. Just do the best you can and move on.) After you create your list, if you find that you have more than ten items listed, circle the ten you most want to use in your next career.

You don't have to know how these tools and materials will combine with your skills to create your next career. For now just focus your attention on whether you'd like to use these tools and materials in your work if given an opportunity.

Your Favorite Tools, Equipment, and Raw Materials		
Tools and equipment:		
Airplanes Audio equipment Automotive repair tools Boating equipment Camera equipment Camping gear Carpentry hand tools and power tools Catering equipment Cleaning equipment Clocks Collectibles and antiques Communication gadgets Computers and peripherals Cooking utensils and appliances Craft equipment, such as scissors or a glue gun	Fitness equipment Framing equipment or matting materials Furniture making and repair tools Game stations Gardening tools Glass blowing equipment Hi-tech gadgets Household appliances Laboratory equipment Machinery Medical testing equipment Metalsmithing tools Musical instruments Office equipment Organizing items Paint brushes, canvases, and an easel	Sewing machine, pins, needles, and patterns Shipping supplies Sports equipment Telescopes, microscopes, or binoculars Vehicles Video equipment Woodworking tools Writing tools
Raw materials:		
Beads Chemicals Clay Concrete Fabrics, threads, and notions Food, spices, and condiments Flowers and vases Gemstones	Glazes Metal Minerals Paper Pictures and photographs Plants and soil Plastics Silicon Stones	Rubber Wood Wrapping paper Yarn, sequins, and ribbons

Worksheet 8-3: Listing tangible things you like to use.

Identifying Industries That Light Your Fire

Each company falls within a particular industry. By identifying industries that interest you, you effectively narrow your search for a new career.

Place a check mark in front of the industries included in Worksheet 8-4 that you're most interested in. Cross out any you absolutely know you aren't interested in. Leave the remaining industries as they are.

Intriguing Industries	
Accounting	Journalism
Advertising	Legal services
Aerospace and defense	Machinery
Agriculture	Manufacturing
Air transportation	Marketing
Alternative health	Medical devices
Apparel and accessories	Mining or quarrying
Architecture	Movie industry
Auditing	Motor vehicle manufacturing and
Automotive	dealers
Banking	Music and recording industry
Beauty and cosmetics	Office equipment and furniture
Biotechnology	Oil and gas
Broadcasting	Packaging and containers
Cable and television	Paper and paper products
Casinos and gaming	Personal and household products
Chemical manufacturing	Pharmaceuticals
Cleaning and maintenance services	Philanthropy
Coaching	Photography
Commercial banking	Precious stones and gems
Communications	Printing and publishing
Computer hardware	Public relations
Computer networking	Public transportation
Computer security	Public utilities
Computer software and programming	Railroad
Computer services	Real estate
Computer storage devices	Recreation activities
Computer peripherals	Recreation products
Construction, services	Restaurants
Construction, raw materials	Retail
Construction, supplies and fixtures	Risk management
Consumer electronics	Savings and loan
Consumer products	Scientific and technical
Counseling	instruments
Data processing	Security
Education	Securities and commodities
Electronic equipment manufacturing	Semiconductors
Energy or utilities	Shipping
Engineering	Ship building and repair
Entertainment	Social services
Environmental management	Sports
Financial and investment services	Steel manufacturing
Food processing	Telecommunications
Government	Toys and games
Health care, facilities	Transportation
Health care, managed care	Travel
Health care, pharmaceuticals	Trucking or warehousing
Health care, products and supplies	Venture capital
Heavy manufacturing	Veterinary medicine
Hospitality	Waste management
Housewares and furnishings	Water transportation
Import/export	Wellness
Industrial automation	Wholesale trade
Insurance	Wine and spirits
Internet and new media	Wireless industry

Worksheet 8-4: Exploring industries that interest you.

Understanding the attributes of an industry helps you get a feel for whether that industry and its occupations are a good fit for you. After you narrow your focus to a particular industry, turn to Chapter 14 for more information on how to research an industry.

Recording Your Favorite Interests

Take a moment to review all of the interests you identified in the following worksheets:

- ✔ Worksheet 8-1: Your Favorite Topics of Interest
- ✔ Worksheet 8-2: Uncovering More Topics of Interest
- ✔ Worksheet 8-3: Your Favorite Tools, Equipment, and Raw Materials
- ✔ Worksheet 8-4: Intriguing Industries

Your task, if you choose to accept it, is to identify your top 20 interests that you'd most like to include in your work. As you record your favorite interests in Worksheet 8-5, you create a valuable list of clues that consists of topics, equipment, and industries.

In Chapter 9 you combine this list (Items 21–40) with your favorite skills from Chapter 7 (Items 1–20) to stimulate your creativity as you brainstorm a variety of possible career ideas.

Please note that if you don't choose an item, you aren't abandoning that interest completely. In fact, if you have an interest that you know is more of a hobby than a focus for your next career, don't include it in this list.

The key is that every entry in Worksheet 8-5 reflects the interests you'd like to incorporate into your work. Keep in mind that you don't, in this moment, need to know how the topic fits into your career picture. (Chapter 9 shows you how to combine your favorite interests with your list of favorite skills from Chapter 7 to create a list of concrete career ideas.)

As you complete this worksheet, take the opportunity to fine-tune your list by removing any duplicate topics, adding any interests that are missing from your list, eliminating anything you've listed only because your mother always thought you enjoyed it, and modifying the wording to make each item as accurate and informative as possible.

When considering a career change, you need to focus on your present wishes, rather than on what you've done in the past or what you think you should do. To help you break free of restrictive thoughts, consider the following possibility:

If you knew you'd be well taken care of financially no matter what career you chose, how would you answer the following questions?

- ✔ Would you rethink any of the interests you listed in Worksheet 8-5?
- ✔ Would you drop a topic you dislike even though it's practical?
- ✔ Would you delete an entry you're tired of even though you spent years attaining that expertise?
- ✔ Would you add an artistic and aesthetic passion to your list in Worksheet 8-5?

Make whatever changes necessary to make Worksheet 8-5 as true to your interests as possible.

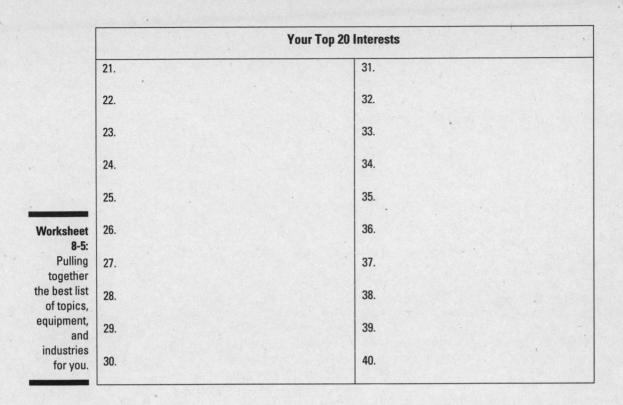

Worksheet 8-5: Pulling together the best list of topics, equipment, and industries for you.

Your Top 20 Interests	
21.	31.
22.	32.
23.	33.
24.	34.
25.	35.
26.	36.
27.	37.
28.	38.
29.	39.
30.	40.

Chapter 9

Brainstorming Intriguing
Career Ideas

As you think about your next career, you may use what you've done in the past as your guide to your next position. Although this linear approach may yield results, it may also limit you if you're at all frustrated with your current career. Focusing on only your recent past, rather than on your true career passions, can severely limit your opportunities.

The fun, nonlinear creativity worksheets in this chapter help you use a broader range of passions and interests as the basis for brainstorming potential career ideas. You'll get the most out of this chapter if you do the brainstorming activities after you've completed the worksheets in Chapters 7 and 8, which help you create lists of your favorite skills and interests, or if you use other sources to create those lists.

Use this chapter to expand your career horizons. Have fun playing with the worksheets in this chapter; the more you work with them, the more you get out of this chapter. Dream big. Be outrageous. Give all of the ideas you come up with equal weight in your brainstorming process. You have plenty of opportunities to evaluate and enhance the feasibility of your ideas in Chapter 10.

Preparing the Way for New Ideas

Before you begin brainstorming, you may want to take a good look at your favorite skills in Worksheet 7-7 and your favorite interests in Worksheet 8-5 (ideally, you've already filled out those worksheets). Verify that you thoroughly enjoy every element on both of your lists. If you feel any sense of hesitation, dislike, or dread associated with an item — no matter what the reason — let that item go. You need to make your list as strong as you possibly can by deleting or modifying elements that don't quite work for you.

If you cross out an item on either list or you didn't fill out the worksheets completely the first time around, take another look. Do you see anything from the other worksheets in Chapters 7 or 8 that you'd like to add to fill in the empty spaces in these worksheets? If so, now is the time. If you find more than 20 skills or topics you absolutely love, don't hold back. Just add them to the end of the appropriate list.

If you list more than 20 skills or topics, you need to do one more step before you start brainstorming. For the brainstorming activity to work properly, every item on your lists must have a unique number. The skills on Worksheet 7-7 are numbered 1 through 20. The interests on Worksheet 8-5 are numbered 21 through 40. Begin numbering your additions at 41 and keep going until each item you've added has its own number. To retain the richness and depth of your list, do not group or combine your items.

Recording Career Ideas Already on Your Mind

Before you begin brainstorming, record on paper any careers you may already be thinking about. By jotting your ideas down in Worksheet 9-1, you don't have to work so hard to keep them in mind while you're brainstorming. When you're ready to assess which ideas are your favorites in Worksheet 9-7, remember to include this list in your evaluation.

If, at this point, you don't have any idea what your next career might be, don't sweat it. Just move on to the next section.

Career Ideas Already on Your Mind
☆
☆
☆

Worksheet 9-1: Recording career ideas you already have.

Dreaming Up New Career Ideas

Imagine that you have a deck of cards and each card in the deck represents one of the skills or interests included in Worksheets 7-7 and 8-5. Imagine further that you can deal out the cards from this deck in various combinations that represent different dream careers. As you shuffle this deck in your mind, consider how many exciting combinations exist. The possibilities are endless.

Although you may get some career ideas by scanning your lists, playing with various combinations allows you to see specific ideas more easily. First read over this three-step approach. Then take a look at the example in Figure 9-1. Use the steps and example to brainstorm your own intriguing career ideas in Worksheet 9-2.

1. **Choose four numbers at random between 1 and 40.**

   Write the numbers you choose on the blanks provided in the first row of Worksheet 9-2. Avoid reusing these numbers in a future worksheet.

   If you added items to either worksheet, replace the number 40 with the largest number you came up with when you numbered the new items on your worksheets.

2. **Refer to Worksheets 7-7 and 8-5 to discover what skills and interests correspond with the numbers you chose.**

   Write the description associated with each number in the space under the numbers in Worksheet 9-2.

3. **Brainstorm as many career ideas as you can that include at least three of the four elements in your list. You might come up with a job title, a project, a job task, or a business idea.**

   Stretch your mind. Think creatively. An idea may come to you in a flash, or you might try telling yourself a story, weaving in as many of the words as you can. Look at each word from various angles to see what other directions your brainstorming can take. At this stage, any idea is a good idea! Don't censure your flow of creativity. Do what you can to fill in the ten career blanks provided in Worksheet 9-2. Chapter 10 can help you refine your ideas and narrow your focus.

Jill, a frustrated administrative assistant with artistic talents from Seattle, chose numbers 12, 14, 32, and 6. After writing down the numbers, she referred back to her worksheets and learned they corresponded with the phrases listed under each number in Figure 9-1. In her next step, she brainstormed some career ideas that incorporated the elements from her original lists of favorite skills and interests. Notice that some of her ideas are job titles while others are projects or job tasks. At this stage of the game, her main goal is to get her ideas down on paper — the exact form isn't all that important.

On your first pass through each worksheet, plan to spend about ten minutes coming up with possible career ideas; you can always come back later to round out your lists of career ideas for each "hand." Don't fret if you don't reach ten careers; the worksheets are helpful even when you don't fill in all the blanks.

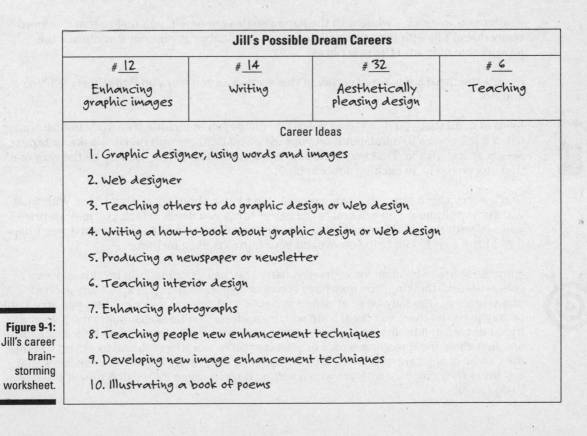

Jill's Possible Dream Careers			
# 12 Enhancing graphic images	# 14 Writing	# 32 Aesthetically pleasing design	# 6 Teaching
Career Ideas			

1. Graphic designer, using words and images

2. Web designer

3. Teaching others to do graphic design or Web design

4. Writing a how-to-book about graphic design or Web design

5. Producing a newspaper or newsletter

6. Teaching interior design

7. Enhancing photographs

8. Teaching people new enhancement techniques

9. Developing new image enhancement techniques

10. Illustrating a book of poems

Figure 9-1: Jill's career brainstorming worksheet.

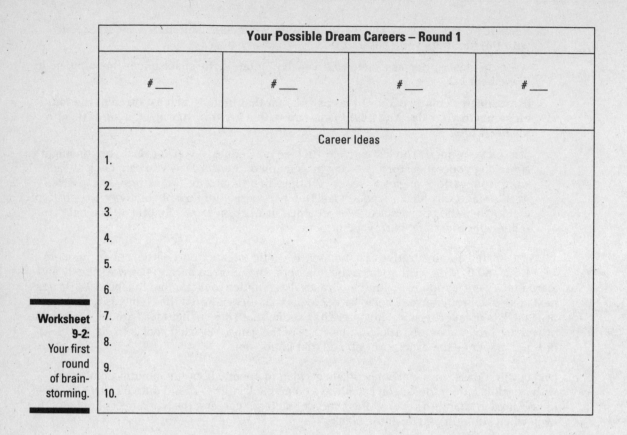

Your Possible Dream Careers – Round 1			
# ___	# ___	# ___	# ___
Career Ideas			
1.			
2.			
3.			
4.			
5.			
6.			
7.			
8.			
9.			
10.			

Worksheet 9-2: Your first round of brainstorming.

If, after you work for a while with the hand you dealt yourself, you realize that one word really doesn't fit with the others, choose another number at random and replace the unworkable item with the new phrase.

Repeat the three steps listed earlier in this section as you work on Worksheets 9-3, 9-4, and 9-5.

Keep in mind that you don't have to want to do the job to include it on your brainstorming list. If a job comes to mind, put it on your list no matter how outlandish, kooky, or bizarre it seems at first glance. That very idea you consider leaving off the list may be the very one that steers you in an exciting new direction.

Don't worry about how much you know or don't know about what's out there. With what you know right now, you can create the career ideas you need. In fact, you may surprise yourself with the ideas you come up with! After you've had a chance to brainstorm, Chapters 11 through 13 can help you expand your horizons even further.

Sometimes brainstorming for yourself is hard. You may get caught up in "this-is-never-going-to-work" thinking. You may have convinced yourself that you aren't any good at brainstorming. You may be so attached to how it's all going to work out that you aren't able to stay in the moment to play around with your ideas. Don't despair. Enlist the help of a friend or two. Tell them that you are working on a project and need some help brainstorming. Just show them the four words or phrases you're working with and ask them whether they know of any careers that incorporate three or four of the ideas. Let them know that any ideas they come up with are worth writing down — even if they don't think you'd like to do the job.

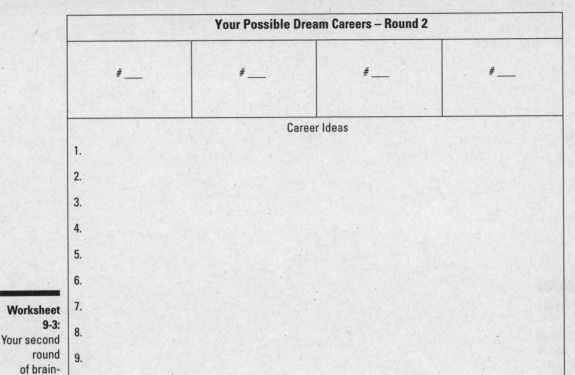

Your Possible Dream Careers – Round 2

# ___	# ___	# ___	# ___
	Career Ideas		

1.
2.
3.
4.
5.
6.
7.
8.
9.
10.

Worksheet 9-3: Your second round of brainstorming.

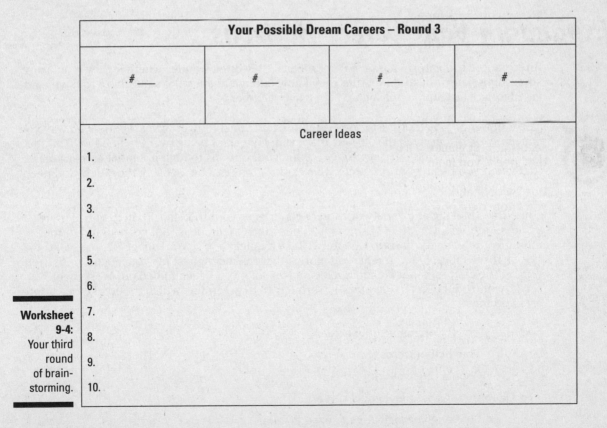

Your Possible Dream Careers – Round 3

# ___	# ___	# ___	# ___
	Career Ideas		

1.
2.
3.
4.
5.
6.
7.
8.
9.
10.

Worksheet 9-4: Your third round of brainstorming.

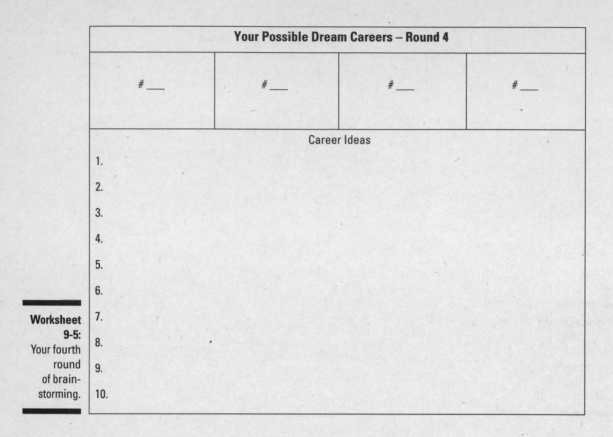

Your Possible Dream Careers – Round 4			
# ___	# ___	# ___	# ___
Career Ideas			

1.

2.

3.

4.

5.

6.

7.

8.

9.

10.

Worksheet 9-5: Your fourth round of brainstorming.

Expanding Your Career Horizons

After people brainstorm possible career ideas, they often wonder whether they're missing something. They question whether they know enough about what's out there to have made an adequate attempt at coming up with a list of career ideas.

The number of jobs that exist today is infinite and constantly growing. There is no way you can know or research all the options that exist. Instead of being overwhelmed with all the possibilities, shift your strategy to narrowing your options to high-potential career areas so that when you begin your research, your explorations can be focused, thorough, and deep in the fields that count.

Sometimes looking at a variety of careers can trigger your thinking. To help you explore what is out there, Chapters 11 through 13 describe career ideas that correspond to the multiple intelligence charts in Chapter 7. Take a quick look at Worksheet 7-2 to recall the two or three multiple intelligence categories that ranked highest for you. Focus your attention on the chapters that are most relevant to you. If you haven't filled out Worksheet 7-2, read the introductions to Chapters 11 through 13 to determine which group of careers interests you most.

✔ Chapter 11: Communicating careers

- Thinking in words

- Connecting well with others

✔ Chapter 12: Scientific/logical careers

- Thinking in a logical, organized fashion

- Appreciating nature and its creatures

↙ Chapter 13: Creative careers

- Having a good eye

- Having a good sense of your body

- Having an ear for music

As you read through the chapters, make note of any careers that intrigue you. You don't have to know how you'd move into these careers at this point. The most important thing is that the description of the career area grabs your attention and makes you want to know more. As you find interesting careers, use Worksheet 9-6 to record the chapter, page number, and heading of each find. While you're there, note any job titles you'd like to investigate further.

More Intriguing Career Ideas		
Chapter: Page Number	Heading:	Interesting Job Titles:
Chapter 11: Page 123	Technical writing	Scientific writer Manual writer Medical writer Technical editor

Worksheet 9-6: Expanding your list of career ideas.

George, a talented writer in his personal time, was intrigued by several job titles included in the technical writing section in Chapter 11 on page 123. Follow this same pattern as you add careers that interest you.

Don't feel that you must look under every heading to search out career ideas or that you must have the solution to your career dilemma before you can move on to Chapter 10. If an idea is missing from the list you create in this chapter, the process in the next few chapters can help you fill in any gaps. Remember that you're in the middle of the brainstorming process at this point — not the end of it.

Recording Your Top Ten Intriguing Careers

To take your discovery process to the next level, review all the career ideas you've come up with in this chapter.

- ✔ Worksheet 9-1: Ideas you had already thought of
- ✔ Worksheets 9-2 through 9-5: Ideas you brainstormed by using your favorite skills and interests
- ✔ Worksheet 9-6: Ideas you found while exploring the careers listed in Chapters 11 through 13

Circle any careers or business ideas that appeal to you. Shoot for a total of ten ideas. Then copy them into Worksheet 9-7. You don't have to be sold on the feasibility or practicality of your career ideas to include them in this list. You just need to feel interested in, drawn to, or intrigued by the idea or some aspect of it.

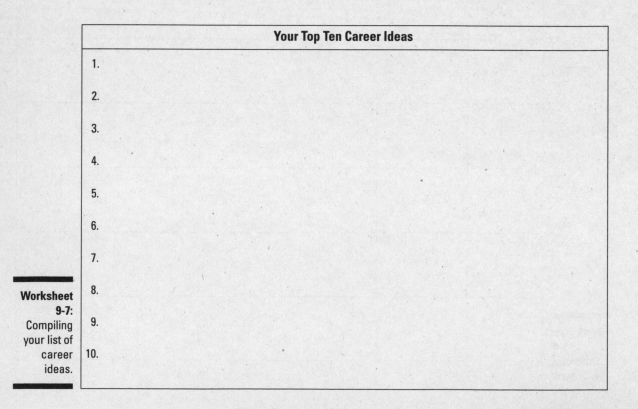

Your Top Ten Career Ideas
1.
2.
3.
4.
5.
6.
7.
8.
9.
10.

Worksheet 9-7: Compiling your list of career ideas.

You may end up doing one of the careers that you list in Worksheet 9-7. And then again, you may not! You may ultimately choose a career that combines several of your ideas. As you explore your intriguing career ideas, you may also be drawn in an entirely different direction. For now, don't stress yourself out by trying to figure out which direction is right. Instead, relax.

If you want to proceed directly to Chapter 10, that's where you begin taking a deeper look at your top ten career ideas, refining your focus, and identifying the themes that best describe your career interests. By the end of that chapter, you take your top ten careers and narrow your focus to your top two career ideas.

Chapter 10

Sifting Out Your Most Intriguing Dream Careers

- -

In This Chapter

▶ Considering the pros and cons of your favorite career ideas

▶ Looking for themes

▶ Searching for the keys to your career decisions

▶ Checking out creative ways to combine your talents

▶ Narrowing your focus to two careers

- -

*I*f you've been thinking about your career options, either by working through the previous chapters of this book or on your own, you may be a bit overwhelmed with all of your options. You aren't sure which ideas are likely to work; you aren't sure how to identify your best ideas. The activities in this chapter help you narrow your top ten career ideas (from Chapter 9) to the two career ideas you want to investigate in more detail.

This process works best if you've worked through Chapters 7 and 8 to create your lists of favorite skills and interests and then used those lists in Chapter 9 to brainstorm your favorite career ideas. Even if you haven't done those chapters, you can still benefit from this chapter by sitting down now and making a list of the ten careers you're considering.

Instead of looking at your Top Ten list and trying to figure out which one is going to be "it," look at each career idea on the list as a clue to what you find interesting and appealing. Instead of sitting right there in broad daylight, your next career may be waiting in the shadows — a combination or a modification of what's on your list that you'll have to do a little searching to discover.

Making the Most of This Chapter

The process of converting your Top Ten list into your Top Two list is more like a logic puzzle with multiple solutions than a simple equation with only one answer.

You begin this chapter by considering a wide range of possibilities. As you settle on each piece of information and confirm, "yes, that's something I want," another part of the logic puzzle comes into focus. Until the entire solution is clear, finding a new clue may require you to take a step back to reconfigure how everything fits together as a whole.

To clarify your thinking and fine-tune your career puzzle, you swing back and forth between the specific aspects of your career list and the topics and skills your career ideas are built on and the overarching themes and goals that begin to come into focus. Whether you're looking at broad themes or specific details, always keep your eye on the prize: your ideal career.

Finding the solution to your career puzzle is likely to move forward in fits and starts. You may move along smoothly for a while and then notice a potential conflict between two aspects of your puzzle. Perhaps you revel in the idea of working from home but know that you'll go a bit stir-crazy if you don't have contact with other people each day, or you discover that working with your favorite population means your busiest times are when you had hoped to be off the clock. When this happens, back away for a time to see the broader picture again. Look for creative ways to get the two pieces to fit together. You may need to try several configurations before you find the ones that are most promising.

As you explore your ideas, you may see that you're attracted to careers with common job titles, such as accountant, marketing communications specialist, software engineer, salesperson. Or you may be attracted to careers that aren't so easy to label, such as the job of traveling around the world scouting for places to shoot movie scenes (is that all this person does?). Although you may feel pressure to find a job title for your new career right away, don't push too hard to find one. The absence of a name doesn't mean the opportunity doesn't exist; it may just be that your career idea is on the cutting edge.

Exploring Your Career Ideas in Depth

The first step in narrowing your focus to your top two career ideas is to record your current thoughts about each of your top ten career ideas. To prepare for the worksheet in this section, copy your top ten career ideas from Worksheet 9-7 into the first column of Worksheet 10-1.

As soon as your list of careers is in place, begin your exploration by taking a closer look at the pros and cons of each career on your list. The more clues you uncover about what intrigues you and what concerns you about each career idea, the more your future direction comes into focus.

In the top section for each career listed in Worksheet 10-1, write down several phrases to describe what excites you about each career idea on your list. It may be one or more of the following:

- ✔ **A feeling:** It can be a feeling of freedom, independence, or responsibility.

- ✔ **The work format:** This can include working alone, part-time possibilities, or travel.

- ✔ **The work itself:** You can include tasks, topics, or roles.

- ✔ **The lifestyle:** You may want to include things like the vacation schedule, the ability to get home early, or more time with friends and family.

Each career or business idea you list in Worksheet 10-1 has both an upside and a downside. Based on what you know right now, what worries you about each of your career ideas? Jot down the phrases that come to mind in the appropriate section associated with each career listed in Worksheet 10-1. Again, think about the work tasks involved in this career and how this career might impact your ideal work arrangements and your lifestyle.

	Exploring Your Top Ten Career Ideas
Career Idea #1	What excites you about this career idea? ☆ ☆ ☆
	What worries you about this career idea? ☆ ☆ ☆
Career Idea #2	What excites you about this career idea? ☆ ☆ ☆
	What worries you about this career idea? ☆ ☆ ☆
Career Idea #3	What excites you about this career idea? ☆ ☆ ☆
	What worries you about this career idea? ☆ ☆ ☆
Career Idea #4	What excites you about this career idea? ☆ ☆ ☆
	What worries you about this career idea? ☆ ☆ ☆
Career Idea #5	What excites you about this career idea? ☆ ☆ ☆
	What worries you about this career idea? ☆ ☆ ☆

Worksheet 10-1: Investigating the pros and cons of careers that interest you.

Career Idea #6	What excites you about this career idea? ☆ ☆ ☆
	What worries you about this career idea? ☆ ☆ ☆
Career Idea #7	What excites you about this career idea? ☆ ☆ ☆
	What worries you about this career idea? ☆ ☆ ☆
Career Idea #8	What excites you about this career idea? ☆ ☆ ☆
	What worries you about this career idea? ☆ ☆ ☆
Career Idea #9	What excites you about this career idea? ☆ ☆ ☆
	What worries you about this career idea? ☆ ☆ ☆
Career Idea #10	What excites you about this career idea? ☆ ☆ ☆
	What worries you about this career idea? ☆ ☆ ☆

If you find the same issues surfacing again and again, don't despair — celebrate, instead! Repetitive clues are a gift because they illustrate what is truly important to you. Note any repetitive clues you discover by recording them in Worksheet 10-2.

Repetitive Clues from Worksheet 10-1	
Clues from What Excites You	Clues from What Worries You
☆	☆
☆	☆
☆	☆
☆	☆
☆	☆
☆	☆
☆	☆
☆	☆
☆	☆

Worksheet 10-2: Discovering what's important to you.

Don't be overly concerned about the worries you record for each career on your list. By listing the concerns that are circling in your mind, you discover more about what's important to you. In some cases, your worries help guide you to a new work arrangement or a new angle on a profession. In other cases, your concerns become a catalyst for some deeper thinking about trade-offs and your priorities. Any way you look at it, your worries are a rich source of clues about you and your needs. Rather than brush them under the rug, bring them out in the open for a frank look at your options. Keep in mind that some of your worries are likely to evaporate as you find out more about each career in Chapters 14 and 15.

Searching for Themes

By looking at your list of top ten careers from a different perspective, you gain access to another valuable window into understanding what intrigues you. Discovering the overlying themes associated with your list gives you crucial information that simultaneously narrows your focus and expands your options.

Because the process of working your list of top ten careers down to your top two career options unfolds differently for each person based on the content of his or her Top Ten list, I include two examples to demonstrate this process. You find references to both of these examples throughout this section.

✔ Figure 10-1: Belinda is currently a consultant from British Columbia.

✔ Figure 10-2: Joanne is currently a claims adjuster from Arizona.

Belinda's Career Themes	
Belinda's List of Top Ten Careers	Themes Belinda Identified
1. Helping people create a new career/life for themselves	✱ Change/transition
2. Working with an outplacement firm	✱ Facilitating Groups
3. Facilitating employees who are undergoing change in organizations, to come up with a personal strategy	✱ Working in corporations
4. Facilitating support groups for people in change	✱ Coaching individuals
5. Life coaching	✱ Doing things a different way – to improve life
6. Developing processes/challenging questions to help people get beyond the way they've always done things	✱ Career coaching
7. Helping others simplify their lives by rethinking how they do things	
8. Supporting people who are retiring to downsize and find ways to do things in ways that they physically/mentally can	
9. Developing "self-help" workbooks/guides for people in change situations	
10. Organization coach, for home or office	
Belinda's Observations and Conclusions	
WHAT (Topics): Transitions and Careers WHO/HOW/FORMAT: Individuals outside organizations, Group work – in organizations, Group work – outside organizations	
Belinda's Umbrella Statement: Supporting people in discovering different ways to do what they do with the ultimate goal of improving, simplifying, and transforming their lives	

Figure 10-1:
Belinda's
career list.

Joanne's Career Themes	
Joanne's List of Top Ten Careers	Themes Joanne Identified
1. Physical therapist 2. Sports massage 3. Therapist 4. Personal trainer 5. Grief counselor 6. Counselor 7. Sports psychologist 8. Forest/park ranger 9. Working for a sports/running magazine 10. Teacher	☆ Therapy ☆ Sports ☆ Training ☆ Pets/nature ☆ Physical ☆ Emotional ☆ Working one-on-one with clients

Joanne's Observations and Conclusions		
Working with the body: Physical therapist Sports massage Personal trainer	Working with emotions/mind: Therapist Grief counselor Counselor	Working with both: Sports psychologist
Outliers: Working for a sports/running magazine, teacher, forest/park ranger		
Joanne's Umbrella Statement:		

Figure 10-2: Joanne's career list.

After you read through the following steps to help you complete Worksheet 10-3, be sure to study the two examples before searching for your own themes.

Step 1: Copy your list of top ten careers (from the first column of Worksheet 10-1) into the first column of Worksheet 10-3. This is the last time I'll ask you to do this, I promise! If you'd like to add a new spin to this task, begin to group similar careers together as you go. This step isn't required. In the examples, Belinda sorted her list as she wrote them down, while Joanne copied them directly from her Worksheet 10-1.

Step 2: Identify the themes that are represented in your list. Jot your themes in the second column of Worksheet 10-3. A number of different kinds of themes may surface during this process. Don't worry about what category your themes fall into; just list as many themes as you see. In the examples you find the following:

✔ **Topics or focus:**

> Belinda: Change/transition, careers
>
> Joanne: Sports, pets/nature, physical, emotional

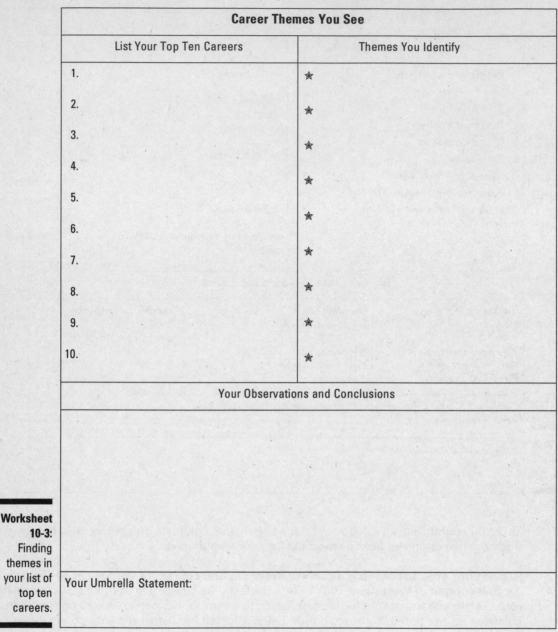

Career Themes You See	
List Your Top Ten Careers	Themes You Identify
1.	☆
2.	☆
3.	☆
4.	☆
5.	☆
6.	☆
7.	☆
8.	☆
9.	☆
10.	☆
Your Observations and Conclusions	
Your Umbrella Statement:	

Worksheet 10-3: Finding themes in your list of top ten careers.

✔ **Function:**

Belinda: Coaching, facilitating

Joanne: Therapy, training

✔ **How to provide service:**

Belinda: Working in corporations, facilitating groups, coaching individuals

Joanne: Working one-on-one

Use the categories I provide as starting points for your own theme exploration. If other theme categories emerge from your list, go with them. You might find themes that appear around your target client or whether the work is indoors or outdoors. Don't try to force-fit your list into the categories described in this example because that approach won't work. You must run with what your list is showing you.

If you have trouble seeing how to categorize your ideas, write each idea on a separate slip of paper and move the papers around until you see similarities. You can probably sort the careers in your list in several different ways — by skills you use, by work arrangement, by ultimate customer — so don't be concerned about doing it right. As you find themes that make sense, write them down in Worksheet 10-3 so you can study them later.

Step 3: Sort your careers according to the themes that make the most sense to you. Grouping your career ideas helps you begin to see the patterns that are emerging. As you see in the examples, all your ideas may fall under one broad category (Belinda), or they may cluster around two or three distinct themes (Joanne).

- ✔ **Belinda:** For the most part, all the entries on Belinda's list fall under one broad category of helping others improve their lives. Within that category, Belinda identified several useful clues to help her restructure her ideas.

- ✔ **Joanne:** Joanne organized her career ideas into three categories. Take a look at how she structured her conclusions.

Sometimes you'll find careers that don't really fit the overall themes. That's fine. For instance, Belinda's list had one outlier (organization coach), while Joanne's list had several (forest/park ranger, working for a sports/running magazine, and being a teacher).

Step 4: Create an umbrella statement that describes your overriding mission or goal. This step is easiest if all of your career ideas fall under one broad category or if your categories are related. If you have a wide variety of themes, make an attempt at creating an umbrella statement, but don't force it.

- ✔ Belinda's umbrella statement is "Supporting people in discovering different ways to do what they do with the ultimate goal of improving, simplifying, and transforming their lives."

- ✔ Although Joanne didn't state hers, she might have said her umbrella statement was "Improving people's relationship with their bodies and minds." Notice that she came to clear conclusions without stating her overall goal.

Step 5: Notice the careers that are floating to the top.

- ✔ **Belinda:** With her new level of clarity gained from Worksheet 10-3, Belinda can continue playing with her ideas to define how she'd like to fulfill her purpose while working with her favorite topics in these formats/settings. The fact that she didn't have a clear-cut career at the end of this process didn't bother Belinda. In fact, because she'd never seen her passions described in this way before, she was excited to explore possible positions and business ideas.

- ✔ **Joanne:** From Worksheet 10-3, Joanne easily identified three areas she wanted to learn more about: counseling, physical therapy, and teaching.

As you move through Steps 1 through 5, you may need to flip back and forth between the steps, the examples, and your Worksheet 10-3. Take it one step at a time. Sit with your own list to discover the clues it has for you about your next career. There's no hurry. Take the time you need to feel comfortable with your themes, the way you categorize your careers, and your umbrella statement.

In case you're wondering, here's what Belinda and Joanne decided:

- Belinda is in the process of creating a composite career — working full time as an organizational consultant and creating a part-time business on the side to work with individuals as a career change/transition coach. (For an explanation of composite careers, see the section "Contemplating Various Career Forms," later in this chapter.)

- Joanne is in school working toward a degree in occupational therapy, a career that's similar to physical therapy.

Isolating Your Key Career Criteria

At this point, you're quite familiar with your top ten career ideas. Something about each one intrigues you. What you don't know is how you'll ever narrow down your options. The worksheet in this section helps you identify the criteria that are most important to you as you make decisions about your next career.

For some people, one element or characteristic of their career or lifestyle is so important to them that it is the cornerstone of their new career. For others, several characteristics play a role in how they prioritize their career choices.

May, a former volunteer coordinator and a newly trained therapist in New Jersey, is embarking on her third career. Although she knows that she wants to use her new skills in her work, she's not quite sure what form her work will take because her Top Ten career list includes everything from working for social services to being a child advocate to having her own practice. As she reads the key criteria in Worksheet 10-4, she is able to clearly articulate what is most important to her as she makes decisions about the form her career takes. You see, May is a new grandmother. Suddenly her priorities have shifted. Although she still knows it's important to her that her work has meaning and makes a difference in the lives of those she works with and that she thrives when she does therapy with clients, her key criteria is her lifestyle. Because her grandchildren live in Indiana, she places high priority on being able to take time off to visit them for 10 to 14 days, several times a year. With this new clarity, she suddenly finds it a lot easier to narrow down her choices to those that give her the freedom to travel and possibly do her work from out of town if the need arises.

Think about your lifestyle, your style, and what you've written about your intriguing career ideas in Worksheets 10-1 and 10-3. Do you see the key to making a decision about your career? Are there any features of your career that must be in place for your life to work the way you'd like it to? Use the questions in Worksheet 10-4 to help you sort this out.

Read through the questions and put one slash through the box if your answer to the question is a strong, emphatic "yes." Then look at all the statements with one slash and think about what you value most about your life and your career. Choose the two or three statements that best reflect what's most important to you as you make your career decisions and make a slash in the opposite direction to create an X.

In May's case, having a career that allowed her to travel to see her grandchildren was the first brick she needed to keep in mind as she built her new career. If she ignored that feature, the work format and the eventual career would run counter to her needs.

Keys to Your Career Decisions	
	Is there a particular passion or interest you want to pursue in your work?
	Are you enthralled by a particular industry?
	Is there a certain company you want to work for?
	Is there a specific task or function that's the ticket?
	Is there a distinct topic you feel drawn to incorporate into your work?
	Do you thrive when you use a particular process?
	Is your work environment the most important factor for you?
	Are the people you work with a crucial piece of the puzzle?
	Is your work format the clincher?
	Is an aspect of your personal style/needs/desires the deciding factor?
	Must your work have definite meaning?
	Is there an aspect of your lifestyle that defines what you need?

Worksheet 10-4: X marks the spot of your career decisions.

As you proceed with your discovery process, keep your "keys" in mind. They can help you stay focused as you put the pieces of your career puzzle in place. In fact, by identifying your keys, you may be able to identify, with more certainty, the cornerstones of your career puzzle. After these important pieces are in place, you can begin to build your career around them.

Contemplating Various Career Forms

As you tie your career ideas and your key career decision criteria together, you may be bumping into elements that don't seem to work together. Although it's too soon to finalize your next career, it's not too soon to begin broadening your perspective about how your career ideas may take form. As you read this section, use the ideas to help you think outside the box about how you might create a career that truly works for you. Take the ideas in, work them around in your mind, but don't feel you need to identify the final form of your career just yet. Instead, use the ideas to spark new creative options you may not have known about before now.

As you begin to search for your next career, you can easily fall into the trap of thinking, and hoping, that your career is going to have a simple title and a singular focus: pilot, nurse, doctor, secretary, lawyer. You get the idea. The truth is that many careers are as diverse and multifaceted as people are. Although these careers aren't easy to cubbyhole, they are rich, interesting, and amazing in their diversity. In fact, opportunities abound!

If you have several ideas you really like, you might consider combining your favorite themes to create a unique career. The following examples show how people have found success in their careers by combining a variety of talents into a single career:

- A writer who is also a counselor combines his skills to create a practice that helps clients break through their creative blocks.

- An artist with a postgraduate degree in forensics and physical anthropology combines her talents to help a law enforcement agency reconstruct a face for a recently discovered skull.

- A social worker with clowning talents works as a therapeutic clown in a health-care setting to bring laughter, play, and empowerment to hospitalized children and their families.

- A biologist with advanced programming skills has his pick of jobs as companies search for bioinformatics programmers to analyze the human genome for potential configurations that can lead to drug discoveries.

Although finding the exact combination of skills to create a multifaceted career like this may take some deep thought, begin the process by playing with your ideas. As you look at your list of themes in Worksheet 10-3, daydream about how you might combine them. Don't get pulled down by the logistics or feasibility of your combinations — just explore the possibilities. Have fun with it!

Another option to consider, if you have multiple interests, is a composite career, a term introduced by William Bridges in his book *JobShift: How to Prosper in a Workplace without Jobs*, published by Perseus Books. In a *composite career,* you weave several careers together to create a fulfilling professional life that meets your personal and financial goals. The format of a composite career can be designed to meet your specific needs. For example, a composite career might have any of the following formats:

- A full-time job with occasional part-time projects on the side

- Two part-time jobs

- One part-time job and a business

- Two businesses

In addition to giving you added flexibility and variety in your work, you also gain a surprising sense of security with this arrangement. With multiple sources of income, you're no longer dependent on one paycheck. If one income stream dries up, you aren't a sitting duck because you can always rely on the other one(s) to tide you over. Consider how a composite career could change how you think about structuring your new career.

Choosing Your Top Two Career Ideas

After reading this chapter and working through each section, what career ideas keep rising to the top of your list? Your favorites may be careers you included in Worksheet 10-1, conclusions you made in Worksheet 10-3, a career you came up with by combining several of your career ideas together, or a career that came into focus when you identified your key career criteria (from Worksheet 10-4) or your umbrella statement (from Worksheet 10-3).

Focus on the two careers that seem the most interesting or promising to you at this time. By identifying these two careers, you aren't making a commitment to enter these fields; you're just highlighting these two careers as the ones you're most interested in exploring.

Record your top two career ideas in Worksheet 10-5. Even if you don't yet have a complete picture of these careers, make an effort to describe them the best you can.

Are you frustrated that you're being asked to choose only two careers from your list? Are you disappointed that you must turn away from careers that really do interest you? If so, you may find some relief in the section "Contemplating Various Career Forms," earlier in this chapter, which shows you how to combine your favorite elements of various careers into one workable idea. Also, keep in mind that if one of your first career choices doesn't pan out as you explore it in more detail in Chapters 14 and 15, you'll return to your Top Ten career list again to choose another career to investigate.

Describing Your Top Two Careers	
Career Idea #1	Career Idea #2

Worksheet 10-5: Identifying the two careers you want to learn more about.

Although you have a couple of promising career ideas on your list, you are, in actuality, still in the middle of your creative process. Nothing is yet set in stone. Before you dive in and activate your job search, use Chapters 14, 15, and 16 to verify that your career ideas are in fact good matches for you. As soon as you confirm that they're viable options for you, you can proceed to launch your job search, your business planning process, or your return to school in Chapters 18 and 19.

Part III
Exploring Possible Career Directions

The 5th Wave   By Rich Tennant

"When choosing a career I ignored my heart
and did what my brain wanted. Now all my
brain wants is Prozac."

In this part . . .

After you have a seed of a career idea, use this part to help you convert your idea into any number of creative career options.

Instead of seeing these chapters as complete lists of possible careers, think of them as springboards that trigger you to think of your idea in entirely new ways. Use your Multiple Intelligence Profile in Chapter 7 to determine which of the chapters in this part align with your interests. As you scan each career box, find the career areas that appeal to you. After you identify a few intriguing options, use the related job titles and professional associations as the first clues in your career exploration.

Chapter 11

Considering Communicating Careers

. . . .

In This Chapter

▶ Checking out careers with a focus on the written word

▶ Finding careers that involve your ability to speak

▶ Tapping into careers with education potential

▶ Using your skills to help people heal physically and emotionally

▶ Exploring ways to help others enjoy life more

▶ Assisting others in the workplace

▶ Keeping people safe as your line of work

. . . .

*W*hether you're in the process of brainstorming possible career ideas in Chapter 9, investigating your top two career ideas in Chapter 14, or dipping into the book right here just to take a look, you can use the career descriptions to expand your options. Although this chapter can't possibly list every single career, the descriptions that are included serve as a launching pad for creative thinking and exploration.

All of the career categories described in this chapter involve communicating in some way. The section "If You Thrive on Words" offers careers that capitalize on your desire and ability to use written and spoken words in your work. The section "If You Connect Well with Others" lists careers that tap into your ability to interact well with others.

If you're unsure whether these two categories are a good fit for you and your skills, refer back to Worksheet 7-2 in Chapter 7 to see whether your Multiple Intelligence Profile highlights these two career categories. Depending on your Multiple Intelligence Profile, you may also be interested in exploring the logical/scientific careers in Chapter 12 or the creative careers in Chapter 13.

Don't worry if you don't find a description of one of your ideal careers. The best way to explore any career, whether it's included in these pages or not, is to use the Internet. Chapter 14 provides a number of resources to help you explore the careers you want to learn more about.

Making the Most of This Chapter

Within each career category in this chapter you find descriptions of various career areas. See Figure 11-1 for an explanation of the career descriptions you find in this chapter.

If you're using this chapter to enhance your list of possible careers as you work through Chapter 9, record all the career categories that catch your attention in Worksheet 9-6. Although your exploration opens a number of possible avenues of discovery, don't get distracted. For now, use these descriptions to build your list of possible careers. After you use Chapter 10 to narrow your focus to your top two careers, you can return to this chapter to explore those ideas in more depth.

Career area title	Related jobs
A brief description of the career area with tips, explanations, and requirements. As you move through this chapter, skim the career descriptions to see if anything catches your eye.	A list of related job titles are in alphabetical order. Use these jobs to expand how you think about this career area. Notice that some job titles show new directions you can take within this career area.
For more information: Use the contact information to connect with a relevant professional association. Don't worry if the professional association isn't quite a good fit for your target career. In Chapter 14, you can access several online resources that help you find professional associations that are on target.	**Explore this career?** Yes / No Circle or highlight "yes" to indicate that you'd like to take more time to explore this career in depth.

Figure 11-1: Finding your way around career area descriptions.

If you've already identified your top two careers in Chapter 10 and are now working in Chapter 14, use the career descriptions in this chapter to better understand your two favorite options. The professional association contact information is your best source for current information related to your target careers and industries. The list of related jobs may open a window to an option you hadn't considered before. After learning what you can from the career descriptions, return to Chapter 14 to find other ways to discover more about the careers that interest you most.

Scanning the careers in this chapter may help you think of or discover other careers that fit your Multiple Intelligence Profile and your interests. Keep track of ideas that come to mind so that you can follow up on your discoveries later. And if an insight about a possible career comes to you while you read, snag it! Get it in writing in Worksheet 9-6 as soon as possible because spontaneous Aha! ideas have a way of fading fast if not acted upon in the moment.

If You Thrive on Words

If you think in words and enjoy expressing your thoughts, feelings, and knowledge with words, check out the careers in this section. Whether you want to write or work with the words that others have written, you can find various ways to inform, entertain, and convince others through the use of words.

Writing

Words are ubiquitous. Aside from words exchanged in personal correspondence, nearly every word you read each day — from your cereal box to the daily newspaper to the parking ticket so thoughtfully left on your windshield — has been crafted by a paid professional. Indeed, words are the currency of the information age and the technology age. If you enjoy writing, one of the careers in this section may intrigue you.

Technical writing	Related jobs
As a technical writer, you explain complex scientific information in a way that makes sense to readers, whether they're novices or experts. In addition to having good writing skills and an interest and aptitude in science, you must be an especially clear thinker who can communicate complex technical information in a well-organized, easy-to-comprehend way.	Legal analyst Manual writer Medical writer Scientific writer Specifications writer Technical editor Technical speech writer Technical writer
For more information: Society of Technical Communication, Inc. (STC): 901 N. Stuart St., Suite 904, Arlington, VA 22203; phone 703-522-4114; Web site www.stc.org	**Explore this career?** Yes / No

Reporting information	Related jobs
Use your way with words to inform and educate others on the issues of the day. Accurate, objective reporting is your primary goal. Although each story is unique, the process you follow is similar. After investigating leads to find a story, you gather the facts; observe what you can; interview relevant, trustworthy sources for quotable material; and do background research. After you have the information you need, you organize it into a concise, well-written, engaging piece and submit the story in time to meet your deadline.	Abstractor Broadcast journalist Correspondent Investigative reporter Journalist News writer Radio writer Reporter Researcher
For more information: Society of Professional Journalists, Eugene S. Pulliam National Journalism Center, 3909 N. Meridian St., Indianapolis, IN 46208; phone 317-927-8000, fax 317-920-4789; Web site www.spj.org	**Explore this career?** Yes / No

Writing opinions	Related jobs
In sharing your opinions about current events or experiences with your audience, your intention may be to stir the pot to get people thinking about the topic from a different perspective. Or you may be interested in giving them a preview of a movie, play, restaurant, art exhibit, or travel destination. Incorporate your personal perspective to add color and interest to your pieces. One way to expand your reach is to syndicate your columns so that they appear in more than one publication.	Book or movie reviewer Columnist Commentator Critic Editorial writer News analyst Newspaper critic Reviewer Travel writer
For more information: American Society of Journalists and Authors, 1501 Broadway, Suite 302, New York, NY 10036; phone 212-997-0947, fax 212-768-7414; Web site www.asja.org	**Explore this career?** Yes / No

Sales writing	Related jobs
You write to persuade your audience to buy a product or service, give a donation or a grant, or hire your client. Such writing tends to be catchy, convincing, and concise. It takes practice, and lots of it, to produce such results in a fast-paced, deadline-oriented environment. With the advent of new technologies, you may also use your talents to write scripts for infomercials, multimedia, and interactive media.	Advertising editor Advertising writer Copywriter Grant writer Publicity director Public relations Resume writer
For more information: American Marketing Association, 311 S. Wacker Dr., Suite 5800, Chicago, IL 60606; phone 312-542-9000; Web site www.ama.org	**Explore this career?** Yes / No

Writing for various audiences	Related jobs
Writing broadcast copy, scripts, lyrics, speeches, jingles, plays, and jokes are all possible as well. To be a successful freelance writer, you must be persistent, always looking for possible angles and publications to submit your work to. Some surprisingly lucrative markets for writers include greeting cards, newsletters, filler articles for publications, specialty cookbooks, and encyclopedia articles. The writing profession has great potential for flex-place employment arrangements. Have laptop and Internet connection, can travel and write!	Comedy writer Lyricist Non-fiction author Novelist Poet Reference writer Scriptwriter Speech writer Storyteller Writing instructor
For more information: National Writers Union, National Office East, 113 University Place, 6th Floor, New York, NY 10003; phone 212-254-0279; e-mail nwu@nwu.org, Web site www.nwu.org	**Explore this career?** Yes / No

Working with other people's words

After words have been written or spoken, another set of professionals swings into action. They publish or produce pieces based on these words, organize them, retrieve information from them, translate them, or transcribe them. If you enjoy working with the written word, one of the careers in this section may intrigue you.

Editing	Related jobs
As an editor, you read, query, and rewrite what writers produce to create a more powerful final piece. You may also manage the big picture, including how the articles and pictures come together in a newspaper or magazine, or how the chapters hang together to produce a book. You use your knowledge of the publications' readership to determine what gets included and what gets cut. You recommend changes to text, make corrections, modify the document length, plan the layout, and coordinate the production of the final document.	Acquisitions editor Assistant editor Fact checker Managing editor News editor Production editor Proofreader Publisher Technical editor
For more information: Editorial Freelance Association, 71 W. 23rd St., Suite 1910, New York, NY 10010; phone 212-929-5400, fax 212-929-5439; e-mail info@the-efa.org, Web site www.the-efa.org	**Explore this career?** Yes / No

Managing information	Related jobs
The role of librarian may seem obsolete given that information is so accessible these days, but the world of virtual libraries, remote databases, and the Internet may need your information management and retrieval skills now more than ever. Without clear, organized information structures, finding a piece of information in this ever-growing sea of data can be downright frustrating and fruitless. An alternative is to become an information broker who searches out, analyzes, interprets, and synthesizes information for businesses, agencies, investigators, and politicians.	Academic librarian Archivist Corporate librarian Database consultant Digital library manager Independent researcher Information architect Information broker Public librarian
For more information: American Library Association, 50 E. Huron St., Chicago, IL 60611; phone 800-545-2433, fax 312-440-9374; e-mail ala@ala.org, Web site www.ala.org	**Explore this career?** Yes / No

Translating	Related jobs
Whether you take documents in one language and translate them into another language or you interpret conversations from one language into another, you must know two or more languages, have good verbal and linguistic aptitude, have an understanding of the pertinent cultures, and be extremely attentive to the detail involved in translation. With the globalization of the marketplace, the Internet, and multilingual cultural groups, more and more businesses must make their materials and products, both online and offline, accessible to people who speak other languages.	Closed caption writer Court interpreter Interpreter Legal terminologist Literary translator Medical terminologist Reviser Sign language interpreter Technical translator
For more information: American Translators Association, 225 Reinekers Lane, Suite 590, Alexandria, VA 22314; phone 703-683-6100, fax: 703-683-6122; e-mail ata@atanet.org, Web site www.atanet.org	**Explore this career?** Yes / No

Transcribing	Related jobs
You create a verbatim record of what transpires in meetings, during courtroom proceedings, or as a result of medical situations. To do this work effectively, you must be familiar with the profession-specific terminology used by your clients, whether it is legal or medical in nature. You must hear well and type what you hear accurately and precisely. On occasion, your work setting requires that you remain calm and focused on your tasks, even in highly-charged situations. Technological advances in this field make the transcribing process less cumbersome then it once was.	Closed-caption writer Court recorder Court reporter Court stenographer Legal secretary Litigation secretary Medical transcriptionist
For more information: American Association of Electronic Reporters and Transcribers, Inc., 23812 Rock Circle, Bothell, WA 98021-8573; phone 800-233-5306; e-mail AAERT@blarg.net, Web site www.aaert.org	**Explore this career?** Yes / No

Using the spoken word to inform or educate

Some word-based careers focus on using the spoken word to educate, inform, inspire, and motivate audiences.

Newscasting or reporting	Related jobs
To make it in this profession, you must have the voice, personality, confidence, and looks to attract a large, loyal following. Ratings run the show. Your working conditions are one of a kind. Tight, unpredictable schedules punctuated with ongoing deadlines add to the stress of producing concise, top-notch stories. Although consolidations at the network level tighten the market, new digital technology and alternative media make it easier and faster to produce shows. To enhance your employability, gain experience with the technical side of producing your own show. A show can do without a technician, but it can't do without the host!	Disc jockey Network reporter News anchor Newscaster News correspondent Radio host Sports announcer Talk show host Traffic reporter Weathercaster
For more information: National Association of Broadcasters, 1771 North Street, NW, Washington, DC 20036; phone 202-429-5300, fax 202-429-4199; e-mail nab@nab.org, Web site www.nab.org	**Explore this career?** Yes / No

Teaching	Related jobs
As a teacher, you create projects, initiate interactive discussions, and offer hands-on learning opportunities to help your students think, solve problems, and become active, successful members of the workforce after graduation. In addition to having a good grasp of the subjects you teach, you must evaluate your students' needs and communicate with each of them in a way that is motivating, effective, and matched to their abilities. Using your creativity to work around limited budgets and tight resources is a valuable talent. Schools are looking for teachers who are qualified in math, science, and computer science.	Curriculum specialist English-as-a-second- language teacher Reading specialist Schoolteacher Special education teacher Substitute teacher Teacher's aid Teaching assistant Training specialist
For more information: American Federation of Teachers, 555 New Jersey Ave. NW, Washington, DC 20001; phone 202-879-4400; Web site www.aft.org	**Explore this career?** Yes / No

Using words to convince

If you have a strong command of the language, you may enjoy persuading others to follow your lead or agree with your point of view. Whether you make your convincing arguments in writing, in conversations, or during presentations, you may find the following careers to be exciting and challenging.

Law	Related jobs
In this profession, you interpret the existing laws to help your clients understand and successfully navigate whatever legal circumstances they face. Regardless of whether you serve as your client's advocate in a criminal or civil trial, or in the role of advisor, suggesting a proper course of action for a business-related situation or a personal matter, you take the relevant case law together with the facts of the case and distill it all into a convincing argument or strategy for your client. Or you might consider a law-related position within a corporation, the government, or a nonprofit organization.	Corporate attorney District attorney Judge Legal analyst Lobbyist Mediator Paralegal Politician Public defender Trial lawyer
For more information: American Bar Association, Service Center, 321 N. Clark St., Chicago, IL 60610; phone 312-988-5522; Web site www.abanet.org	**Explore this career?** Yes / No

Marketing	Related jobs
After a product is made, and before it goes to market, the marketing team must make customers aware of the product. As a marketer, you create such a recognizable brand that your customers think of your product whenever they have the need. Due to the nature of this career, a blend of strong communications skills, sharp analytical abilities, creativity, and interpersonal skills make you a good candidate. Your niche may be product development, market research, direct mail, public relations, advertising, or Internet marketing.	Brand manager Graphic designer Marketing assistant Marketing communications Market research analyst Promotions specialist
For more information: American Marketing Association, 311 S. Wacker Dr., Suite 5800, Chicago, IL 60606; phone 312-542-9000, fax 312-542-9001; e-mail info@ama.org, Web site www.ama.org	**Explore this career?** Yes / No

Public relations	Related jobs
You make sure that the public sees your client or company in the best possible light. You attract the attention of the press with riveting press releases, unusual events, and breaking news, so that they run pieces that communicate your client's or employer's message. You work hard to make sure that the message is clear and carried consistently across the multitude of media channels. When events or errors cause negative or damaging publicity, you use your communication skills to turn the situation around as quickly.	Fundraiser Information officer Media spokesperson Press agent Press secretary Public affairs Publicist Public relations consultant
For more information: Public Relations Society of America, 33 Maiden Lane, 11th Fl., New York, NY 10038-5150; phone 212-460-1400, fax 212-995-0757; Web site www.prsa.org	**Explore this career?** Yes / No

Sales	Related jobs
For every product and service offered, someone must make a sale before the money rolls in. No matter what the product or service, the sales process is essentially the same. Closing the deal is based on what you know about your client's needs and the product, and your ability to listen, explain, and create unique solutions. Anything you can do to enhance your credibility is a plus. Your work style and need for structure and contact with co-workers help you decide how you want to sell: inside sales, on the road, telemarketer, or retail sales.	Account executive Broker Financial services sales Insurance agent Manufacturer's sales rep Real estate agent Retail sales Sales manager Wholesale sales rep
For more information: National Association of Sales Professionals, 11000 N. 130th Pl., Scottsdale, AZ 85259; phone 480-951-4311; Web site www.nasp.com	**Explore this career?** Yes / No

If You Connect Well with Others

All of the careers that I describe in this section require you to enjoy working closely with patients, clients, co-workers, guests, customers, or the general public. To do this work well, you must have strong interpersonal skills that allow you to sense what others need, to encourage them, and to guide them.

Helping others heal physically

Some people with interpersonal skills enjoy helping people who are ill or facing health challenges. With your knowledge and care, you help others heal.

Nursing care	Related jobs
As you work directly with patients, helping them through their diagnosis, treatment, and rehabilitation, your empathy and compassion are essential. Your job includes following instructions, providing patients with proper care, and making quick, sound decisions about when to call in others for consultation and assistance. The records you keep, your discussions with patients, and the hands-on care you give must be done meticulously to prevent errors. Due to the aging population, technological advances, and people's desire to heal at home, growth is expected to escalate in home health, long-term care, ambulatory care, outpatient hospital centers, rehabilitation, chemotherapy, and surgicenters. The high demand also results in rapid growth in salaries as well.	Emergency medical technician (EMT) Home health nurse Hospice nurse Licensed vocational nurse Nurse practitioner Paramedic Physician Physician assistant Public health nurse Registered nurse
For more information: American Nurses Association, 8515 Georgia Ave., Suite 400, Silver Spring, MD 20910; phone 800-274-4ANA; Web site www.nursingworld.org	**Explore this career?** Yes / No

Rehabilitation	Related jobs
Within rehabilitation specialties, you help patients improve how they function in their work, home, school, and social environments. You bring out their creativity, confidence, and problem-solving abilities while teaching them new social and life skills. You evaluate what patients can and can't do, review their medical histories, and create treatment plans to bring about the desired outcome, whether it's a greater range of motion, the ability to use a computer, techniques to alleviate pain, or ways to compensate for a permanent loss of function. Over time, you assess your patient's progress and modify the treatment plan as needed.	Audiologist Ergonomic specialist Occupational therapist Physical therapist Recreation therapist Rehabilitation specialist Respiratory therapist Special education counselor Speech pathologist Speech therapist
For more information: National Rehabilitation Association, 633 S. Washington St., Alexandria, VA 22314; phone 703-836-0850, fax 703-836-0848; e-mail info@nationalrehab.org, Web site www.nationalrehab.org	**Explore this career?** Yes / No

Holistic medicine	Related jobs
As a chiropractor, acupuncturist, or other alternative medicine practitioner, you combine your extensive knowledge of the systems that make up the human body, your compassion, and your ability to listen to find ways to ease your patients' pain. Using the diagnostic system and devices preferred in your specialty, you evaluate your patient to determine what is out of alignment based on the symptoms the patient shares with you. Then you use treatments, such as chiropractic manipulations, acupuncture, herbs, biofeedback, or massage, to strengthen the body's weaknesses.	Acupuncturist Biofeedback specialist Chinese medicine practitioner Chiropractor Massage therapist Midwife Naturopath physician Nutritionist Osteopath Sound healer
For more information: Complementary Alternative Medical Association, P.O. Box 373478, Decatur, GA 30037; e-mail cama@mindspring.com, Web site www.camaweb.org	**Explore this career?** Yes / No

Helping others make the most of life

Sometimes a little extra boost of support can go a long way. As a member of one of the following professions, you're in a fine position to help children and adults live full lives.

Counseling and supporting individuals	Related jobs
If you enjoy listening to people and helping them resolve personal, family, relationship, educational, and mental health situations, consider a counseling career. Regardless of the setting, you begin by getting a picture of your client's situation and what isn't working. From what they say, how they say it, and what they don't say, you discern their needs and help them gain the perspective, the skills, and possibly the medication they need to resolve their difficulties. Confidentiality, trust, and objectivity are essential elements of your work. Besides establishing a private practice, consider working in hospitals, home health agencies, social service agencies, employee assistance programs, and rehabilitation settings.	Art therapist Clergy Clinical psychologist Counselor Dance therapist Drug/alcohol counselor Hypnotherapist Professional coach Psychiatrist School psychologist Social worker Sports psychologist Therapist
For more information: American Counseling Association, 5999 Stevenson Ave., Alexandria, VA 22304-3300; phone 800-347-6647, fax 800-473-2329; Web site www.counseling.org	**Explore this career?** Yes / No

Childcare	Related jobs
You help children develop and grow physically, emotionally, socially, and intellectually through play, cooperative activities, and instruction. To accomplish this goal, you plan a series of events for the day, knowing, of course, that those plans may change as the day unfolds. Tracking your charges' progress, creating a plan to work with their special needs, and sharing your ideas with parents are integral aspects of your job. To succeed in this work, you must have the physical stamina and energy to keep up with active children; the imagination, wonder, and patience to participate in their activities; and the common sense and knowledge to respond appropriately in times of crisis.	Child care worker Child psychologist Daycare operator Developmental psychologist Family child care provider Guidance counselor Nanny Preschool teacher School counselor Tutor
For more information: National Association for Education of Young Children, 1509 16th St. NW, Washington, DC 20036-1426; phone 202-232-8777 or 800-424-2460, fax 202-328-1846; e-mail naeyc@naeyc.org, Web site www.naeyc.org	**Explore this career?** Yes / No

Helping others enjoy their leisure time

If you like giving people the times of their lives, you may enjoy the following careers in the travel and recreation industries.

Recreation	Related jobs
If you're creative and outgoing and you enjoy organizing events, consider working in recreation. As a recreation leader, you plan events, teach necessary skills, facilitate activities, and encourage participants to engage in activities. Your motivational skills and your ability to sense who needs an extra boost of confidence can go a long way toward making you a success. The increased interest in health and fitness and the need for recreation activities for older adults increase the demand for people in this profession. Look for opportunities on cruise ships, in health clubs, apartment complexes, corporate wellness programs, and summer camps.	Activity specialist Camp counselor Craft specialist Director of recreation and parks Lifeguard Personal trainer Recreation leader Recreation supervisor Recreation therapist Resort social director
For more information: National Recreation and Park Association, 22377 Belmont Ridge Rd., Ashburn, VA 20148; phone 703-858-0784, fax 703-858-0794; e-mail info@nrpa.org, Web site www.activeparks.org	**Explore this career?** Yes / No

Travel	Related jobs
Your clients depend on your organizational skills, research abilities, and knowledge of the travel industry to book them on the best, most economical trips available. You ask a series of questions to come up with options that best fit their desired parameters and book the arrangements they choose. Although the Internet gives travelers unprecedented opportunity to make their own travel arrangements, global business, travel tours for foreign tourists, and baby boomers retiring with money and a desire to travel indicate a need for travel agents. Creating specialized tours for targeted markets is one way to niche yourself in this field.	Adventure travel organizer Cruise director Entertainment director Location tour guide Member services counselor Relocation specialist Reservation agent Ticket agent Travel agent
For more information: American Society of Travel Agents, 1101 King St., Suite 200, Alexandria, VA 22314; phone 703-739-2782, fax 703-684-8319; e-mail askasta@astahq.com Web site www.astanet.com	**Explore this career?** Yes / No

Hospitality	Related jobs
Working within a hotel, you put in long days completing the myriad of tasks that keep the property in tiptop shape. You may obtain fresh flowers for the lobby, choose furnishings for the next upgrade, plan the restaurant menus, orchestrate on-site meetings, or verify that repairs have been completed. Your ability to interact easily with a diverse group of guests and team members, manage your time and multiple projects, and solve problems in a timely manner contribute to your success. Many hotel managers are self-employed, owning the establishment they manage. Others act as property managers, looking after a property for long-distance owners.	Bed-and-breakfast owner Concierge Convention service manager Front desk clerk General manager Hotel manager Property manager Resident manager Restaurant manager Sommelier Spa manager
For more information: American Hotel & Lodging Association, 1201 New York Ave. NW, #600, Washington, DC 20005-3931; phone 202-289-3100, fax: 202-289-3199; e-mail infoctr@ahla.com, Web site www.ahla.com	**Explore this career?** Yes / No

Helping others in a business or public setting

The careers in this section allow you to use your interpersonal skills to locate the best employees for your company, to support employees, to manage your own company or department, or to keep your community safe.

Staffing	Related jobs
As a recruiter, you use your ability to put people at ease and your aptitude to discern what the employer wants and what skills and experience each applicant brings to the party. You find and hire the best candidate for each job. To do your job well, you must judge people impartially and communicate your assessments effectively to executives and hiring managers. Recruitment and staffing functions may be outsourced, which means that opportunities exist to work independently or in small agencies.	Casting director Employment manager Headhunter HR coordinator Interviewer Personnel recruiter Placement manager Staffing specialist Temporary agency rep
For more information: Recruiters Network, 5464 N. Port Washington Rd., Suite #196, Milwaukee, WI 53217; phone 414-357-8350, fax 414-357-8333; e-mail info@recruitersnetwork.com, Web site www.recruitersnetwork.com	**Explore this career?** Yes / No

Supporting employees	Related jobs
If you have strong interpersonal and communication skills, the desire to help employees make the most of their work experience, and the ability to juggle multiple tasks, consider a career in human resources (HR). Depending on your interests, you may work with compensation issues, labor issues, benefits, or the allocation of resources. You help the company utilize the skills of its personnel in a cost-effective and quality way. To do this, you must be well informed about the company's strategy, goals, and constraints. Two specialties are emerging in this field: global and culturally diverse workforce and information systems for managing human resource programs.	Benefits specialist Compensation specialist Corporate coach Employee relations manager Group facilitator HR specialist Labor relations specialist Management consultant Organizational development consultant Safety specialist Trainer
For more information: Society for Human Resource Management, 1800 Duke St., Alexandria, VA 22314; phone 703-548-3440, fax 703-535-6490; e-mail shrm@shrm.org, Web site www.shrm.org	**Explore this career?** Yes / No

Managing businesses	Related jobs
Managers and executives create strategies, policies, and procedures to achieve a company's long-term and short-term goals. To do the job well, you must be able to scan and synthesize an infinite amount of information from sources inside and outside the company to help you make sound decisions. After seeing what needs to be done, you must clearly articulate what you want and delegate tasks to appropriate members of your staff. Depending on the size of your company, you may be accountable for a narrow aspect of the operations, such as marketing, purchasing, finance, or property management or several or all of these areas.	Business manager Chief executive officer Education administrator Entrepreneur Executive director General manager Governor Management consultant Mayor Operations manager Volunteer coordinator
For more information: American Management Association, 1601 Broadway, New York, NY 10019; phone 212-586-8100, fax 212-903-8168; e-mail mworld@amanet.org, Web site www.amanet.org	**Explore this career?** Yes / No

Keeping the public safe	Related jobs
Your communication skills; your ability to handle sensitive, perhaps even explosive, situations with a calm demeanor; and your talent for thinking well on your feet make you a good candidate for a career in public safety. Because a fair amount of the work in this field is physical, you must be in exquisite shape, both strong and agile, fast and enduring. Whether you direct traffic during an emergency, respond to a call, or investigate a crime, you protect the safety of those in the community. In each situation, you use as little force as necessary to turn a difficult situation into a peaceful resolution.	Airport security officer Correctional officer Fire marshal Highway patrol officer Police officer Private investigator Probation officer Security guard Sheriff State police officer Store detective
For more information: American Federation of Police, 6350 Horizon Dr., Titusville, FL 32780; phone 321-264-0911, fax 321-264-0033; e-mail policeinfo@aphf.org, Web site www.aphf.org	**Explore this career?** Yes / No

Chapter 12

Exploring Scientific/Logical Careers

● ●

In This Chapter

▶ Exploring your scientific and technical career options

▶ Transforming your way with numbers into viable financial careers

▶ Discovering ways to use your planning skills

▶ Identifying work that employs your green thumb

▶ Connecting with careers that include animals

▶ Finding careers to aid the earth itself

● ●

*W*hether you flip here from Chapter 9, where you're brainstorming possible career ideas, or Chapter 14, where you're exploring your top two career ideas, use the career descriptions in this chapter to discover and explore careers that interest you. Even if you haven't yet read Chapter 9 or 14, focus your attention on the career areas that catch your eye.

All of the career categories described in this chapter involve the ability to think logically. The section "If You Think in a Logical, Organized Fashion" offers careers based on scientific and strategic thinking. The section "If You Love Nature and Its Creatures" lists careers that use these same skills while also tapping your affinity with nature.

Review Worksheet 7-2 in Chapter 7 to determine whether these two categories are a good fit for you and your skills. A quick look at your Multiple Intelligence Profile tells you whether these two career categories are relevant expressions of your skills. You may also find that you're interested in exploring the communication careers in Chapter 11 or the creative careers in Chapter 13.

Making the Most of This Chapter

Within each career category in this chapter you find descriptions of various career areas. See Figure 12-1 for an explanation of the career descriptions you find in this chapter.

Career area title	Related jobs
A brief description of the career area with tips, explanations, and requirements. As you move through this chapter, skim the career descriptions to see if anything catches your eye.	A list of related job titles are in alphabetical order. Use these jobs to expand how you think about this career area. Notice that some job titles show new directions you can take within this career area.
For more information: Use the contact information to connect with a relevant professional association. Don't worry if the professional association isn't quite a good fit for your target career. In Chapter 14, you can access several online resources that help you find professional associations that are on target.	**Explore this career?** Yes / No Circle or highlight "yes" to indicate that you'd like to take more time to explore this career in depth.

Figure 12-1: Finding your way around career area descriptions.

If you're working in Chapter 9 and using the careers in this chapter to expand your list of possible careers, record all the career categories that interest you in Worksheet 9-6. Don't let the multitude of options distract you into researching every career that catches your eye. For now, stay focused on using these descriptions to enhance your list of possible careers. After you narrow down the field a bit in Chapter 10, you can return to this chapter to explore your top two career ideas in more depth.

If you're working in Chapter 14 and using this chapter to gain a deeper understanding of your top two careers, refer to the contact information about the professional association. The association can give you current information about your possible profession and industry. After learning what you can from the professional association and list of related jobs, be sure to return to Chapter 14 to discover other ways to gain more information about the careers that interest you most.

Scanning the careers in this chapter may help you think of or discover other careers that fit your Multiple Intelligence Profile and your interests. Keep track of ideas that come to mind so that you can follow up on your discoveries later.

If You Think in a Logical, Organized Fashion

Your ability to think in a logical and organized fashion can open the door to a variety of careers in the scientific world, technical venues, financial circles, and planning situations. Read the introductory paragraph in each section to assess whether the careers in that section are a good match for your skills.

Working in the sciences

Whether you want to conduct research to further the theories of science, or take what others have discovered and use it to find solutions to practical problems, you may be intrigued by the pure science careers that I describe in this section.

Biology and medicine	Related jobs
As a biologist, you study life itself, from the smallest cell to the largest ecosystem. You apply your expertise to solving problems in health-related fields, agriculture, and environmental preservation. Whether you focus on research and development, applied research, product development, or manufacturing, your dedication, inquisitive nature, attention to detail, and stamina contribute to your success. Regardless of your specialty, the increasingly complex instrumentation, research methods, and production techniques used in this field require that you have well-developed technical skills.	Bacteriology technician Biological scientist Cardiovascular technologist Geneticist Immunologist Marine biologist Microbiologist Molecular biologist Pharmacy technician Toxicologist
For more information: The American Institute of Biological Science, AIBS Headquarters, 1444 I Street NW, Suite 200, Washington, DC 20005; phone 202-628-1500, extension 253, fax 202-628-1509; Web site www.aibs.org	**Explore this career?** Yes / No

Chemistry	Related jobs
How you apply your knowledge of chemistry depends on what you want to produce. As a basic researcher, you investigate chemicals to understand how they function and to find compounds with certain characteristics. Or you apply the findings of other researchers to produce products and processes. Another option is to work in manufacturing plants to make sure the products and processes are sound and of good quality. In all likelihood, you perform one of these functions in a specialty area, such as analytical, organic, inorganic, or physical chemistry.	Analytical chemist Biochemist Chemical engineer Chemist Food scientist Hazardous waste manager Production chemist Quality control chemist Research chemist Toxicologist
For more information: American Chemical Society, 1155 16th St. NW, Washington, DC 20036; phone 202-872-4600 or 800-227-5558; Web site www.acs.org	**Explore this career?** Yes / No

Mathematics	Related jobs
You use mathematical theory and computational techniques to find solutions to practical problems in financial and business settings, the social sciences, or the hard sciences. Because so much of your work uses computers, knowledge of computer programming is essential, as are good reasoning skills and the ability to discuss and explain your solutions to others who may not have the extensive mathematical background that you do. Most employees using mathematics in their jobs do not have the word "mathematician" in their job titles. Look to engineering, computer science, statistics, physics, atmospheric science, and economics for additional careers that use math extensively.	Actuary Atmospheric scientist Computer scientist Demographer Economist Epidemiologist Market research analyst Mathematician Math teacher Statistician Theoretical mathematician
For more information: American Mathematical Society, 201 Charles St., Providence, RI 02904-2294; phone 800-321-4AMS, fax: 401-331-3842; e-mail ams@ams.org, Web site www.ams.org American Statistical Association, 1929 Duke St., Alexandria, VA 22314; phone 703-684-1221 or 888-231-3473, fax 703-684-2037; e-mail asainfo@amstat.org, Web site www.amstat.org	**Explore this career?** Yes / No

Physics	Related jobs
Your inquisitive nature, your ability to think through complex, abstract ideas, and your exceptional mathematical ability allow you to become a physicist. Use what you know to conduct basic research to understand the laws of nature, apply research findings to solve practical real-life problems or create devices, equipment, and materials. A specialty may give you the background to combine two fields, such as biophysics, geophysics, and astrophysics. If you plan to move into applied physics, broaden your knowledge by studying economics, business management, or computer science.	Acoustics physicist Aerodynamicist Astrophysicist Biophysicist Cosmologist Medical physicist Optics physicist Physicist Physics teacher Solid-state physicist
For more information: American Institute of Physics, One Physics Ellipse, College Park, MD 20740-3843; phone 301-209-3100; Web site www.aip.org	**Explore this career?** Yes / No

Working in engineering and computer science

Careers in engineering allow you to use scientific findings to create viable products or find solutions to technical or structural problems. As a result, most of the work that engineers and computer scientists do is quite practical and focused on solving specific problems.

Civil engineering	Related jobs
This career allows you to build large-scale projects from start to finish or rebuild outdated parts of the infrastructure, including roads, tunnels, the power grid, public buildings, and bridges. You start each project with preconstruction planning, which includes surveying, assessing needs, determining budgets, and designing. Then you coordinate all aspects of the actual construction, handling and making decisions about any problems on the spot. After the work is finished, you evaluate the project and maintain it. As you work to bring the project in on time, your patience may be tested as you encounter delays due to bureaucratic stalls, politics, and the weather.	Bridge engineer Civil engineer Construction engineer Environmental engineer Hydraulic engineer Public works engineer Structural engineer Surveying engineer Traffic engineer Water management engineer
For more information: American Society of Civil Engineers, 1801 Alexander Bell Dr., Reston, VA 20191-4400; phone 703-295-6300 or 800-548-2723; Web site www.asce.org	**Explore this career?** Yes / No

Mechanical engineering	Related jobs
Mechanical engineering entails designing, manufacturing, and testing mechanical parts; machines that produce power, such as engines and turbines; or machines that use power to run, such as refrigeration and production equipment. Your ability to look at problems analytically and from different vantage points allows you to find new solutions to mechanical problems. As you gain experience, you may have greater independence, but remember that the overall project may be a team event, making good communication skills a must for success. Focusing on a specialty builds your expertise and boosts your employability.	Acoustics engineer Agricultural engineer Biomedical engineer Fluid mechanics engineer Heating engineer Mechanical engineer Nuclear engineer Petroleum engineer Power generation engineer Tool engineer
For more information: American Society of Mechanical Engineering International, Three Park Ave., New York, NY 10016-5990; phone 800-843-2763, fax 973-882-1717; e-mail infocentral@asme.org, Web site www.asme.org	**Explore this career?** Yes / No

Electrical engineering	Related jobs
You design, develop, troubleshoot, test, and maintain electronic and electrical equipment, ranging from computers and communication systems to electric motors and radar systems. Although you spend most of your time working out the technical aspects of your project, you can also expect to spend up to 40 percent of your time in meetings with team members, developing strategic plans and tracking project progress. As a result, communication skills are crucial to your success in this field. Pay attention to devices hitting the market and track the industry buzz about upcoming products to spot the next trend.	Analog engineer Avionics engineer Control systems engineer Digital design engineer Electrical engineer Electronics test engineer Hardware engineer Power systems engineer Radio systems engineer Telecommunication engineer
For more information: Institute of Electrical and Electronics Engineers, Inc., 445 Hoes Lane, P.O. Box 1331, Piscataway, NJ 08855-1331; phone 732-981-0060 or 800-678-4333, fax 732-981-1721; Web site www.ieee.org	**Explore this career?** Yes / No

Industrial engineering	Related jobs
You help companies produce a higher quality product in less time while using all human and material resources as efficiently as possible. To do this, you must combine your expertise in manufacturing, your observations of how the work is currently being done, and a keen understanding of the company's culture and business needs. After communicating recommendations to the management team, you implement the changes to produce the desired results. Employers tend to hire people with specialties in production, manufacturing, administrative paperwork practices, assembly, or raw-product processing.	Industrial designer Industrial engineer Industrial engineering technician Logistics engineer Manufacturing engineer Mechanical engineer Packaging engineer
For more information: The Institute of Industrial Engineers, 3577 Parkway Lane, Suite 200, Norcross, GA 30092; phone 770-449-0460 or 800-494-0460, fax 770-441-3295; e-mail cs@iienet.org, Web site www.iienet.org	**Explore this career?** Yes / No

Computer engineering	Related jobs
Whether you help a company design a new computer system, or attempt to squeeze more resources out of an existing one, you must understand the company's goals, future needs, budget, and existing system in great detail. After the company gives its approval, you build the system, test it, and configure it for optimal use. In addition to having strong problem-solving skills, practical hands-on experience, and the ability to attend to details while multi-tasking, you also need to be able to work effectively with end-users. A growing demand for networking, online security, and e-commerce creates great career opportunities.	Communication specialist Computer consultant Computer engineer Computer security analyst Hardware engineer Systems administrator Systems analyst Systems architect Systems developer
For more information: Institute of Electrical and Electronic Engineering Computer Society, 1730 Massachusetts Ave. NW, Washington, DC 20036-1992; phone 202-371-0101, fax 202-728-9614; e-mail membership@computer.org, Web site www.computer.org	**Explore this career?** Yes / No

Software engineering	Related jobs
Use your strong analytical skills, patience, and attention to detail, along with your ability to conceptualize and solve abstract problems to create code that allows computers to function and perform myriad tasks. Throughout development you must participate on teams and endure the long development phase. Apply your skills in a key software market: system software, utilities, education, personal productivity, finance, Web site, games, or reference materials. Keep your skills from becoming obsolete by staying up to date on the ever-changing tools and technology that make up this profession.	Bio-infomatics programmer Database administrator Game developer Software architect Software designer Software developer Software engineer Software tester Web programmer
For more information: Institute of Electrical and Electronics Engineers, Inc., 445 Hoes Lane, P.O. Box 1331, Piscataway, NJ 08855-1331; phone 732-981-0060 or 800-678-4333, fax 732-562-5445; Web site www.ieee.org	**Explore this career?** Yes / No

Working with money

With a good head for figures, you can excel in any number of financial careers. Depending on your interests, you may track money, invest money, loan money, or advise others on how to handle their money. Take a look at these careers to see what fits you best.

Keeping the books	Related jobs
As you audit a company's financial records, prepare taxes, or take care of bookkeeping tasks, you provide an honest picture of a company's or individual's financial picture. To do this job well, you must keep an eye on the accuracy of the smallest detail, while remembering the big picture and large-scale implications of the company's financial decisions. The skill with which you can communicate sometimes difficult technical information to clients and peers adds to your success. As borders melt in the globalization of business dealings, the move to establish international accounting rules is heating up. This globalization may have an impact on your work.	Accountant Auditor Bookkeeper Certified public accountant Cost accountant Enrolled agent Government accountant Investigative accountant Management accountant Tax preparer
For more information: American Institute of Certified Public Accountants, 1211 Avenue of the Americas, New York, NY 10036-8775; phone 212-596-6200, fax 212-596-6213; Web site www.aicpa.org	**Explore this career?** Yes / No

Making loans	Related jobs
If you are highly motivated, can develop good working relationships with clients, and feel comfortable with computers and finances, consider becoming a loan officer for a bank or mortgage broker. In this business, you develop a customer base, work to understand your customers' financial needs, and guide your customers through the loan application process. Then you use your computer to analyze the risk associated with granting the loan. Your hours need to be flexible enough to meet your customers' needs, which may mean working long hours, especially when interest rates are low and your business booms.	Business loan broker Business loan officer Commercial loan officer Consumer loan officer Credit specialist Loan collection officer Loan counselor Loan officer Mortgage loan officer Venture capitalist
For more information: National Association of Mortgage Brokers, 8201 Greensboro Dr., Suite 300, McLean, VA 22102; phone 703-610-9009, fax 703-610-9005; Web site www.namb.org	**Explore this career?** Yes / No

Managing money	Related jobs
Use your understanding of finances, your analytical skills, and your sense of in-house operations and the state of the economy to help your company reduce financial risks and maximize profits. Whether you oversee your company's financial functions and formulate plans and policies, or you invest funds and manage cash, your creative problem-solving skills, your clear communication style, and your knowledge of computers contribute to your success. As the global economy takes hold, financial managers must have a good feel for international finance and may even need to speak another language.	Banker Branch manager Cash manager Chief financial officer Controller Credit manager Entrepreneur Insurance manager Treasurer Vice president of finance
For more information: Financial Management Association International, University of South Florida, College of Business Administration, 4202 E. Fowler Ave., BSN 3331, Tampa, FL 33620-5500; phone 813-974-2084, fax 813-974-3318; e-mail fma@coba.usf.edu, Web site www.fma.org	**Explore this career?** Yes / No

Investing	Related jobs
To succeed as an investment broker, you must use your mathematical aptitude to evaluate stocks based on research with the goal of making profits for your company and clients. You need a thorough understanding and gut sense of the market, and you must possess a high tolerance for risk. Be prepared to take the blame if your client's portfolio takes a significant dive in value as a result of market moves. The investment landscape has changed tremendously over the last decade and is likely to continue with the advent of electronic trading, large discount brokerage operations, and changes to security exchanges.	Account executive Financial planner Investment advisor Investment banker Investment broker Investment manager Portfolio manager Retirement consultant Stockbroker Venture capitalist
For more information: National Association of Security Dealers, 1735 K Street NW, Washington, DC 20006-1500; phone 202-728-8000 or 301-590-6500; Web site www.nasd.com	**Explore this career?** Yes / No

Analyzing financial research	Related jobs
Whether you predict the performance of specific stocks, evaluate the impact of economic policies, or screen business plans for possible venture capital funding, expect to spend time studying financial trends, crunching numbers, and reading annual reports. To handle your intense workload and strict deadlines, you must prioritize, work well alone or as part of a team, and have an innate ability to work with numeric patterns. With the global economy, increased competition, and a greater reliance on analyzing financial data, people with analytical skills are in a fine position for employment in this career.	Claim adjuster Credit analyst Economist Financial analyst Financial planner Insurance underwriter Loss-control specialist Market research analyst Market researcher Risk manager
For more information: CFA Institute, 560 Ray C. Hunt Dr., Charlottesville, VA 22903-2981; phone 800-247-8132, fax 434-951-5262; e-mail info@cfainstitute.org, Web site www.cfainstitute.org	**Explore this career?** Yes / No

Organizing people, data, and things

Even if you aren't enthralled with scientific or technical topics, your logical, organized way of thinking can position you well for careers that range from planning events to investigating crimes.

Event planning	Related jobs
You plan and produce events that fit your clients' needs, making sure that each event runs smoothly and comes in on budget. This work entails tracking myriad details associated with site selection, negotiations, travel arrangements, registration, food and entertainment, audio-visual equipment, public relations, and marketing. One hitch can spell disaster, so it pays to be well organized and efficient. Your oral and written communication skills also contribute to your success by helping you head off potential misunderstandings with clients or subcontractors and negotiating the best deals for your clients.	Association manager Convention planner Event/meeting planner Festival producer Media escort Professional organizer Relocation specialist Reunion planner Trade show coordinator Wedding planner
For more information: Meeting Professionals International, 3030 LBJ Freeway, Suite 1700, Dallas, TX 75234-2759; phone 972-702-3000, fax 972-702-3070; Web site www.mpiweb.org	**Explore this career?** Yes / No

Collecting	Related jobs
Use your ability to organize, your flair for design, and your desire to maintain documents and objects of historical value. In this field, you acquire items for a collection, preserve and restore pieces, classify and inventory items, and design and plan exhibits. Due to the detailed and sensitive nature of your work, you must have extensive training in a particular specialty to get into this line of work. Although specific protocols are still evolving, specialists in this field expect computers, multimedia, and the Internet to revolutionize how collections are stored and shared with the public. Stay tuned for details as they emerge.	Anthropologist Antiques dealer Archeologist Artifacts conservator Botanist Curator Document controller Genealogist Museum technician Zoologist
For more information: Society of American Archivists, 527 South Wells St., 5th Floor, Chicago, IL 60607; phone 312-922-0140, fax 312-347-1452; e-mail info@archivists.org, Web site www.archivists.org	**Explore this career?** Yes / No

Buying	Related jobs
If you are a strong negotiator, hard worker, good planner, and quick decision maker who can act effectively on fast-changing data, you may have a future as a buyer. Whether you buy products for a retail store or purchase parts for a manufacturer, your goal is to get the highest quality merchandise at the best possible price. To succeed in the long run, you must continually track inventories, review sales figures, and be aware of factors that impact the supply and demand of the products and materials you buy. Another key to success is building a reliable, trustworthy network of suppliers.	Buyer Commodity manager Contract specialist Inventory specialist Merchandise manager Planner Purchasing agent Purchasing manager Scheduler Supply manager
For more information: American Purchasing Society, North Island Center, Ste. 203, 8 East Galena Blvd., Aurora, IL 60506; phone 630-859-0250, fax 630-859-0270; e-mail propurch@mgci.com, Web site www.american-purchasing.com	**Explore this career?** Yes / No

Investigating	Related jobs
As long as you don't mind a bit of confrontation on the job, your ability to follow leads, interview, interrogate, and think on your feet make you a prime candidate for doing detective or investigative work. You use surveillance, computer research, searches, and interviews to verify facts, gather information, or solve crimes. You can expect to work irregular hours, some of which you spend out in the field doing surveillance and conducting interviews. If you are intrigued by detective work, you can build a viable specialty based on a previous career in finance, accounting, investigative reporting, law, or insurance.	Accident reconstructor Forensics Inspector Investigative accountant Investigative reporter Investigator Medical examiner Police detective Polygraph operator Store detective
For more information: International Crime Scene Investigators Association, PMB 385, 15774 South LaGrange Rd., Orland Park, IL 60462; phone 708-460-8082; e-mail info@icsia.org, Web site www.icsia.org	**Explore this career?** Yes / No

If You Love Nature and Its Creatures

If you enjoy being outdoors, studying nature, and preserving the environment, you may be intrigued by the career ideas in this section that allow you to apply your skills to plants, animals, or the earth as a whole.

Working with plants

If you have a green thumb, you no doubt know it. Plants grow and flourish in your care. The career ideas in this section help you use your talent and knowledge in a variety of ways.

Botany	Related jobs
As someone who understands and is fascinated by plants and their functions, you may be interested in discovering new plants, classifying plants, keeping plants healthy, or understanding how plants work. Your ability to observe, classify, and ask good questions makes you a valuable researcher in your field. Your knowledge puts you in a good position to address issues related to the global food supply by improving crop yields and minimizing the effects of stresses such as drought and pests on crops.	Agricultural engineer Agricultural scientist Agronomist Botanist Crop scientist Food chemist Plant collector Plant explorer Plant taxonomist
For more information: Botanical Society of America, P.O. Box 299, St. Louis, MO 63166-0299; phone 314-577-9566, fax 314-577-9515; e-mail bsa-manager@botany.org, Web site www.botany.org	**Explore this career?** Yes / No

Growing plants	Related jobs
If you want to live close to the land and have a hands-on business, growing plants may serve you well. Do your research to find a crop that flourishes in your climate and then identify growing methods to maximize your production. Your hard work, your knowledge of plants, and your ability to track your business contribute to your success. The work tends to be seasonal, so combine this work with other jobs to create a viable composite career. To boost your employability in this area, focus on a specialty such as floriculture, nursery operations, arboriculture, or turf care.	Farm crew leader Farmer Farm manager Flower grower Horticulturist Hydroponics farmer Nursery manager Organic farmer Vineyard manager Viticulturist
For more information: American Society for Horticulture Science, 113 South West St., Suite 200, Alexandria, VA 22314-2851; phone 703-836-4606, fax 703-836-2024; e-mail webmaster@ashs.org, Web site www.ashs.org	**Explore this career?** Yes / No

Designing landscapes	Related jobs
By becoming a landscape architect, you have a unique opportunity to combine your love of nature, your creative sense, your communication skills, and your ability to work with your hands. Each project begins by assessing the soil, sunlight, water, drainage, and slope of the property, while gaining a clear understanding of the purpose and needs for the site. After analyzing the information, you create a preliminary design and present it to your clients for review. As with architecture, your ability to accurately articulate your vision and work with other professionals on the team are crucial to your success.	Architect Environmental planner Interiorscaper Landscape architect Landscape architectural technician Landscape consultant Landscape designer Urban planner
For more information: American Society of Landscape Architects, 636 Eye St. NW, Washington, DC 20001; phone 202-898-2444, fax 202-898-1185; Web site www.asla.org	**Explore this career?** Yes / No

Managing forests	Related jobs
You use your knowledge of trees to manage forests by balancing the ecology of the area with the harvest of the trees. Your tasks include maintaining an inventory of the trees in the forest, reforesting, harvesting, preventing fires, controlling insects and invasive plants, and managing conservation programs. You must have a solid scientific background, exceptional health and a strong constitution, and good planning and problem-solving skills to excel. In addition to working alone, you also interact with landowners, farmers, loggers, government officials, special interest groups, and the public.	Appraisal forester Consulting forester Forest economist Forest engineer Forester Forest firefighter Forestry technician Range conservationist Range ecologist Range manager
For more information: Society of American Foresters, 5400 Grosvenor Lane, Bethesda, MD 20814; phone 301-897-8720, fax 301-897-3690; e-mail safweb@safnet.org; Web site www.safnet.org	**Explore this career?** Yes / No

Working with animals

Whether you work with pets, farm animals, wild animals in captivity, or animals in their native habitats, you want to strengthen your connection with the animal kingdom. The careers in this section give you the opportunity to do so.

Zoology	Related jobs
You observe animals in their natural setting, conduct experiments in a controlled setting, or dissect animal specimens to gain a thorough understanding of how animals function, why they behave as they do, where they came from, and what sort of habitat they need to thrive. For this career, basic research skills in observation, experimentation, and analysis create a strong foundation for future career growth. Launch your career with a broad education in zoology and then specialize in a specific species or topic area that intrigues you.	Animal biologist Developmental scientist Herpetologist Icthyologist Mammalogist Marine biologist Morphologist Ornithologist Physiologist Zoologist
For more information: Society for Integrative and Comparative Biology, 1313 Dolly Madison Blvd., Suite 402, McLean, VA 22101; phone 703-790-1745 or 800-955-1236, fax 703-790-2672; e-mail SICB@BurkInc.com, Web site www.sicb.org	**Explore this career?** Yes / No

Training animals	Related jobs
Combine your love of animals with your patient nature to help animals learn new behaviors. To succeed in this work, you must enjoy working with and being around animals as you spend much of your time repeatedly training, rewarding, and caring for your charges. Your specific working conditions depend on the animals you train. Numerous niches exist in this profession, including training animals for entertainment purposes, protection, service, show, law enforcement, or rescue operations.	Animal behaviorist Animal handler Animal keeper Animal trainer Drug dog trainer Exotic animal handler Jockey Obedience instructor Pet therapist Search and rescue dog trainer
For more information: The Professional Handlers' Association, 17017 Norbrook Dr., Olney, MD 20832; phone 301-924-0089; Web site www.infodog.com/misc/pha/phainfo.htm	**Explore this career?** Yes / No

Caring for animals	Related jobs
If you want to spend your days surrounded by animals, you may find care-taking of interest. Although you can expect strenuous, long days, you may be rewarded with lots of love and affection from your animal clients. Patience, physical strength, and an even temper are essential for success. By the way, don't forget that communicating with human owners is an inherent part of the package. Look to animal shelters, vet hospitals, vet clinics, stables, labs, zoos, pet stores, aquariums, wildlife management facilities, kennels, and rehabilitation centers as possible places for employment or volunteer experience.	Animal caretaker Animal control officer Boarding kennel operator Curator Groomer Pet sitter Pet store owner Ranch hand Zoo manager Zookeeper
For more information: National Dog Grooming Association of America, P.O. Box 101, Clark, PA 16113; phone 724-962-2711, fax 724-962-1919; e-mail ndga@nationaldoggroomers.com, Web site www.nationaldoggroomers.com	**Explore this career?** Yes / No

Healing animals	Related jobs
You combine your love for animals and your ability to sense what they are experiencing with your scientific knowledge to treat the animals in your care. To prepare, you must undertake extensive training and then devote time to keeping up with constant medical and technological advances. In addition to attending to the health of animals, you also provide support to the people who own the animals, so your bedside manner must calm both the pets and their owners. Look beyond a private practice to wildlife management, aquatic animal medicine, zoos, food hygiene and safety, private research firms, and colleges.	Animal nutritionist Avian veterinarian Exotics veterinarian Veterinarian Veterinarian dentist Veterinary inspector Veterinary pathologist Veterinary physiologist Veterinary surgeon Vet tech
For more information: American Veterinary Medical Association, 1931 North Meacham Rd., Suite 100, Schaumburg, IL 60173; phone 847-925-8070, fax 847-925-1329; e-mail avmainfo@avma.org, Web site www.avma.org	**Explore this career?** Yes / No

Managing wildlife	Related jobs
You tend to the needs of wildlife, both game animals that are harvested for sport or for food and non-game species. Through research and careful data collection, you discover and solve problems for species in your area while striving to maintain the habitat that the species needs to survive. For the long-term survival of wildlife, you spend a considerable amount of time educating the public about animals and their needs. Translating scientific details into entertaining, everyday language that the public can understand is a key talent in your line of work. You may also spend a considerable amount of time lobbying, testifying, advocating, and creating legislation for wildlife.	Game warden Interpretive docent Naturalist Park ranger Refuge manager Wildlife conservationist Wildlife educator Wildlife expert/manager Wildlife management specialist
For more information: International Association of Fish and Wildlife Agencies, 444 North Capitol St. NW, Suite 725, Washington, DC 20001; phone 202-624-7890, fax 202-624-7891; e-mail info@iafwa.org, Web site www.iafwa.org	**Explore this career?** Yes / No

Nurturing nature and the earth

The earth's systems and resources need management and care. If the state of the earth interests you, explore the careers in this section.

Working with land and water	Related jobs
Use your scientific expertise and extensive knowledge of geological formations to explore the earth's surface for natural resources (such as water, oil, gas, and minerals), clean up the environment, guide appropriate land use and construction, and predict future earth-changing events. To do this work well, you must visualize the earth's structure and movements in three dimensions. Although some of your work takes place inside, you also do extensive fieldwork, on land or at sea, anywhere on the surface of the globe, which requires stamina, physical strength, and a flexible lifestyle.	Engineering geologist Geochemist Geologist Geophysicist Ground water geologist Hydrologist Oceanographer Reservoir engineer Seismologist Water quality engineer
For more information: Geological Society of America, P.O. Box 9140, Boulder, CO 80301-9140; phone 303-447-2020, fax 303-357-1070; e-mail gsaservice@geosociety.org, Web site www.geosociety.org American Society of Limnology and Oceanography, 5400 Bosque Blvd., Suite 680, Waco, TX 76710-4446; phone 254-399-9635 or 800-929-2756, fax 254-776-3767; e-mail business@aslo.org, Web site www.aslo.org	**Explore this career?** Yes / No

Ecology	Related jobs
Use your natural science background to understand the interactions between organisms and their environment. Not only do you strive to understand how nature works, but you also teach others, help communities solve environmental problems, manage resources, and restore ecosystems. Your work may include field observation as well as laboratory research. Strong writing and presentation skills, well-thought-out research methods, and accurate statistical analysis are required in your field. A working knowledge of social sciences, such as geography and economics, can enhance your work.	Ecologist Environmental consultant Environmental planner Field ecologist Lobbyist Natural resource manager Outdoor educator Park naturalist Wildlife biologist Wildlife specialist
For more information: Ecological Society of America, 1707 H St. NW, Suite 400, Washington, DC 20006; phone 202-833-8773, fax 202-833-8775; e-mail esahq@esa.org, Web site www.esa.org	**Explore this career?** Yes / No

Working with the weather and air	Related jobs
Your observation, measurement, and computer skills allow you to observe, understand, analyze, and forecast the weather. Your work guides key decisions for builders, farmers, travelers, land managers, and those in the path of extreme weather. To excel in this field, you must have strong analytical and mathematical skills, good map-reading skills, and the ability to visualize in three dimensions. Combine atmospheric science with other specialties such as astronomy, civil engineering, environmental engineering, electrical engineering, computer science, physics, mathematics, or biology for a multidisciplinary career.	Air quality engineer Air quality meteorologist Atmospheric scientist Climatologic geographer Climatologist Consulting meteorologist Meteorologist Weather service specialist Weather station officer-in-charge
For more information: American Meteorological Society, 45 Beacon St., Boston, MA 02108-3693; phone 617-227-2425, fax 617-742-8718; e-mail amsinfo@ametsoc.org, Web site www.ametsoc.org	**Explore this career?** Yes / No

Waste management	Related jobs
Managing waste of all varieties — from household garbage to toxic industrial waste — requires a strong background in the sciences, including geology, chemistry, physics, ecology, or some combination. Whether you work in the field finding and implementing a solution to an ongoing waste problem, cleaning up a recent spill, or working in a governmental agency devoted to waste management, you prepare written statements and give presentations to pitch project proposals and provide status updates. To excel in this field, you must adhere to safety regulations and find your way through government guidelines to make the impact you strive to make.	Decommissioning and decontamination worker Emergency responder Environmental engineer Recycling plant operator Sanitary landfill operator Treatment plant operator Treatment, storage, and disposal (TSD) worker Waste management engineer Water pollution biologist
For more information: Air and Waste Management Association, One Gateway Center, Third Floor, 420 Fort Duquesne Blvd., Pittsburgh, PA 15222; phone 412-232-3444, fax 412-232-3450; e-mail info@awma.org, Web site www.awma.org	**Explore this career?** Yes / No

Chapter 13

Thinking Outside the Box with Creative Careers

*W*hether you're in the process of brainstorming possible career ideas in Chapter 9 or you're investigating your top two career ideas in Chapter 14, you can use the career description in this chapter to expand your thinking, spark your creativity, and further your career exploration.

If you have just turned to this chapter, without reading Chapter 9 or 14, scan the career areas in this chapter to identify any that interest you.

All of the career categories described in this chapter involve creativity in some form. The section "If You Have a Good Eye" offers careers that capitalize on your eye for beauty and perspective. The section "If You Want Your Work to Be Physical" lists careers that use your body in some way. The section "If You Have an Ear for the Sound of Music" describes careers that put your musical abilities to work.

If you're unsure whether these three categories are a good fit for you and your skills, refer back to Worksheet 7-2 in Chapter 7 to see whether your Multiple Intelligence Profile highlights these three career categories. You may also find you're interested in exploring the communicating careers in Chapter 11 and the logical/scientific careers in Chapter 12.

Making the Most of This Chapter

Each of the following sections contains descriptions of different careers related to that particular category. See Figure 13-1 for an explanation of the information you find in each section of the career description.

Career area title	Related jobs
A brief description of the career area with tips, explanations, and requirements. As you move through this chapter, skim the career descriptions to see if anything catches your eye.	A list of related job titles are in alphabetical order. Use these jobs to expand how you think about this career area. Notice that some job titles show new directions you can take within this career area.
For more information: Use the contact information to connect with a relevant professional association. Don't worry if the professional association isn't quite a good fit for your target career. In Chapter 14, you can access several online resources that help you find professional associations that are on target.	**Explore this career?** Yes / No Circle or highlight "yes" to indicate that you'd like to take more time to explore this career in depth.

Figure 13-1: Finding your way around career area descriptions.

If you're going through Chapter 9, and looking at the careers in this chapter to expand your list of possible careers, record all the career categories that appeal to you in Worksheet 9-6. Don't stop to investigate every career that catches your eye. For now you just need to focus on using these career descriptions to enhance your list of possible careers. After you've reduced your options a bit in Chapter 10, you can return to this chapter to explore your top two career ideas.

If you're reading Chapter 14, and using this chapter to understand your top two careers in more depth, you may find the professional associations good sources of current information about the profession. You can visit an association's Web site or call or write for more information. After finding out what you can from the professional association and list of related jobs, head back to Chapter 14 to discover other ways to gain more information about the careers that interest you most.

As you read the career descriptions in this chapter, you may be struck by a career area or a particular job title. Although this insight feels incredibly obvious in the moment, don't bank on the details sticking with you unless you write it down!

As you scan each section, skip over any career areas that don't interest you.

If You Have a Good Eye

The careers in this section may intrigue you if you think in pictures, translate visual images into physical form, manipulate three-dimensional structures in your head, or have a good sense of direction.

Working on a two-dimensional "canvas"

Although visual images have always had a place in society, the explosion of new technological media has caused a surge in the use of visual imagery. You see photographs, video clips, and animation just about anywhere and everywhere you look. These visual images, which you see in entertainment, education, and advertisements, were designed by a person with artistic capabilities.

Graphic design	Related jobs
You use images, type, color, and various two-dimensional media to create distinctive and descriptive logos and Web images. Your work conveys information or establishes a recognizable brand for your clients' products or companies. You translate your clients' ideas into results that fit within their purpose, budget, time frame, and design limitations. In addition to producing images, often with computer manipulation, you spend a considerable amount of time talking with your clients at key points in the development process. After each discussion, you take their thoughts into account as you brainstorm solutions to create finalized images.	Animator Art director Computer artist Demonstrative evidence specialist Graphic designer Illustrator Layout designer Medical illustrator Production artist Web designer
For more information: Graphic Artists Guild, 90 John St., Suite 403, New York, NY 10038; phone 212-791-3400; Web site www.gag.org	**Explore this career?** Yes / No

Photography	Related jobs
You blend artistic sense with technical knowledge to capture photographic images that evoke a certain mood or feeling about a person, place, or event. No matter what your subject, being in the right place at the right time is the name of the game. The explosion of new media outlets in entertainment, education, communication, and marketing creates a growing and constant demand for more visual images. Digital cameras and scanners allow photographs to be processed, manipulated, edited, and enhanced more readily than ever before. This change impacts the work process and the creative parameters of the work. Photography has many niches. Choose a niche that appeals to you and fits your lifestyle, and then build your expertise!	Camera operator Cinematographer Commercial photographer Freelance photographer Motion picture photographer Photo editor Photographer Photographic restorer Photographic retoucher Photojournalist Videographer
For more information: Professional Photographers of America, Inc., 229 Peachtree St. NE, Suite 2200, Atlanta, GA 30303; phone 800-786-6277; e-mail csc@ppa.com, Web site www.ppa.com	**Explore this career?** Yes / No

Working on a three-dimensional "canvas"

Not all creative design happens on a two-dimensional surface. Some people with artistic talents visualize and work in three dimensions. For example, artists and people in the fashion industries are masters at thinking in and working in 3-D. If this form of creativity is in your blood, you can't ignore it!

Self-expressive art	Related jobs
Create unique pieces that express a feeling, vision, thought, or notion, using one or more media. To create a profitable art career, you need to know how to price, promote, and sell your art. Finding ways to get your pieces into galleries and museums or noticed by collectors helps you build your career and a name for yourself. Think about incorporating several of your talents into a composite career that allows you to have the time and mental space to be creative in a self-expressive manner. Some of the most lucrative avenues to pursue as an artist include graphic design, commercial photography, advertising, product design, art direction, and computer art.	Floral designer Glass blower Installation artist Lithographer Metal arts worker Mosaic designer Neon sign maker Painter Sculptor Stained glass artist Textile artist Woodworker
For more information: Artists Equity, P.O. Box HG, Pacific Grove, CA 93950; e-mail mdart2u@aol.com, Web site www.artists-equity.org	**Explore this career?** Yes / No

Fashion design	Related jobs
You translate the pulse of the culture, times, and trends into clothing and accessories the public wants to buy. You have strong technical training; a good eye for color, line, and style; excellent pattern-making skills; and a sense of what is functional for your customers. For the majority of designers, the road to success starts with learning the ropes and paying dues in low-paying assistant positions. If you aren't interested in the high-stakes game of fashion design, but love the industry, look into some of the more stable careers within the industry, including fabric buyer, textile designer, merchandiser, sample maker, quality control specialist, and image consultant.	Accessories designer Clothing buyer Costumer Designer Image consultant Pattern maker Seamstress Tailor Textile designer Wardrobe specialist Wearable artist
For more information: Council of Fashion Designers of America, 1412 Broadway, Suite 2006, New York, NY 10018; phone 212-302-1821; e-mail info@cfda.com, Web site www.cfda.com	**Explore this career?** Yes / No

Creating environments

One form of 3-D creativity takes a sense of design and mixes it with spatial reasoning and building. Most people with this combination of talents work with buildings and structures in some way, through design, construction, or decorating.

Architecture	Related jobs
To design a building, you must use your sense of design and spatial relationships to balance a number of factors, including aesthetics, functionality, safety, economic limitations, and the desires of those who are to occupy the space. From the initial conversation with your client until the building is completed, you play an active role. During the initial phases, design and engineering are your key functions. After building begins, you supervise the construction and verify that the plans are built to your specification. Technological advances have changed this industry and made it easier to make and communicate revisions.	Architect technologist Drafter Entertainment architect Industrial designer Kitchen and bath designer Landscape architect
For more information: American Institute of Architects, 1735 New York Ave. NW, Washington, DC 20006; phone 202-626-7300 or 800-AIA-3837, fax 202-626-7547; e-mail infocentral@aia.org, Web site www.aia.org	**Explore this career?** Yes / No

Carpentry	Related jobs
Although you must have stamina, ability, and balance to build structures, you must also read blueprints accurately, have good spatial perception, and have the ability to visualize how something needs to be put together. Your knowledge of the tools and methods required to transform a pile of materials into a building according to the architect's plans minimizes errors, costs, and delays. To encourage steady work, develop a set of well-rounded skills so that you can take work in a variety of areas. The variable work schedule makes this profession work as part of a composite career.	Cabinetmaker Carpenter Detail carpenter Electrician Finisher Home inspector Home remodeler Installer Plumber Steel structure worker
For more information: National Association of Home Builders, 1201 15th St. NW, Washington, DC 20005-2800; phone 800-368-5242, ext. 0; e-mail info@nahb.com, Web site www.nahb.com	**Explore this career?** Yes / No

Interior design	Related jobs
You take empty spaces and design them to be both functional and aesthetically pleasing to the owners, while coming in under budget within the stated time frame. You rely on your artistic abilities and your knowledge about materials, construction methods, and safety regulations. Because creating a space is often a joint effort, communication and coordination are crucial. As with any design field, you must stay up-to-date with trends and be open to incorporating new influences into your designs. Begin each job with a "before" picture and then follow up with vivid "after" pictures to demonstrate your style.	Display designer Exhibit designer Feng Shui specialist Furniture designer Interior decorator Interior designer Office space planner Retail space designer Set designer Stager
For more information: American Society of Interior Designers, 608 Massachusetts Ave. NE, Washington, DC 20002-6006; phone 202-546-3480; Web site www.asid.org	**Explore this career?** Yes / No

Mapping and navigating the world

The careers I list in this section tap a different aspect of visual intelligence, one that relies less on a sense of design and more on spatial reasoning abilities, mapping expertise, and navigational skills.

Surveying	Related jobs
Use your ability to visualize distances and shapes and to measure, calculate, and plot the terrain to provide civil engineers, architects, and local authorities with the surveying measurements they need to build projects and establish legal boundaries. Because your work is the first step in long-term projects, precision and accuracy are crucial. Although new technology makes surveyors more accurate than ever, work in the field still requires stamina, strength, and coordination. Surveying is a team event, so your ability to cooperate and communicate — verbally and with hand signals — is vital.	Cartographer Geologist Geophysical prospecting surveyor Land surveyor Licensed surveyor Marine surveyor Surveying engineer Surveying technician Topographer
For more information: American Congress on Surveying and Mapping, 6 Montgomery Village Ave., Suite 403, Gaithersburg, MD 20879; phone 240-632-9716; Web site www.acsm.net	**Explore this career?** Yes / No

Urban planning	Related jobs
You help communities determine long-term and short-term plans for land usage, especially in times of growth and community revitalization. You must take the needs and ideas of various groups and visualize and develop spatially sound and inviting plans for the area. At key points in the planning process, you must effectively communicate the newest version of the picture to the city's citizens and officials to work through any potential conflicts and to enhance the plans. Political diplomacy and the ability to build consensus among various groups are crucial skills in this profession.	City planner Civic leader Community planner Community planning director Land developer Public sector planner Regional planner
For more information: American Planning Association, 122 S. Michigan Ave., Suite 1600, Chicago, IL 60603; phone 312-431-9100; e-mail CustomerService@planning.org, Web site www.planning.org	**Explore this career?** Yes / No

Piloting	Related jobs
Whether you fly planes, helicopters, or balloons, you deposit your passengers or cargo in their final and desired destination. Your extensive training, experience in the air, and knowledge of the equipment, controls, weather patterns, and emergency procedures are crucial to your success, as are flawless eyesight and good spatial reasoning skills. Aside from flying as a commercial airline pilot, consider one of the following flying niches: charter, sight-seeing, cargo delivery, air-taxi service, flight instructor, rescue service, agricultural, mail delivery, firefighting, aerial inspections, test pilot, or traffic monitoring.	Air traffic controller Balloonist Captain Check pilot Co-pilot Driver Flight dispatcher Flight engineer Navigator Ship captain
For more information: Air Line Pilots Association International, P.O. Box 1169, Herndon, VA 20172; phone 703-689-2270; Web site www.alpa.org	**Explore this career?** Yes / No

If You Want Your Work to Be Physical

For some people, the thought of sitting at a desk all day can send them into the doldrums. They prefer to be in motion throughout the day, using their bodies to perform their work.

As you read about the four career categories in this section, notice any jobs that appeal to you. Make note of what interests you, even if it's just one aspect of a job. Each clue you discover helps you build a picture of the career you want.

Doing precision work

Your eye for detail and your ability to produce precision results make you a candidate for any of the following careers. Decide on your medium of choice and specialize.

Metal working	Related jobs
If you have fine vision, a passion for doing precision work with your hands, and excellent eye-hand coordination, you may be cut out to be a machinist. After reading the blueprints, you plan the steps necessary to produce the specified pieces. Then you use an extensive collection of devices to shape the metal and sophisticated lasers or optical measuring devices to verify the precision of your work to the one-ten-thousandth of an inch. In the final phase of each project, you assemble the pieces that you make and polish the surfaces as required.	Blacksmith Die maker Instrument maker Locksmith Machinist Metal pattern maker Metal worker Mold maker Welder
For more information: National Institute for Metalworking Skills, Inc., 3251 Old Lee Highway, Suite 205, Fairfax, VA 22030; phone 703-352-4971, fax 703-352-4991; e-mail NIMS@nims-skills.org, Web site www.nims-skills.org	**Explore this career?** Yes / No

Jewelry work	Related jobs
Combine your eye for detail and design with fine dexterity, good eye-hand coordination, and concentration to become a jeweler. Whether you specialize in design, repair, or cutting, setting, and polishing stones, you can include appraisals as one of your services if you can identify stones and assess their value. Physical stress is a daily part of this career because you do very fine, precise handwork for hours at a time. Technology has made its mark in this field as more and more jewelers use lasers to cut stones or engrave jewelry, and use computer-aided design to design and manufacture jewelry.	Appraiser Clock repairer Engraver Etcher Jeweler Jewelry designer Jewelry maker Locksmith Polisher Watchmaker
For more information: Jewelers of America, 52 Vanderbilt Ave., 19th Floor, New York, NY 10017; phone 646-658-0246; e-mail info@jewelers.org, Web site www.jewelers.org	**Explore this career?** Yes / No

Dentistry	Related jobs
Use your fine dexterity to help others care for their teeth and gums. Whether you are a hygienist, who cleans teeth, takes and develops x-rays, applies fluoride and sealant, and educates patients; a dental assistant, who prepares patients and works alongside the dentist; or the dentist, who fills cavities, prepares crowns, and evaluates overall dental health, you must work with a variety of tools and interact with patients who may be more than a little bit nervous. For certain tasks, you work as part of a team, so communication and cooperative work patterns are essential.	Dental assistant Dental ceramist Dental hygienist Dental laboratory technician Dental technician Dentist Oral surgeon Orthodontics technician Prosthetics technician
For more information: American Dental Hygienists' Association, 444 North Michigan Ave., Suite 3400, Chicago, IL 60611; phone 312-440-8911; e-mail mail@adha.net, Web site www.adha.org	**Explore this career?** Yes / No

Working with your hands

For some people who like to work with their hands, precision work is too meticulous and intricate. They prefer working on a larger scale, repairing, building, or creating objects of various forms.

Equipment repair	Related jobs
Combine your ability to work with your hands, your knowledge of electronics, and your passion for troubleshooting to repair electronic and mechanical equipment. When a machine goes down, you arrive in a timely manner, assess what is wrong, and make repairs on the spot or in the shop by replacing the defective parts, resetting the machine, or reinstalling new parts or software. To perform your work, you use a variety of diagnostic and repair tools. As more and more businesses and individuals depend on computers and computerized equipment, they increasingly need immediate, high-quality repair service.	Aircraft mechanic Bench technician Computer repairer Engine repairer Home appliance repairer Installer Instrument repairer Line installer Mechanic Office machine repairer
For more information: Electronics Technicians Association, 5 Depot St., Greencastle, IN 46135; phone 765-653-8262, fax 765-653-4287; e-mail eta@tds.net, Web site www.etasda.com	**Explore this career?** Yes / No

Culinary work	Related jobs
Chefs train hard and work long, unusual hours under considerable pressure to do what they love best, which is to create aesthetically pleasing dishes that provide their patrons with unique eating experiences. Having endurance, an eye for detail and design, a keen sense of taste and smell, and the dexterity to work effectively with kitchen tools and food are essential to success in your trade. While you learn to cook, spend time honing your ability to create as a member of a team. Specialization is a key to success in this field, whether you are known for pastries, regional cuisine, or a style of entrée.	Assistant chef Baker Caterer Chef Industrial baker Institutional chef Pastry creator Pastry chef Preparation chef Specialty food producer
For more information: American Culinary Federation, 180 Center Place Way, St. Augustine, FL 32095; phone 904-824-4468, fax 904-825-4758; Web site www.acfchefs.org	**Explore this career?** Yes / No

Working with your body

Some careers require you to throw your entire body into the job. Although the work tends to be strenuous, the personal satisfaction of seeing what you've created is great.

Construction	Related jobs
Whether you're framing a house, installing the electrical or plumbing system in an office, or roofing a commercial building, you must be fit enough in mind and body to handle the strenuous work and perform precision tasks accurately. Your ability to read blueprints; use your knowledge of construction to come up with sound, workable solutions on the fly; and work safely contribute to your success. Because any construction project is a team effort, taking directions well and working cooperatively are essential. Use your creativity to find niches that help even out the dips in employment during the year.	Bricklayer Carpenter Cement mason Electrician Floor finisher Painter Plumber Roofer Stonemason Stucco mason
For more information: National Electrical Contractors Association, 3 Bethesda Metro Center, Suite 1100, Bethesda, MD 20814; phone 301-657-3110, fax 301-215-4500; Web site www.necanet.org	**Explore this career?** Yes / No

Training and coaching	Related jobs
Use your fitness experience and knowledge of your sport, your understanding of how the body functions, and your enthusiastic nature to help your clients and class participants become more fit. Depending on your interests, you may specialize in some combination of weight training, assessing fitness, or consulting on weight management and general lifestyle issues. You must be able to explain in very specific terms how your clients can improve their form. Helping them articulate their goals and keeping them motivated are also key skills in this work.	Aerobics instructor Athletic trainer Clinical exercise specialist Coach Exercise physiologist Fitness consultant Personal trainer Physical education teacher Physical therapist Yoga instructor
For more information: American Fitness Professionals & Associates, P.O. Box 214; Ship Bottom, NJ 08008; phone 609-978-7583; e-mail afpa@afpafitness.com, Web site www.afpafitness.com	**Explore this career?** Yes / No

Firefighting	Related jobs
If you can keep your mental and physical edge while vacillating between the extreme adrenaline rush of an emergency and the ultimate boredom of a day with no alarms, you may succeed as a firefighter. You must perform physically strenuous tasks during long shifts under potentially dangerous working conditions, all the while thinking decisively enough to protect people and their property from risk. You must be a team player; your life and the lives of those around you depend on it. If you want to break into the field, move to a fast-growing area.	Fire captain Firefighter Firefighter academy instructor Fire investigator Fire marshal Fire safety consultant Guard Police officer
For more information: International Association of Firefighters, 1750 New York Ave. NW, Washington, DC 20006; phone 202-737-8484, fax 202-737-8418; Web site www.iaff.org	**Explore this career?** Yes / No

Creating with your body

If your body is your instrument of creativity, consider exploring the careers described in this section.

Acting	Related jobs
Use your body and your ability to express emotions, verbally and nonverbally, to entertain and inform your audience. Starting out, you must do what you can to get experience and build a set of favorable reviews. Your hours are long and irregular, and you may need to travel to film on location or to perform on the road, which requires a great deal of stamina. Through it all, you need talent, creativity, the ability to transform yourself into a character, and a degree of stage presence.	Acting coach Actor Clown Comedian Director Impersonator Juggler Mime Narrator Stunt double
For more information: Screen Actors Guild, 5757 Wilshire Blvd., Los Angeles, CA 90036-3600; phone 323-954-1600; Web site www.sag.org	**Explore this career?** Yes / No

Dancing	Related jobs
You rely on your body's grace, flexibility, and stamina to express yourself with movement to music. The practice required to perform well is time consuming and physically taxing and takes discipline and dedication. Whether you perform in theaters, concert halls, amusement parks, music videos, or commercials, you work with a choreographer and other performers to achieve the desired effect. Due to the nature of the field, rejection and periods of unemployment are part of daily life in dancing. A composite career allows you to bring in money in the down times, while giving you the time you need to practice and perform.	Artistic director Choreographer Dance coach Dance critic Dance instructor Dancer Dance therapist Expressive dance Ice skater Movement therapist
For more information: National Dance Association, 1900 Association Dr., Reston, VA 20191; phone 703-476-3400 or 800-213-7193; Web site www.aahperd.org/nda	**Explore this career?** Yes / No

If You Have an Ear for the Sound of Music

This section consists of three career categories, each devoted to a different musical career category.

Making music

If you can compose or perform music, or help others do so, bring music into your career and the lives of others by exploring the career ideas in this section.

Playing an instrument	Related jobs
Although your musical abilities may not guarantee fame, they're an essential component of your success in the music industry. Although some musicians make a living using their music as a form of self-expression, most musicians perform to the specifications set out by a conductor, director, or producer. Practicing, sight-reading music, and taking musical direction are essential to your success. In many careers, establishing a defined niche or specialty ensures success, but for musicians, versatility is the key. The more musical styles and instruments you can play, the better your chances of getting work.	Accompanist Church organist Floor show band member Instrumentalist Instrumental soloist Musician Orchestra member Piano tuner Theater musician
For more information: American Federation of Musicians, 1501 Broadway, Suite 600, New York, NY 10036; phone 212-869-1330, fax 212-764-6134; Web site www.afm.org	**Explore this career?** Yes / No

Teaching music	Related jobs
You help students create music of their own. You may focus on music theory and history, arranging, or performance. The specifics of what you teach depend on the age and skill level of your students as well as the education guidelines specified by the institution that pays your salary. In addition to teaching students, you may be responsible for planning concerts, parades, music festivals, or recitals. Creativity and innovative teaching methods bring results and an air of excitement to each session.	Choir director Conductor Conservatory professor Copyist Music department head Music professor Music supervisor Private music instructor School music teacher
For more information: Music Teachers National Association, The Carew Tower, 441 Vine St., Suite 505, Cincinnati, OH 45202-2814; phone 513-421-1420, fax 513-421-2503; e-mail mtnanet@mtna.org, Web site www.mtna.org	**Explore this career?** Yes / No

Music therapy	Related jobs
Combine your love of music with counseling skills to help people of all ages navigate a variety of life situations, including rehabilitation, age-related disorders, and physical, mental, and emotional disabilities. By encouraging clients to write, create, and listen to music, you assist them in enhancing their self-esteem and developing key motor skills, life skills, and socialization skills. To support clients, most music therapists work as part of an interdisciplinary team, which includes medical professionals, teachers, therapists, and the patient's family.	Art therapist Audiologist Creative arts therapist Dance therapist Drama therapist Music therapist Music therapy consultant Music therapy supervisor Occupational therapist Speech pathologist
For more information: American Music Therapy Association, 8455 Colesville Rd., Suite 1000, Silver Spring, MD 20910; phone 301-589-3300, fax 301-589-5175; e-mail info@musictherapy.org, Web site www.musictherapy.org	**Explore this career?** Yes / No

Enhancing and appreciating sound and music

If you enjoy music and have a good ear for it but aren't cut out to be a musician yourself, consider using your talents to enhance the music that others create. In the following careers, you play an important role in getting high-quality music to those who enjoy it.

Sound technician	Related jobs
As a sound technician for live performances or broadcasts, you make the musicians and performers sound great by blending voices and music to create a pleasing, balanced sound. Your ear for sound, your knowledge of acoustics and the venue, and your ability to identify solutions to eliminate problems on the spot lead to your success. For a successful career, you must understand the traditional tools of the trade as well as the latest analog and digital technologies. Clearly, an aptitude for working with electronic equipment is a plus! Growth in the cable industry and enhancements to Internet access mean an increased demand for audio.	Assistant engineer Audio control engineer Audio technician Broadcast engineer Live sound engineer Location recording engineer Resident sound technician Sound designer Sound technician Touring technician
For more information: Audio Engineering Society (AES), 60 East 42nd St., Room 2520, New York, NY 10165-2520; phone 212-661-8528, fax 212-682-0477; Web site www.aes.org	**Explore this career?** Yes / No

Recording	Related jobs
You record tracks for CDs, films, television, and other media to meet specifications set by the producers and artists. For films or television, you re-record numerous tracks of dialogue, music, sound effects, foley, and narration, adjusting the volume and balance while also producing fade-ins and fade-outs. Clear communication and accurate artistic translation of your client's vision are the name of the game. Your hours in the studio may vary, possibly lasting for long stretches. Advances in equipment, recording, and distribution media mean that you must keep up with the ever-changing technical side of your work.	Audio engineer Audio engineer for video Audio specialist Dialogue editor Digital audio editor Foley artist Post-production engineer Re-recording engineer Sound FX editor Sound mixer
For more information: Society of Professional Audio Recording Services, 9 Music Square South, Suite 222, Nashville, TN 37203; phone 800-771-7727, fax 615-846-5123; e-mail spars@spars.com, Web site www.spars.com	**Explore this career?** Yes / No

Producing	Related jobs
If you know a hit song when you hear one, you may have a future as a record producer. As a producer, you take raw talent and make the necessary decisions and choices to produce a well-arranged, well-recorded hit. If you don't have the technical skills to create the recording yourself, you must communicate with the engineer to articulate the feeling and sound you desire. Aside from the creative side of producing, you also manage the business side of the equation. That means bringing the project in on time, within budget, and with as few technological problems and personal disputes as possible.	Film producer Independent producer Music executive Production coordinator Radio producer Record producer Staff producer Synthesist Talent scout Television producer
For more information: National Academy of Recording Arts and Sciences, 3402 Pico Blvd., Santa Monica, CA 90405; phone 310-392-3777, fax 310-399-3090; Web site www.grammy.com/about.aspx	**Explore this career?** Yes / No

Using your voice

If you have a wonderful singing or speaking voice, you can use your voice as the corner-stone of your career. Consider the careers described in this section.

Singing	Related jobs
By mixing your vocal talent with determination and perseverance, you can create a viable singing career. To do so, you must have a versatile voice, be able to sing any style of music, have the ability to sight read, and exude confidence while performing. The key to success is building a reputation for excellence and dependability. As with most music careers, the hours are irregular, and travel is frequent. Many vocalists make singing part of a composite career, which lets them stabilize their income while still allowing them to utilize their greatest asset.	Background vocalist Backup singer Cantor Jingle singer Opera singer Performing artist Recording artist Rock star Singer Vocal soloist
For more information: American Guild of Musical Artists, 1730 Broadway, 14th Floor, New York, NY 10018; phone 212-265-3687, fax 212-262-9088; e-mail AGMA@MusicalArtists.org, Web site www.musicalartists.org	**Explore this career?** Yes / No

Voiceover	Related jobs
Combine your voice, sense of timing, and acting ability to do voiceovers for television, radio, cartoons, and non-broadcast, industrial narration. To excel in this profession, you must modify the tone, pacing, and quality of your voice on command. The money you spend to have your own voice coach is a worthwhile investment. Just as actors and singers continue their training throughout their careers, with a coach you can continue to enhance your skills, which helps you land bigger and better assignments. Doing voiceovers can be a good element of a composite career as long as your other work is flexible.	Actor Cartoon voice Master of ceremonies Narrator Radio announcer Voice coach Voiceover talent
For more information: Great Voice, 616 East Palisade Ave., Englewood Cliffs, NJ 07632; phone 800-333-8108, fax 201-541-8608; e-mail info@greatvoice.com, Web site www.greatvoice.com	**Explore this career?** Yes / No

Part IV
Bringing Your Dream Career to Life

The 5th Wave   By Rich Tennant

"Look — you want a new career as a fireman, that's fine. But I wouldn't wear that thing around here in the meantime."

In this part . . .

After you have a good career idea or two in hand, this part tells you how to investigate your options, using online resources, offline materials, and conversations with those in your field of interest. When you have a clear understanding of what's entailed in your dream career, it's time to blend your ideal vision with the realities of how you live. The last two chapters in this part help you chart your course to bring your dream career to life.

Chapter 14

Researching Your Top Two Career Ideas

After you have an intriguing career idea or two in mind (see Parts I through III of this book to help you formulate some ideas), it's time to deepen your understanding of each one of them. Having an accurate perspective of your target careers is essential to verifying that the careers match your needs.

The world is far too complex and changing far too fast to rely solely on your assumptions, written material, or one person's opinion about a career. To get an up-to-date picture of a potential career, you need to gather information about the job tasks and the possible industries where those job tasks are needed from several online or hard copy sources.

The job profiles you develop in this chapter help you get a sense of the tasks, educational requirements, and salary related to your top two career ideas. The next step is to explore and profile the industries that hire people in your target field. For example, if you want to write, you might start by looking at job titles that involve writing, such as technical writer, copy editor, public relations, or sitcom writer. Then to get a full sense of these jobs, you'd turn your attention to understanding the industries you might work in. As you'll see, each industry has its own character and culture. For instance, the publishing industry has a different culture, different requirements, and different opportunities than the news industry or the entertainment industry.

Building your job and industry profiles is also likely to open up new avenues of exploration. As you read various job profiles, you may discover a job title you hadn't seen before, or you may run into information about a trend that highlights an industry you hadn't considered before.

In Chapter 15 you expand your investigation by conducting informational interviews with those who are part of your target professions and target industries.

 Although you may already feel like you've hit pay dirt with one of your career ideas, devote the time required to verify that your career idea does in fact fit you and your lifestyle. In the long run, doing this double check *before* you launch your job search, accept a job offer, or start a business saves you time and money. In reality, it's much easier to make a course correction while you're still exploring your options than after you've already started implementing your idea.

Keeping Your Eye on the Prize

As you move through this chapter, you explore your top two career ideas from several angles. In addition to exploring related job profiles, you examine salary information, industry descriptions, and input from relevant professional associations.

The more information you take in, the more insights you gain about the true nature of your top two career ideas and their viability. On one hand, the information you find may absolutely confirm your impressions about your target careers. On the other hand, you may be in for the shock of your life when you discover your picture of a career was totally off base. (At this point you'll be thanking your lucky stars that you did the research *before* you launched into that career.) A third middle option is probably more likely to occur: You discover some information that excites you about the possibilities within a career and some information that leaves you feeling a bit concerned. This mixed bag is common and nothing to be alarmed about at this stage of the game.

I'll be honest with you. This exploration phase can be overwhelming for several valid reasons. I describe those reasons here, along with an antidote so you know how to focus your energy when you feel so overwhelmed that you want to give up.

- ✔ **Reason 1:** You're introduced to a vast new world of information with an infinite number of side roads, dead ends, and scenic routes that lead nowhere.

   Antidote 1: Keep your focus on your top two career ideas to start your exploration. Know that you can come back later to dabble in side road excursions.

- ✔ **Reason 2:** You're stepping into the big unknown. Somewhere, out there, is *your* career, but you have no idea where it is or how to find it.

   Antidote 2: Have trust and faith that each consciously chosen click on a Web site link takes you closer to the career of your wildest dreams. Paying close attention when something inside you signals interest and excitement is a good way to stay on target. Listening to yourself when you feel repelled by an aspect of a career is another important element of your exploration process. Revisit Chapter 2 for more details about these internal focusing tools.

- ✔ **Reason 3:** You're bombarded with new tidbits of information constantly. Each piece that comes your way may sway you this way or that. One minute you feel this is the best career ever. The next moment you think it's the worst idea possible.

   Antidote 3: Remember that you're in the beginning of your exploration phase. Although you'd love to have the final answer yesterday, you don't know enough to make a good decision yet. Your best bet is to stay in an observing and recording mode, calmly and consciously taking in all of the information and writing it down. Feel free to start making connections and seeing patterns and themes, but don't — I repeat, don't — jump to any conclusions in this chapter.

- ✔ **Reason 4:** You're anxious to get on with things. You want to get your resume out there and start talking to people — even though you aren't at all clear about your direction. This scenario is a recipe for disaster. What happens when you get a job interview or, worse, an offer for a job that turns out to be exactly the wrong move for you?

   Antidote 4: Don't spin your wheels like this. The time you invest in your exploration saves you huge amounts of time, energy, sweat, and tears later in the journey. When you're ready to take action, you'll feel clear, focused, and confident about your direction.

Your first pass through this chapter is exploratory in nature. Your goal is to get a broad enough view of each career idea to assess whether it's a viable possibility to consider. Stay open and alert as you do your research. This isn't just a school assignment — it's the foundation of your new life. Honor the mix of discomfort and excitement that you feel. That mix of emotions is common at this stage, honestly reflecting where you are at this stage of the process. Keep an open, curious mind and practice sitting in the space of the unknown. Very soon the clues start coming together, and your future comes into focus.

If your top two career ideas are business ideas or project descriptions, you may not be able to find an online job profile or industry profile that spells out exactly what you want to do. For example, you aren't likely to find a profile for a business to help others through the necessary paperwork after a loved one dies or for a business that uses horse training to help managers develop their leadership skills. Yet both these businesses exist. Your best path is to do a broader Web search using keywords to see whether you can find anyone else doing something similar to what you want to do. Piece together as much information as you can in the sections of this chapter and then head to Chapter 15 to start talking with others.

You may need to change tracks midway through the chapter if you find that one of your target career ideas dead-ends or leads in a direction that won't work for you or your lifestyle. For example, if you discover that your ideal career requires you to travel 80 percent of the time, you (and your toddlers) may quickly determine that this isn't the job for you after all. If that happens, draw another one of your top ten career ideas forward or follow the trail of a job profile or industry profile you've already looked at. By the end of the chapter, your top two career ideas may or may not be the same ones you started with. The key is that they're the most viable, exciting, interesting, and intriguing ideas you've found so far.

If you want, after you've selected your top two contenders, you can read more profiles and industry information to get as thorough a foundation as possible. At some point, however, the Web resources will get repetitive, telling you what you already know. At that point, you're ready for Chapter 15.

In Chapter 15, you do some more in-depth, hands-on research in the form of conversations and observations. One benefit of taking the time to explore your career ideas in this chapter is that you have ample opportunities to acquaint yourself with pertinent profession-specific terminology. This knowledge is a plus during the next phase of your exploration. The more comfortable you become with the language and nuances of your career ideas, the more credibility you have as you talk with people about your target professions in Chapter 15.

Jotting Down Your Unanswered Questions

As you complete the job and industry profiles throughout this chapter, pay close attention to questions that pop into your mind. Use Worksheet 14-1 to record the following:

- Anything that's confusing or contradictory
- Anything you aren't finding enough information about
- Things you've heard about the profession but aren't able to confirm

Although you may find answers to some of your questions before you complete your career exploration, recording your questions gives you a jump-start as you build your questions for informational interviews in Chapter 15.

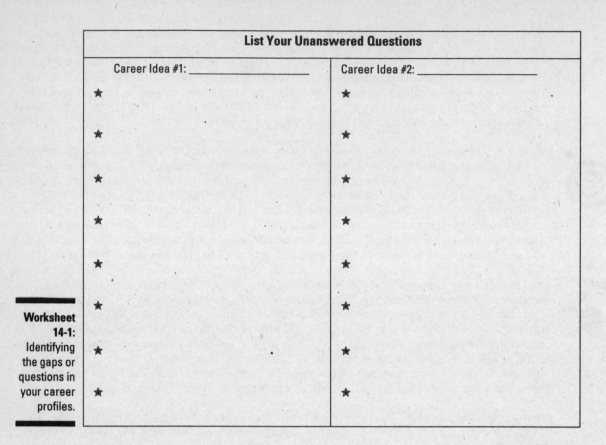

Worksheet 14-1: Identifying the gaps or questions in your career profiles.

Creating Job Profiles for Your Top Career Ideas

As you spend time exploring your career ideas, your main purpose is to confirm that you have a clear idea what's entailed in each profession. To do this, use the resources described in the following sections to begin building your job profiles in the worksheets that I provide.

What to look for

As you build each profile, focus on confirming what you know and discovering what you don't know about your career ideas. Researching what you don't know is an obvious strategy, but to be successful, you must also admit to yourself what you don't yet know. Dig deep to get the full scoop. As you gather information about the field, pay extra attention to any new information that shows you angles you haven't thought of before.

A number of elements go into building a profile of your career ideas. Each resource you access provides another layer of information. Keep adding details until you're confident that you have a full understanding of the job you're researching. Here's the info you'll need to research in order to complete the job profiles in Worksheets 14-2 and 14-3. You may want to make a few extra copies of these worksheets in case your discovery path takes you to other job titles.

✔ **What the job entails:** Describe the main tasks and responsibilities of the job.

✔ **Skills you need:** Identify the skills required to do this job.

✔ **Recommended training:** Make note of the training requirements for this job.

✔ **Employment outlook:** Record whatever information you find about the outlook for this profession. Note the date the forecast was written so you can evaluate its current relevance. If questions arise about future trends, add these questions to your list of unanswered questions in Worksheet 14-1.

✔ **Related job titles:** Track related job titles to get a fuller picture of your options.

✔ **Salary information:** Record what you learn about the salary potential for this job. (In addition to the salary information you find in online job profiles, see the section "Taking a closer look at salary information," later in this chapter.)

✔ **Professional associations and other valuable resources:** Keep a list of professional associations and other valuable resources as you do your exploration. New books, people, Web sites, businesses, and conferences you just happen to hear about in passing may be just the things that open the door to your future.

✔ **Your impressions of this job:** When your job profile is filled out, take a moment to spell out your first impressions. Be sure to articulate the good, the bad, and the ugly. This isn't the time to gloss over warning signs.

Don't let any single piece of information flip you out. You may run across salary information, employment outlook projections, education requirements, or workload descriptions that either don't fit your picture or make you very nervous. Always corroborate key information through several current sources before you react. In addition, if you're excited about almost everything else about the job, hang in there. In Chapters 16 and 17, you find creative ways to resolve trade-offs and possible conflicts. Don't try to resolve these issues now. Just note how you feel and keep exploring the possibilities.

Dawn, an art teacher from Pennsylvania, wants to use her creative talents to design something. Her biggest quandary is that she's not sure what she wants to design. Because she has to start somewhere, she's decided to begin her investigation with the job of architect. As she explored the Web sites in the following section, "Where to find job profiles," she started building a profile of the profession. Take a look at Figure 14-1 to review the way she summarized the research she did. Notice that Dawn referenced certain key sites in her notes so that she could go back later for more detail if she decided to explore this path. Based on how she expressed her impression of this profession, I suspect she's going to keep exploring her options before she makes a final decision about her future as an architect.

Job Profile for __Architect__	
What the job entails (Best job description is Occupational Outlook Handbook.)	Design and plan residential and commercial buildings to be functional, economical, and safe. Depending on level, draft plans using CAD. Sell and explain design ideas. Understand building codes and zoning in great detail. More time attending meetings and consulting with clients than designing(!). Coordinate and manage design and building processes, also conduct feasibility and environmental impact studies.
Skills and knowledge you need	Coordination skills; attention to detail; critical thinking; complex problem solving, time and people management skills, design, mathematical, and computer skills; working knowledge of CAD; ability to work with 3D and perspective; ability to communicate vision and persuade others to see value in design; engineering.
Recommended training	1. Must be licensed in state where I practice. Must get a degree in architecture from accredited university — only 100 in US. 2. Then intern with licensed architect for three years. 3. Then pass 4 day exam by National Council of Architectural Registration Boards (NCARB) or National Architectural Accrediting Board (NAAB). 4. After licensing, continuing education courses required.
Employment outlook	Average growth through 2012. Competitive field. Best strategy = summer internships, getting National CAD Standards. Employment is good when economy is good. Possible self-employment options.
Related job titles (See Wet Feet site for details on each various job levels.)	Design architect, project architect, project managers, construction administrator, draftsperson, CAD technicians, architecture consultant, landscape architect, civil engineer, urban and regional planners, interior designer, industrial designer, graphic designer, furniture/exhibit designer, marine architect, civil engineer
Salary information	Broad range – Architect $50-75K per year Draftsperson - $30-40K per year
Professional associations and other valuable resources	American Institute of Architects (AIA) www.aia.org National Council of Architectural Registration Boards (NCARB) www.ncarb.org
Your impressions of this job	Wasn't expecting so much training! Thought there would be more opportunity for designing and creating. Need to explore related jobs.

Figure 14-1: Dawn's job profile for her target career.

Job Profile for_____	
What the job entails	
Skills and knowledge you need	
Recommended training	
Employment outlook	
Related job titles	
Salary information	
Professional associations and other valuable resources	
Your impressions of this job	

Worksheet 14-2: Building a profile of your first career idea.

Job Profile for _____	
What the job entails	
Skills and knowledge you need	
Recommended training	
Employment outlook	
Related job titles	
Salary information	
Professional associations and other valuable resources	
Your impressions of this job	

Worksheet 14-3:
Building a profile of your second career idea.

Where to find job profiles

In the past, you had to go to a library or a career center to find thorough job profiles. With the Internet, you're just a click away from many extremely valuable resources.

Although you may be tempted to click on all of the interesting links you come across in your research, focus your first round of research on your top two career ideas. A scattered approach to this exploration quickly leaves you feeling confused and overwhelmed. Record jobs that really catch your attention, and the corresponding Web pages, in Worksheet 14-4 so that you can come back later to explore them in detail.

Job Titles that Catch Your Attention	
Job Title	Web Link or Resource
1.	
2.	
3.	
4.	
5.	
6.	
7.	
8.	
9.	
10.	

Worksheet 14-4: Recording interesting jobs that might deserve a second look.

When you locate a useful job profile, bookmark it or save it to your list of favorites so you can go back to it at a later date. Other options include printing the profiles and putting them in a binder or starting a log of the Web sites you visit. Nothing is more frustrating than knowing you saw a key piece of information somewhere on the Web but not recalling where you saw it or how to find it again.

The following Web sites provide the best online job profiles. Read the description of each site to discover what information is in the profiles. I encourage you to check out several sites to compare and contrast what the various sources say about your target careers.

- ✔ **Occupational Outlook Handbook (www.bls.gov/oco/):** On this site, each career profile includes a description of the nature of the work, working conditions, employment options, training and education requirements, job outlook, earnings, related occupations, and sources of additional information. You can access career profiles on this site using an alphabetical index, the occupational clusters, or the site's search engine.

- ✔ **Wetfeet.com (www.wetfeet.com):** Click on the Careers Profiles link, under Career Research, to find the job title that best fits your career idea, and click on it. Each profile consists of five separate pages: career overview, requirements, job outlook, career tracks, and compensation. Use the links just under the job title to access these pages. To the right of each profile is a list of additional resources, including profiles of related industries, associations, and discussion boards.

- **Princeton Review** (`www.princetonreview.com/cte/search/careerSearch.asp`): Although primarily a resource for students making decisions about their education, this site has 180 detailed profiles that consist of an unusual mix of information. The first page of each career profile gives you a day in the life of a career, paying your dues, and associated careers. Use the links on the left-hand navigational bar to explore quality of life two years, five years, and ten years out; past and future of the field; statistics about who is in the profession; salary information; what professionals read; movies and books that feature the career; major employers; who you're likely to associate with; and key professional associations. If you use the "Search Careers and Internships" search engine to hunt for a particular job title, the results provide all direct hits and other related possibilities. You can also access the profiles through the alphabetical listings. If you sign up as a member of the site, you can save your profiles for later reference.

- **Monster.com** (`http://jobprofiles.monster.com/`): This site has 120 different job profiles that include a description of the job, the necessary skills, the education requirements, employment outlook, related careers, relevant key words, and related articles. Each profile also includes some interesting, and often obscure, factoids.

- **America's Career InfoNet** (`www.acinet.org/acinet/`): This site provides a tremendous amount of information about various facets of career exploration. Begin by clicking on the Occupation Information button on the home page. After clicking on the Occupation Profile link, you can use one of two methods to search for your target job. You can identify the relevant job family, then the occupation, and your state, or you can enter the first few letters of the job title. From there you can check off the parts of the report you want to view. Each profile includes a description of the work; state and national wage information; knowledge, skills, and abilities required to do the job; tasks and activities performed on the job; education and training levels; related occupation profiles; and Web resources, including profiles on other Web sites. Each profile includes a box that leads to related content, including trends and possibly a related video. In the Occupation Information section, you can also access lists of the occupations with the fastest growth, most openings, largest employment, declining employment, and highest salaries. Use these additional lists with caution if you're just starting your research. Too much information can be distracting. After you're clear about your potential direction, check each of these lists to see whether your target career is listed. If, for instance, your targeted career is on the declining employment list, you certainly want to know that.

- **Jobstar** (`www.jobstar.org/tools/career/spec-car.cfm`): This site is a little different from the others in this list. When you reach this Web site, you find a list of career fields. Click on the one of interest to find a list of relevant Web sites. Each link on the list takes you to a Web site created by those in the profession. Some sites are more detailed than others. Some sites include descriptions from individuals who currently work in the field.

- **Cornell University's Career Zone** (`www.nycareerzone.org`): After you pass through the opening screen, run your cursor over each icon to read a brief description of that career cluster. Then click on the career cluster that best matches your interests to find a list of jobs. Under each career cluster you find a list of anywhere from 100 to 500 jobs, but you can make the review process more manageable by sorting the jobs by required education or expected wages by using the Advanced Search link. Each job profile includes a job description, interests, tasks, skills, knowledge, education, school programs, wages, job outlook, additional resources, and similar jobs. Videos accompany some of the profiles. Because this site highlights jobs in New York State, the wages and job outlook are specific to that state, but don't let that deter you. The detailed descriptions of each job and what's entailed are clear and informative no matter where you live.

Plugging keywords, such as job titles, commonly used equipment and supplies, or professional awards, into your favorite Internet search engine can also lead to additional information about a career, such as job announcements (keep track of interesting opportunities, but don't let them seduce you into applying for a job just yet), the Web site or blog of someone who currently does the work, additional professional groups, informative articles about the profession, resources for the tools and equipment these professionals use in their work, and job boards for future reference. If your first set of keywords doesn't give you what you want, try another keyword. Sometimes just a slight variation in the words you use in your search can pull up a different set of links.

The career section of your local bookstore or the reference section in your local library may also have some useful resources to help you gain a more thorough perspective on your career ideas. Look for the following:

- *The Occupational Outlook Handbook:* Published by the U.S. Department of Labor, Bureau of Labor Statistics. This book provides the same information as its Web site (see the preceding list), but in a book format.

- *The Dictionary of Occupational Titles:* Provided by the U.S. Department of Labor, Employment Training Administration. It includes short descriptions of 12,741 occupations, which are organized by occupational categories. Each occupation is also coded according to the work functions performed in each job. If you know from your exploration that you like to work primarily with people, data, or things, paying attention to these codes may expand your horizons.

Cool Careers For Dummies, 2nd Edition, by Marty Nemko and Paul and Sarah Edwards (Wiley), also offers lots of information about great careers.

Locating key professional associations

Professional associations provide another valuable source of career information about occupations and industries. Whether you visit an association's Web site or send for more information, you gain valuable insights about training and education requirements, salary standards, education sources, conferences, and local chapters by connecting with relevant associations.

Start by visiting the associations you've already identified in your exploration thus far. Check out the sites to find out what you can about the professions and industries they serve. Use the information to supplement the job profiles and industry profiles you've been developing.

You might also locate your target career ideas in Chapters 11 through 13 to see if those descriptions point you to a professional association you aren't aware of yet.

If you want to search out associations that are even more closely related to your target career ideas, visit the following Web sites:

- **Weddles** (`www.weddles.com/associations/index.cfm`): Organized by category, this list of associations provides active links to a wide range of professional associations.

- **The Internet Public Library** (`www.ipl.org/div/aon/`): This guide to professional associations begins with a list of broad categories. Begin with the category that is of most interest and keep drilling down through the various levels of subheadings until you reach the list of relevant associations.

- **Jobweb.com** (`www.jobweb.com/Career_Development/prof_assoc.htm`): In addition to being able to access a list of professional associations by category, this site also serves as an access point to a very useful list of associations: the Gateway to Associations. A powerful search tool on the Gateway to Associations site allows you to pull up professional associations by the name of the association, keywords, location, and category. If you don't know the name of the association, scan the drop-down list of categories. After you specify your search criteria, a list comes up on the screen, and you can click through to the most relevant associations.

If you don't have access to the Internet, or you want to do additional offline research, ask the reference librarian in your local library to direct you to the following resources:

- ***Encyclopedia of Associations:*** Published by The Gale Group, this resource lists 22,000 national and international associations. Each entry provides contact information, a description of the purpose of the organization, its publications and affiliations, and convention information. If you're interested in regional, state, or local organizations, look for the volume dedicated to these groups.

- ***National Trade & Professional Associations Directory:*** Compiled by Columbia Books Inc. each year, this index provides information about 7,500 trade associations, professional societies, labor unions, and technical organizations. You can use this book to find contact information and a description of an association even if you only know the acronym, subject area, or location of the organization.

Taking a closer look at salary information

Estimating the salary associated with a particular job title is a very complex operation. Generally, your salary depends on a number of factors, including your job responsibilities, performance, tenure, training, experience, the company's size, company pay scales, the industry, and your geographic location.

Rather than piecing together a salary estimate on your own or depending on the industry grapevine, use one of the following three Web sites to obtain accurate, reliable salary estimates based on the compilation of salary surveys from various research organizations and government sources:

- **Salary.com** (`www.salary.com`): Enter your target job title into the Salary Wizard on the home page or click on the link to All Titles to select from a list. Then enter your zip code or choose from a list of states and cities. Identify your target job title from the list provided. If you need more information to make your choice, read job descriptions by using the link provided under the box listing job titles. Click on View a Basic Report to see a graph showing the base salary for your area. Scroll to the bottom of the report, and with one additional click, you can see how that salary compares to the national average, to the salary for the same job in a different location, or to a related job in the same location.

- **Salaryexpert.com** (`www.salaryexpert.com`): Select a job title or paste in a job description of your target career, enter your location information, and click on Search. On the next page, select View a Basic Report. The page that opens provides a report summary at the top and then more details about the location-specific wages and the national average wages. Scrolling down, you find a description of the job and additional sources of information. You can obtain a more detailed salary survey for more specific job titles, if you're willing to pay for the report.

✔ **America's Career InfoNet** (`www.acinet.org/acinet/`): Begin by clicking on the Occupation Information link on the home page. After clicking on Occupation Profile, you can use one of two methods to search for your target job. You can identify the relevant job family, then the occupation, and your state, or you can search for the career with a few letters or keywords. From there you check off the wages information option. The page that opens up shows you wage information for the state you selected and the nation. Below the table, look for several links that give you an even bigger picture. One link shows you how the wages for this occupation rank by state. You can also compare these wages to those of a different job or compare the wages across states you select.

Your best offline resource for researching compensation trends is the _American Salaries and Wages Survey,_ published by The Gale Group on an annual basis. This book, which you can find in your library or career center, pulls data from over 300 sources to create geographic-specific salary data for 2,660 occupation classifications and 4,800 individual jobs.

Creating Your Industry Profiles

Another facet to knowing your options is gaining more insight about the industries where your favorite job function may be used. In some cases, the fit between the job and industry may be immediately obvious. In other situations, you may need to do some detective work to find the right job/industry match. Furthermore, an industry profile may open up a new line of exploration by pointing out job titles you haven't seen before.

As you explore possible industries by using the resources included in this section, record your discoveries in Worksheets 14-5 and 14-6. (You may want to make extra copies of these worksheets in case you explore more than two industries.) Your profile is likely to include the following pieces of information.

✔ **Description of the industry:** Make note of the key elements that describe this industry.

✔ **Training requirements:** Record the kind of training and experience recommended within the industry.

✔ **Employment outlook:** Describe the employment trends expected for this industry.

✔ **Related job titles:** List job titles that surface in your research.

✔ **Professional associations and other valuable resources:** Keep track of any resources that may extend your knowledge of the industry, whether it's a professional association, a Web site, or an annual conference. In addition to the associations listed in the profiles you read, refer to the section "Locating key professional associations," earlier in this chapter, to identify professional associations for your target industry.

✔ **Your impressions of this industry:** While the information is fresh, make note of your impressions of the industry and what you like and don't like about what you've discovered.

Industry Profile for _____	
Description of industry	
Training requirements	
Employment outlook	
Related job titles	
Professional associations and other valuable resources	
Your impressions of this industry	

Worksheet 14-5: Creating a full picture of one of your favorite industries.

Industry Profile for_____	
Description of industry	
Training requirements	
Employment outlook	
Related job titles	
Professional associations and other valuable resources	
Your impressions of this industry	

Worksheet 14-6: Creating a full picture of another favorite industry.

Use the following resources to familiarize yourself with industries that intrigue you. Explore what looks interesting even if you don't immediately see a way to blend it with your favorite functions.

✔ **America's Career InfoNet (`www.acinet.org/acinet/`):** Begin by clicking on the Industry Information link on the home page. After clicking on Industry Profile, you can use one of two methods to search for your target job. You can locate the appropriate industry sector or type in the first few letters of the industry of interest. From there, choose the most relevant subsector or industry listed. You may drill down through several layers before you reach the profile information. There you find a description of the industry and industry employment trends. At the bottom of the profile you can follow additional links to an occupation profile. In the Industry Information section, you can also access lists of the industries with the fastest growth, largest employment, and declining employment. Use these additional lists with some restraint if you're just starting your exploration. After you're clear about your potential direction, check each of these lists to see whether your target industry is listed.

✔ **Wetfeet.com (`www.wetfeet.com`):** Click on the Industry Profile link, under Career Research, to reach the industry profiles. Each profile consists of four separate pages: industry overview, love-hate or the workplace, major players, job descriptions and tips or job profiles and hiring. To the right of each profile is a list of additional resources, including profiles of related jobs, associations, and discussion boards.

✔ **Career Guide to Industries (`www.bls.gov/oco/cg/home.htm`):** Offered as a companion to the job profiles of the Occupational Outlook Handbook, this site provides detailed career information by industry. You can browse through a list of industries on the right side of the home page or use the CGI Search/A-Z Index in the upper right-hand corner of the screen. Each industry profile includes significant points about the industry, the nature of the industry, working conditions within the industry, employment options, occupations within the industry, training and advancement, earnings, outlook, and additional sources of information.

The career section of your local bookstore or the reference section in your local library may also have some useful resources to help you gain a more thorough perspective on industries. Look for *The Career Guide to Industries,* published by the U.S. Department of Labor, Bureau of Labor Statistics. This guide describes careers from an industry perspective and includes the nature of the work, job qualifications, job outlook, and income potential for 42 diverse industries. This resource provides the same information as the online counterpart.

Paying Attention to Your Gut Reaction

Now that you've researched your career ideas and written down your discoveries, how do you feel when you think about working in this job or industry? Do you feel drawn to one more than the other? Do you hesitate or pull away from one? Just notice how you feel and write down your overall impressions in Worksheet 14-7.

Some feelings of trepidation and nervousness are natural. You are, after all, doing this research to explore the possibility of changing your career. While you're in the process of discovering your future, you're likely to feel a bit uncomfortable with all the unknowns still in the equation. To keep your anxiety under control, stay focused on the step in front of you. For instance, if you're investigating your target careers, you aren't ready to make any decisions. In fact, you *can't* make a good, solid decision about your future until you have a good grasp of your target career.

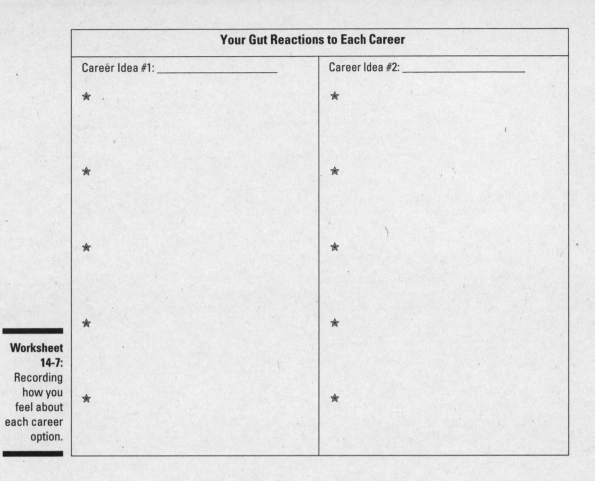

Your Gut Reactions to Each Career

Career Idea #1: _____ | Career Idea #2: _____

Worksheet 14-7: Recording how you feel about each career option.

Use the following list to decide how to proceed from here:

- ✔ **If something about one of your career ideas leaves you cold, bored, or annoyed,** return to your Top Ten list in Chapter 10 to decide what other career you want to explore.

- ✔ **If you've discovered something about a career idea that makes it completely unpalatable to you,** pull another career forward from your Top Ten list.

- ✔ **If you aren't sure about one of your career ideas but are still intrigued by it,** keep exploring. Don't step away too early in the process. You may need to talk with people doing the job to get a good sense of whether it works for you. Investigate the parts of the job that intrigue you. Use Chapter 15 to gather more information about the career by talking with others in the field.

- ✔ **If you're curious about one of the job profiles or industry profiles that you stumbled upon during your exploration,** take some time to look it over. If it's intriguing enough to replace one of your top two career ideas, shift your priorities.

Chapter 15

Asking the Right Questions about Your Top Two Careers

Your objective in this chapter is to expand your knowledge about your target careers, work out any inconsistencies you've uncovered, resolve any mysteries you've run into, and gather more firsthand information about the professions, jobs, and industries you are most interested in. By the end of this chapter, you want to have as full a picture as possible about your top two career ideas.

After you gain a basic understanding of your target careers by reading job profiles, exploring industry descriptions, and finding relevant professional associations (Chapter 14 can help), it's time to bring a human touch to your exploration. The people who work in your target profession or industry offer current, geographically relevant, and personalized information that enriches how you see your target career.

You can use informational interviews for a number of purposes, including trying on a new career, learning about a particular company, exploring a specific work structure, or finding out what it's like to work as a solo entrepreneur. How you approach your informational interviews depends on where you are in your exploration:

✔ If you're exploring whether a profession, occupation, or industry is a good fit for you, proceed with this chapter.

✔ If you think you've decided the direction you want to take, perhaps based on your research in Chapter 14, I encourage you to continue with this chapter. Adding the personal perspective of your contacts gives you a richer, more realistic view of your goal.

Your informational interviews are going to be more successful and meaningful if you conduct them after you have a general base of knowledge about your targeted career interests. If you haven't worked through Chapter 14 yet, I encourage you to take some time to read about your career ideas before you engage in any informational interviews. Those you contact will know whether you've done your homework prior to talking with them by the questions you ask, the words you use, and the questions you don't know to ask. Earn their respect and confidence by being prepared and informed before you approach them.

Later, in Chapters 18 and 19, you may also use informational interviews to ask questions about the more specific aspects of your plan to find a new job, start your business, or return to school for more training.

Building Your List of Questions

The questions you include in your informational interviews depend on the research you've done up to this point. As you begin creating your list of questions in Worksheet 15-1, consider what you've already discovered about your top two careers.

Your Initial List of Informational Interview Questions	
Career #1: _____	Career #2: _____
1.	1.
2.	2.
3.	3.
4.	4.
5.	5.
Industry #1: _____	Industry #2: _____
1.	1.
2.	2.
3.	3.
4.	4.
5.	5.

Worksheet 15-1: Creating your list of questions.

✔ Do you need more information about what a job entails, the skills a job requires, the training you may need, or the outlook for salary or employment (refer to Worksheets 14-2 and 14-3 in Chapter 14)?

✔ Do you need more information about the industry you're interested in (refer to Worksheets 14-5 and 14-6)?

✔ Has your research provided conflicting or confusing information about a job or industry that you'd like to clarify?

✔ Do you have any unanswered questions about a job or industry (refer to Worksheet 14-1)?

✔ Is there anything else you'd like to know to help you answer this question: Is this career a good fit for me?

The following questions may also provide helpful ideas as you build your list of questions for your informational interviews:

✔ **The profession in general**

- What is the outlook for this profession?

- What training or education is required?

- What sort of advancement possibilities exist?

✔ **A specific job**

- What is your day like?

- What are your key job responsibilities?

- What are your most favorite and least favorite parts of your job?

✔ **The industry in general**

- What is the long-term outlook for this industry?

- What is at the cutting edge of this industry?

- What are the pros and cons of working in this industry right now?

✔ **The form of work**

- What are the pros and cons of your schedule?

- How did you negotiate your flexible work arrangement?

- Did you experience any unexpected surprises when you started this schedule?

✔ **The lifestyle**

- How does this job impact your life?

- How much flexibility do you really have?

- How much travel should I expect?

✔ **The contact's career path**

- How did you get into this field?

- What jobs have you held?

- Do you know anyone who entered this field with my background?

Because each informational interview should last only 20 to 30 minutes, you won't be able to ask each contact all of your questions. Instead, you'll need to prioritize your questions and preselect the questions that each contact is likely to be best qualified to answer.

As you gain more insight on your general questions about each profession, turn your attention to more specific elements of your target careers. When possible, ask each question in several informational interviews to obtain different perspectives on the same issue.

Creating a List of Contacts

With a list of questions in hand, you're ready to start locating and talking with people who work in the careers you're investigating. But how do you find those people?

To get the ball rolling, make a list of the people you know, using the prompts in Worksheet 15-2 to stimulate your thinking. As you scan your e-mail inbox and your address book for ideas, think about current contacts, people you knew in the past, and people you know through professional networking groups or social groups. Write down as many names as you can. At this early stage, don't worry about whether they know anything about your target field. Instead, keep your focus on those you know to be well connected, because they're the contacts that are most likely to put you in touch with the largest number of people who can help you most.

Never underestimate who your friends know. For all you know, your friend's uncle is the CEO of a company that specializes in the work you want to do. You never know until you ask!

Keep track of your contacts as your list grows. Later in your journey, you access your network again as you search for job openings or build your new business.

Your List of Potential Contacts		
Friends	Family members	Neighbors
1.	1.	1.
2.	2.	2.
3.	3.	3.
4.	4.	4.
5.	5.	5.
Colleagues	Managers	Professors
1.	1.	1.
2.	2.	2.
3.	3.	3.
4.	4.	4.
5.	5.	5.
Community contacts	Professionals you work with	Vendors
1.	1.	1.
2.	2.	2.
3.	3.	3.
4.	4.	4.
5.	5.	5.
Members of professional associations	Contacts from networking groups	Members of service organizations
1.	1.	1.
2.	2.	2.
3.	3.	3.
4.	4.	4.
5.	5.	5.

Worksheet 15-2: Creating your list of well-connected contacts.

Staying Objective in Your Quest

During your informational interviews, remember that you're meeting with each person to gather information to help you better understand a potential career. Follow this advice to achieve your objective:

- **Confront your worst fears:** Remove your rose-colored glasses and ask the tough questions you don't really want the answers to. Your goal must be to gather as accurate a picture as possible about your target profession, job, or industry. If, for instance, you're worried about salary potential or the long-term outlook for the profession, ask the question and face the truth. Now is not the time to play hide-and-seek from the truth.

- **Test your assumptions:** If you think something is true about your target career, based on your prior investigations, ask questions to confirm or disprove what you think you already know. Perhaps you may have developed some assumptions about the level of education required to do the job. Ask the question so you can confirm your beliefs before you're set to take action.

Whenever possible, conduct at least two or three informational interviews before you make any pivotal decisions about your career. Compare what you hear from different sources and send a follow-up e-mail to your contacts to explore anything that doesn't quite add up.

Stepping into Your First Round of Informational Interviews

Although the thought of asking people to talk with you about their professions may be a bit daunting at first, don't let your fear or discomfort stop you. In my experience, people are generally happy to talk with you as long as you're genuinely interested in listening to them.

To keep from feeling overwhelmed by the process, choose five people from your list in Worksheet 15-2 whom you feel comfortable just calling or e-mailing out of the blue. This first round of informational interviews tends to be quite informal and helps you build confidence in yourself and in the process.

When you reach out to your first five contacts, explain that you're exploring a new career and you'd like to ask them a few questions. Assure them that even if they don't know about the career specifically, they can help you out by listening to you, giving you their honest feedback about your interview style, and pointing you in the direction of contacts who are familiar with your field. Set up a time to meet in person, if possible, for coffee or a walk.

When you get together, open the conversation the same way you would if you were meeting with a professional contact. If the person is familiar with your target career, ask a few questions from your initial list in Worksheet 15-1. In addition to paying attention to the answers, notice how effectively you communicate what you're looking for. If your contact seems confused by anything you've said, reword your question or ask the person what was unclear. The purpose of these interactions is not only to give you information but also to help you practice and polish your spiel.

If your contact doesn't know much about your target field or industry, ask if she'll role-play with you so you have an opportunity to practice asking your questions.

At the end of your interviews, always ask your contacts whether they know anyone who is familiar with your field of interest or might know people in the field. If you get a name, be sure to obtain the person's contact information as well as permission to say you were referred. This one question makes the size of your network snowball. You can even be more direct and ask whether your contact knows anyone who works in a particular company or is a member of a specific association.

Record the results of your first round of interviews in Worksheet 15-3. (Make extra copies of this worksheet so you have one for each of your first-round interviews.) Focus on the content of what you discovered during the interview. Record your contact's pertinent information, the questions you asked, and the answers your contacts gave you. Make note of any contacts they provided you as well.

Summary of Your Round One Informational Interviews	
Contact:	Phone:
Contact's Title/Role:	E-mail:
Contact's Company:	Address:
Questions and Answers	
Question 1:	
Answer:	
Question 2:	
Answer:	
Question 3:	
Answer:	
Question 4:	
Answer:	
Question 5:	
Answer:	
Follow-up Required to Connect with Next-Generation Contacts:	
1.	
2.	
Steps to Complete the Interview with This Contact	
Thank-you note: ____ Update note: _____ Note about your final direction: ____	

Worksheet 15-3: Making notes about your first set of informational interviews.

After you complete your informational interview, write a thank-you note to your contact and mail it — snail mail — within 48 hours. Later, as you shift your focus or make your final decision about your career direction, send another note to keep your contact updated. Use the bottom portion of the worksheet to track which notes you've sent and when you sent them.

One reason to conduct a first round of informational interviews before you talk to your high potential contacts is that you find out what works and what doesn't work with a bit of practice. Take some time to review your first five interviews in Worksheet 15-4. Recording what you learn means that you're less likely to make the same mistakes in the next round of interviews.

Ways to Improve Your Interview Style		
Interview	What Worked?	What Would You Do Differently Next Time?
#1		
#2		
#3		
#4		
#5		

Worksheet 15-4: Recording what worked or didn't work about the interview process.

Moving on to Your Second Round of Informational Interviews

After you smooth out the rough edges and feel more comfortable with the informational interview process, begin your second round of informational interviews. At this stage, you begin talking with people you don't know well or at all.

Use the following steps to set up and conduct your informational interviews:

1. **Think about the information you still need to discover about your target career.**

   Scan your contact list to identify those who are well connected or in a position to provide you with information relevant to your current objective, whether you're trying to find out more about a profession, job, or industry. You can select names from Worksheet 15-1 or begin to contact people whom your first round of contacts referred you to.

   If your personal network doesn't produce the kinds of contacts you need, consider contacting people through an alumni group, sorority or fraternity, or career center. These organizations often offer career networks as part of their services. In addition, online networking systems, such as Ryze (`www.ryze.com`) or Linked In (`www.linkedin.com`), may be of assistance.

2. **Decide how you'll introduce yourself to each contact.**

   Carefully craft your introductory sentence or paragraph so that it conveys who you are and why you're calling or writing. This statement must be clear and concise and tell the contact who you are and why you're contacting them. For instance, you could say, "Jennifer Davey recommended that I contact you. I'm in the process of exploring a new career in dune buggy construction. I understand from Jennifer that you have experience in this field. Would it be possible to arrange a time for an informational interview in the next two weeks?"

   Of course your exact words will reflect your interests and be appropriate for the communication channel you're using to connect with your contact. If you're calling your contact, always have a concise phone message at the tip of your tongue. Nothing makes a worse first impression than a message full of stammers and uhs.

3. **Make your initial contact with a letter, an e-mail, or a phone call.**

   If you're contacting people you've known in the past, include a reference to the location or event where the two of you met. With permission from your original contacts, use their names in your initial communication with contacts they've given you (as in the example in Step 2). If you do need to contact someone cold, be polite yet persistent. Even if you run into what seems like an endless series of nos, just keep reaching out on a regular basis. Your perseverance may pay off in surprising ways in the long run.

4. **Set up a 20- to 30-minute appointment.**

   If given the choice, meet with your contact in person at her workplace. Getting the experience of being in your contact's work environment may provide you with information you couldn't get from asking a question. In fact, the setting may even stimulate a question or two. If meeting in person isn't possible, set up a phone appointment. As a last resort, you can conduct an informational interview by e-mail if that's the only way to obtain the information you need.

5. Prepare for your informational interview.

Take time before your appointment to lay out the questions you want to ask this particular contact based on her background, position, and training. Use Worksheet 15-5 to plan and guide your interview. (Before you begin writing, make a number of copies of Worksheet 15-5 so you can use the worksheet for subsequent interviews as well.) Although you should plan to spend 20 to 30 minutes interviewing any one contact, create a thorough list of questions so that you're prepared if you find that the person's expertise differs slightly from what you expected or you have the unexpected opportunity to talk longer than originally planned.

6. Arrive early, dressed professionally for your informational interview (even if you know your contact personally).

You don't want to arrive rushed and harried, so plan extra time for traffic tie-ups and parking problems. Use your extra time to breathe and take in the environment.

7. Conduct your interview.

Upon meeting your contact, introduce yourself and thank her for agreeing to meet for the informational interview. Your contact is likely to feel more comfortable if she knows that you're sticking to your word and not angling for a job. In one or two sentences, describe the focus of the interview. For instance, you might say, "Thank you for meeting with me to discuss interior design" or you might say "I appreciate the time you've made in your schedule to meet with me. To make the most of our time together, I'd like to focus our conversation on upcoming opportunities within the photography industry." Then begin asking the questions you developed in Worksheet 15-5. If your contact's comments bring up new angles you hadn't considered before, fold a few new questions into the conversation, but don't abandon your original questions entirely. If you can, add the new questions to the bottom of Worksheet 15-5 during the interview so it will be easier to re-create the full content of the interview in Worksheet 15-6.

At the beginning of your interview, ask your contact if she minds if you take notes. If you plan to take notes, come prepared with professional-looking paper and pen. Focus on getting enough of the main points down on paper so that that you can fill in the details on Worksheet 15-6 after the interview. On the other hand, don't take so many notes that you slow the interview to a crawl. Focus on getting the key words or phrases down on your pad of paper to serve as memory triggers.

Before your time runs out, ask your contact if she knows others who might provide you with valuable information. Jot any contacts and their contact information at the bottom of Worksheet 15-5.

If you're still doing informational interviews, it's too early to be making any binding career decisions. Focus your attention on verifying that your target career is a good fit for you. If your contact mentions a job opening in conversation, tell her you'd like to hear more about it after the informational interview is complete. Don't allow the informational interview to become a job interview. Participating in a job interview when you aren't sure the career is a good fit for you is like playing with fire. (However, if you've completed enough informational interviews to know that you're leaning toward this career, explore the opportunity with your eyes and ears wide open. If a fantastic job offer does come your way, evaluate it very carefully before you make a final decision. Refer to Chapters 16 and 19 for help in thinking through whether the career is a good fit for you and your life.)

8. Complete the interview professionally.

Pay attention to the time so that you can bring the interview to a close at the agreed upon time. Thank your contact for her time, shake hands if you're meeting in person, and leave the premises. If you happen to know someone at the location, don't turn your visit into a social call. Leave the location with the same professionalism with which you conducted the interview. Remember to make time in your schedule to sit down immediately to record as many details as possible in Worksheet 15-6 in the next section.

Guide for Your Round Two Informational Interviews	
Contact:	Phone:
Contact's Title/Role:	E-mail:
Contact's Company:	Address:
Referred by:	
Appointment Day/Time:	
Appointment Location:	
List of Potential Questions	
1.	
2.	
3.	
4.	
5.	
6.	
7.	
8.	
9.	
10.	
Questions that Evolve During Your Conversation	
1.	
2.	
3.	
4.	
5.	
Next-Generation Contacts	
1.	
2.	

Worksheet 15-5: Preparing for your informational interview.

9. **Thank those who talk to you, even if your conversation only lasts five minutes.**

Follow up with a handwritten thank-you note (not an e-mail) to your key contacts. Use the note to thank them for taking the time to talk with you, for the information they shared, and for the additional contacts they provided you. If you have progress to report, let them know how they helped you move forward. (You can track whether you've sent your thank-you notes at the bottom of Worksheet 15-6.)

10. **Keep your contacts informed of your progress as you fine-tune your ideas.**

If you refocus your goal, write another note to your contacts. Sharing your new direction may encourage your contacts to think of a new set of referrals for you.

Later, when you're clear about your long-term goal, your informational interview contacts may be some of your best sources for job leads. Because you've already established a pattern of communicating with them, sending a note that describes the kind of position you're looking for is a completely natural next step.

Recording Your Discoveries about Each Career

Immediately after your meeting, record your discoveries in detail in Worksheet 15-6. In your summary include the following information:

- ✔ **The contact you spoke with:** At the top of Worksheet 15-6, record your contact's particulars and something about the interview or interviewer that brings the conversation right back to you. Perhaps it's the fuchsia suit, a picture of the Rocky Mountains, or your contact's wild sense of humor that caught your attention.

- ✔ **The questions you asked:** Although it's obvious in the moment what questions you posed, your mind may not retain the actual content of each informational interview several weeks later. Writing down the questions that you asked also helps you know how to interpret what your contact said during the interview.

- ✔ **The answers you heard:** Immediately after your interview, you may not think that recording everything your contact said is that important, but after you've talked to several contacts, you'll be happy to have a detailed summary of what transpired in each interview. Using your contact's own words, when possible, helps you compare and contrast what various contacts have said. If you run out of space on this worksheet, just add an additional page to capture the thoughts and ideas expressed in the interview.

- ✔ **The contacts you were referred to:** Make a note at the bottom of your summary to indicate what actions you need to take to obtain the contact information for the new referrals. Do you need to send your contact an e-mail to receive the contact information or do you need to call a company to track down the contact?

Fill out a new copy of Worksheet 15-6 for each person you talk with. Keep your summaries in a folder or binder so you can review them after you've spoken with several contacts.

Summary of Your Round Two Informational Interviews	
Contact: Contact's Title/Role: Contact's Company:	Describe something unique that can help you recall the conversation in the future.
Questions and Answers	
Question 1: Answer: Question 2: Answer: Question 3: Answer: Question 4: Answer: Question 5: Answer:	
Follow-up Required to Connect with Next-Generation Contacts	
1. 2.	
Steps to Complete the Interview with This Contact	
Thank-you note: _____ Update note: _____ Note about your final direction: _____	

Worksheet 15-6: Summarizing your informational interview.

Synthesizing What You Know So Far

At a certain point, the information you receive from your contacts confirms what you've already discovered, and the time has come to consolidate what you know.

Set aside some quiet time to reread all of the informational interviews you've conducted thus far. Record new discoveries in Worksheet 15-7 so you can see them all in one place.

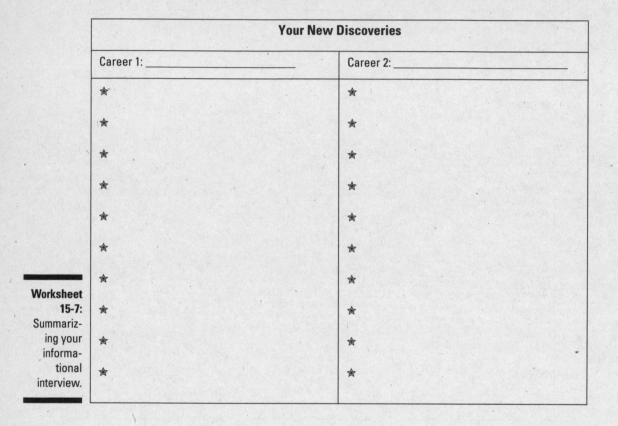

Your New Discoveries	
Career 1: _____	Career 2: _____
☆	☆
☆	☆
☆	☆
☆	☆
☆	☆
☆	☆
☆	☆
☆	☆
☆	☆
☆	☆

Worksheet 15-7: Summarizing your informational interview.

As you review your newfound nuggets of information and your original job and industry profiles, you should have a fairly good understanding of your target careers.

Take stock of how you feel about your options. Are you leaning toward one more than the other, torn between the two ideas, or obsessing over a few lingering questions you have about whether the career will really work for you?

Don't rush into a final decision, just yet. Instead move into Chapter 16 to look for the best way to blend your ideal career idea with your preferred lifestyle and work environment preferences.

Shifting Gears Midstream

If you discover at some point during your informational interviews (or your online research in Chapter 14) that the direction you're moving in causes you to drag your feet, stop and take a good look at what's going on.

To make a successful career change, you must feel the inner drive to go after it, so don't stay committed to an idea just because you've been interested in it in the past.

If your career idea has lost some of its luster, ask yourself the following questions to determine what's going on:

✔ What caused your interests to shift?

✔ Is there a subtle change you can make in your plan to bring it back to life?

✔ What catches your attention these days?

Can you do something to reignite your interest, or is changing your goal the answer?

Changing direction now is better than waiting until you've started a new career or quit your current position. Furthermore, admitting that you want to change your direction doesn't mean you have to start from scratch! You're already way ahead of the game. Based on what you already know about yourself, your needs, your interests, and your ideas, you can easily update your focus and find a direction that better suits you.

If you feel uncomfortable about a particular part of your career puzzle, the best place to start is to revisit the relevant chapter to rethink what you need.

✔ If something has shifted in your personal life, review Chapters 3 and 4.

✔ If you've discovered something new about your work environment needs, revisit Chapters 5 and 6.

✔ If your passions or interests have modified or become clearer, return to Chapters 7 and 8.

✔ If you need to expand your career options because your first picks didn't pan out, take another look at your brainstorming in Chapter 9 and your top ten careers in Chapter 10.

Just a small, subtle shift in your approach may help you get back on track or point you toward a new, more viable path.

Chapter 16

Merging Your Personal Life with Your Dream Career

In This Chapter

▶ Revisiting your personal needs

▶ Reviewing your work environment needs

▶ Comparing your needs with your dream career ideas

▶ Choosing the best career format

▶ Imagining yourself in your new career

▶ Identifying possible conflicts

▶ Finding the blend that works best

Throughout this book, I encourage you to focus on your ideal career and lifestyle, putting aside thoughts of whether any particular idea is feasible or not. In your exploration of potential careers, you've no doubt found aspects of your needs and desires that clash to some degree. This chapter helps you identify where your needs and desires are compatible and where they are in conflict, and then offers advice on how to blend all the pieces into a career picture that works for you both professionally and personally.

One way to visualize this process is to imagine working on a 3D puzzle in which one dimension is your personal needs, another reflects your work environment needs, and the third is the profession that best captures your passions and interests. Your goal is to discover how these three dimensions intersect in a way that fills as many of your needs as possible.

In some cases, all the pieces of your dream career puzzle may fall into place relatively easily. In other cases, you may have a harder time figuring out how it all fits together. Chapter 17 helps you find creative ways to blend your dreams and your reality when pieces of your puzzle are in conflict.

Just as in doing a jigsaw puzzle, synchronizing your ideal with your reality may require you to turn the pieces around several times to get them all to fit. As you work the puzzle, stay as open as you can to seeing solutions that may not be obvious at first.

Updating Your Personal Must-Haves

Before you delve into how to move your ideal career into reality, take a moment to remember what you need for yourself and your family.

The best way to do this is to review what you recorded about your personal style in Chapter 3 and your personal life and needs in Chapter 4. Start with the summaries in the following worksheets and then move to the individual activities in each chapter if you'd like a deeper perspective.

✔ Worksheet 3-11 is your summary of all you discovered about what's uniquely you from your personality traits and your values to your reasons for working.

✔ Worksheet 4-4 is your synopsis of your wish list for your personal life and includes descriptions of how you want to live and how you like to spend your personal time.

If you started this book at the beginning and have worked your way through to this point, you've spent a lot of time reflecting on yourself and what you want, so you may know more about yourself now than you did when you completed Chapters 3 and 4. As you review Worksheets 3-11 and 4-4, add new discoveries, refine the wording of existing comments, and delete things you know aren't true anymore so that the result is a current and complete picture of your needs.

With your needs fresh in your mind, begin creating a picture of how you want your life to be. Your description should include elements of your lifestyle that you've found to be *non-negotiable* — from an ideal point of view, you would not sacrifice these elements of your lifestyle for your career because without them, life just wouldn't work for you. Perhaps you've discovered you want to be home with your children when they get out of school, you want to travel extensively, or you want to split your time between two locations. Whatever your dream, start sketching it out on paper. While you're at it, include any non-negotiable aspects of your personality, whether it's your creativity, your desire to make a difference, or your love of the outdoors. The more you know about what you really want, the more likely you are to craft such a life.

Record your picture as best you can in Worksheet 16-1, using a paragraph format or a series of bullet points. Taking the time to revisit and identify the elements of your personal life that feel non-negotiable helps you update and deepen your understanding of what you want in life. Holding this picture as you proceed through this chapter helps you make good decisions.

For the best results, keep your ideal thinking cap on for this activity, even if you don't think what you want is possible. Chapter 17 helps you make sense of the parts of your picture that seem to be in conflict. Say, for instance, you want to be home with your kids after school *and* you want to travel extensively. Although these desires seem contradictory and impossible to fulfill, don't give up quite yet. With some creativity and ingenuity, you may just find a way to get the best of both lifestyles.

If you haven't yet worked through Chapters 3 and 4, look at the categories listed in Worksheets 3-11 and 4-4 to get a sense of the elements covered in those chapters. Then describe, in Worksheet 16-1, your best picture of who you are and how you want to live.

Don't eliminate or downplay any element of your ideal life at this point just because it seems unlikely that you can create it. The truth is that if you back away from that ideal now, you'll never have an opportunity to experience what you want. If you keep your ideal in mind, you may be surprised by the opportunities that take you a step closer to your dream life.

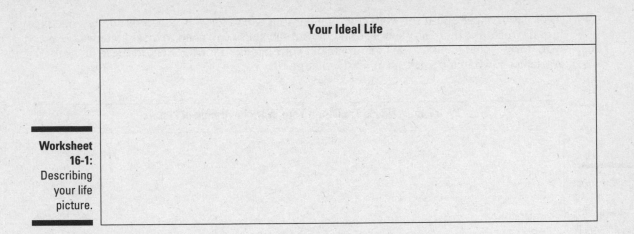

Your Ideal Life

Worksheet 16-1: Describing your life picture.

Refining Your Ideal Work Needs

The next piece of the puzzle is to understand the kind of work environment that supports you at work. To do this, review how you described your ideal work arrangement in Chapter 5 and your ideal workplace in Chapter 6. Start with the summaries in the following worksheets. If you want to do a more thorough review, take yourself through those chapters again, updating and refining your responses as you go.

> ✔ Worksheet 5-7 is your summary of all you discovered about your ideal work format, from your schedule and contract to your pay and benefits.

> ✔ Worksheet 6-13 is your synopsis of your wish list for your workplace, from the company and location to your colleagues and managers.

Begin to pull together an image of your ideal work arrangement and location in Worksheet 16-2. Again, feel free to express your thoughts in a paragraph or a series of bullet points.

If you haven't yet worked through Chapters 5 and 6, look at the categories listed in Worksheets 5-7 and 6-13 to get a sense of the elements covered in those chapters. Then describe, in Worksheet 16-2, your best picture of your ideal work arrangement and environment.

Your Ideal Work Environment

Worksheet 16-2: Summarizing your ideal work picture.

After you're clear about the work environment that works for you, add your family's needs into the mix. Are there any subtle, or not so subtle, shifts you need to make to envision a work format that enables you to flourish and your family to thrive? Record these ideas in Worksheet 16-3 in a paragraph or with bullet points.

How Your Family Needs Transform Your Work Environment Picture

Worksheet 16-3: Identifying changes to your work based on your family's needs.

TIP

If you find a conflict between the environment you need for yourself and the work format you need to meet your family's needs, note your observation in Worksheet 16-6 at the end of the chapter. Don't let your observation of this conflict stop you. Identifying potential conflicts is an inherent part of bringing your dream career puzzle into focus. In Chapter 17 you discover how to work with such clashes.

Finding Compatibility and Conflicts between Your Needs and Your Dream Career

The final element of your dream career puzzle is the career itself. If you worked through Chapter 10, you identified your top two career ideas, and if you read Chapters 14 and 15, you explored those careers in detail to increase your understanding of the realities of your target professions.

If you know the potential upside and downside to each of your career options, you can compare how the two careers fit your needs. (If you don't have this information about your target careers, then you may want to take a look at Chapters 14 and 15 before you proceed.) Use Worksheets 16-4 and 16-5 to evaluate how well each career matches your personal needs and work environment needs. In each worksheet, you find a column for each target career and a list of all the elements you reviewed to get a sense of your personal and your environment needs. By the end of this section, you have a two-page profile of how each career stacks up regarding your needs.

To create a quick visual snapshot, use the following codes to identify the match potential:

✔ If you find a point of compatibility, meaning that your needs and the realities of the career are similar, put a + in the relevant box

✔ If you find a potential conflict where your needs and the realities of the career clash, put a − (minus sign) in the box

✔ If you aren't sure what might happen when you mix your target career with your life, put a ? in the column.

✔ If it's a mixed bag, put a 0 in the column.

Identifying What's Compatible and What's in Conflict with Your Personal Needs		
Your Personal Needs	Career 1: _____	Career 2: _____
Your personality traits		
Your values		
Your definition of success		
Your longings		
Your health		
Your reasons for working		
Your meaning in work		
Your relationship		
Your home		
Your faith		
Your service		
Your hobbies and interests		
Your fun time		
Your location		

Worksheet 16-4: Spotting pluses and minuses of each target career in regard to your needs.

Make notes in each box if doing so helps you keep track of what you're rating.

Be as honest as you can in assessing how well each career matches your needs. Inflating the picture with unrealistic ratings doesn't help you in the end. In addition, keep in mind that all the pieces probably won't match right from the start.

Identifying What's Compatible and What's in Conflict with Your Work Environment Needs		
Your Work Environment Needs	Career 1: _____	Career 2: _____
Your work schedule		
Your contract		
Amount of pay		
Pay options		
Your benefits		
Kind of company		
Company size		
Company purpose		
Company reach		
Company location		
Your work area		
The dress code		
Your co-workers		
Other players		
Your manager		

Worksheet 16-5: Determining how the career lines up with your work environment needs.

As you review Worksheets 16-4 and 16-5, begin by looking at the overall pattern. Does one career seem more compatible with your life than the other? Are the two careers similar or dissimilar in how they match up with your needs?

Then begin a more detailed review by looking at one career at a time. Take note of the conflicts (the minus signs) and the areas where you aren't sure (the question marks) how the career might blend with your life. This is where you start working with individual pieces of the puzzle to see how you might increase the likelihood of the career fitting you and your needs.

Ask yourself the following questions about each target career to begin pulling your puzzle pieces into place:

- **Is your assessment accurate?** Your assessment may be skewed by your assumptions or misinformation. Do what you can to confirm that your assessment is on target by doing a bit more online research or talking with your informational interview contacts to double-check the accuracy of your assumptions. For instance, sometimes my clients are convinced that their target career won't provide the salary they need and that there's no way to make that path work. With further investigation, they discover their target career can be linked with another business to make it more profitable, or they find that a particular niche has great income potential. Even if you think you're right, do your research to be sure. This advice holds true whether you're convinced that your target career is a brilliant idea or a questionable one. You really don't know the truth until you search for it.

- **How critical is your need in this area?** Is this need a must-have or a nice-to-have element of your picture? Are you willing to deal with this trade-off to get the other results that are a great fit?

- **Do you see a conflict arising between two parts of your pictures?** Can you identify a creative way to have the best of both worlds — having your needs met and working in the career of your choice? For now, record any conflicts you find in Worksheet 16-6. Chapter 17 walks you through a brainstorming process to help you find creative solutions for just this situation.

After completing your detailed assessment of how well each career option fits your lifestyle and your work needs, are you coming to any conclusions? Have you narrowed the field to just one option, or are both options still in the running? Regardless of whether you're looking at one option or two (be assured it really doesn't matter at this point), your goal in the rest of this chapter is the same — to juggle the characteristics of each career idea and your lifestyle to discover the best fit. Although the following sections are written as though you're focusing on one career, you may do the same exercises with both of your options to help you refine your thinking on both careers at once.

Homing In on the Right Career Format for You

Now that you have an overall assessment of how well your career options meet your personal and work environment needs, you can see at a glance which areas are rubbing the wrong way. One way to bring your dream career and your personal needs and desires into better alignment is to expand how you think about the work format of your dream career. Sometimes looking at your target career in a different work format alleviates some of the conflicts between your work and your life.

Take a look at the following examples to get a sense of how this works:

- ✔ A scientist can work in a lab, the field, a think tank, a research facility, a start up, or a manufacturing setting. In addition to doing basic research, a scientist might develop a product or process, serve as an expert witness, or assess the quality of the company's output.

- ✔ A writer may work as a freelancer, on staff at a newspaper or magazine, in a public relations firm, in house as a technical writer or editor, or as a marketing consultant for small business owners.

In each case, the career has several work formats to choose from. Each format has inherent pluses and minuses regarding factors such as the work schedule, the company characteristics, and the pay structure. If two people have the same career interests, one might feel quite at home in one setting and like a fish out of water in another, while the other person might feel best in an entirely different setting. By fully exploring the various work formats associated with your target professions, you can choose the option that best fits you personally.

Think about the format options that might be possible with your dream career. As you entertain different formats, see whether one format alleviates more of the conflicts you see in Worksheets 16-4 and 16-5 than the other.

If you base your answer to this question purely on assumptions you've made about your dream career, do yourself a big favor and start talking with others and researching the formats that are possible. Chapters 14 and 15 can provide pointers on how to proceed with this research.

Trying Your Career On for Size

As your picture of your dream career begins to fall into place, don't act on it immediately. Take a couple days to look at your idea from several different angles and do the following:

- ✔ When you wake up in the morning, run your career idea over in your mind.

- ✔ As you daydream about a workday in your dream career, compare and contrast what you do now with what you think you may do in the future. Notice how you feel.

- ✔ Write in your journal about your career idea and its impact on your life.

- ✔ Look at the changes that may happen in your life as a result of making this change in your career. By being aware of how your career change may ripple through your life, you can make some proactive choices to minimize any surprises for yourself and your family.

- ✔ Continue evolving your career idea as insights strike you. For instance, trying on your business idea in your imagination may show you that a particular work schedule or office layout would be better for you than what you'd originally envisioned. (By staying aware of your needs, you can continue to improve your work/life mix even after you start your new venture.)

- ✔ Talk your idea over with someone you trust. Someone else's questions may spark new issues to consider or new ways to resolve your concerns.

As you imagine being in your new career, notice how you feel. Are you excited, motivated, surprised, nervous, or scared? Let your feelings guide you to the best way to move forward. Don't be surprised if you're a little nervous by the magnitude of your vision. It's quite normal to be a bit taken aback as you take your first steps into a new life.

If you come face to face with an idea or a concern you hadn't considered before, talk it over with someone doing the work. It's not too late to do an informational interview to confirm your own ideas or get pointers that can save you time and effort during your transition. Better to have the information you need to make a solid decision than to change your life based on a shaky, unbalanced foundation.

Spotting Potential Conflicts

Throughout this chapter, you see references to Worksheet 16-6, asking you to record any conflicts you find as you think about how your dream career blends with your needs. Although focusing on potential conflicts may be a bit troubling at this stage of the game, facing them now helps you find a way around, through, or over potential deal breakers.

Use the following list of questions to shine light on conflicts that exist in your picture that you haven't voiced as of yet:

- Are your personal needs conflicting with your family's needs?
- Does your career idea clash with your financial needs?
- Does your career idea disregard your family's needs?
- Does your career idea make it impossible to do the things you love to do in your personal time?
- Are your environmental needs not in alignment with your career idea?
- Does your career idea cause a geographic challenge?
- Does your career idea run counter to the current economic trends in your area?
- Does your career idea ignore a key part of your personal style?

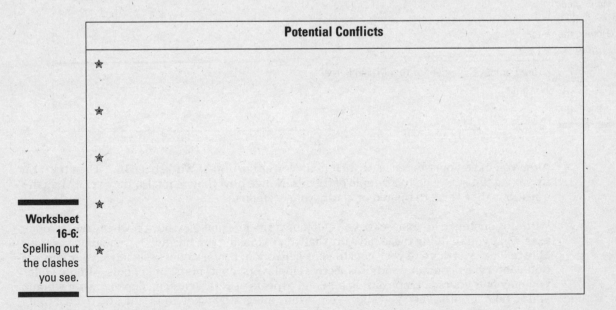

Potential Conflicts

☆

☆

☆

☆

☆

Worksheet 16-6: Spelling out the clashes you see.

If you have one or more conflicts to resolve, jump to Chapter 17 before you try to describe your best scenario in the next section.

Describing Your Dream Career . . . to Date

In this section, you create one sentence to describe your dream career as you know it today. Your statement probably will continue to evolve as your direction becomes clearer and clearer.

Pinpoint your must-haves from Worksheets 16-1, 16-2, and 16-3 and jot them down in the top portion of Worksheet 16-7. Then string your ideas together in various ways until you find the clearest way to describe what you truly want. You may find it helpful to start your sentence with the words "I want to . . . "

You don't have to have a specific job title for your desired work to construct a sentence that says it all. Be as specific as possible as you voice your desires. Take a look at the following examples to get started:

✔ I want to use my accounting skills in a part-time position while working from home.

✔ I want to use my creativity to teach children how to read in a way that is fun.

✔ I want to combine my interests in numeric modeling, tornadoes, and aircraft design in an internal consulting role.

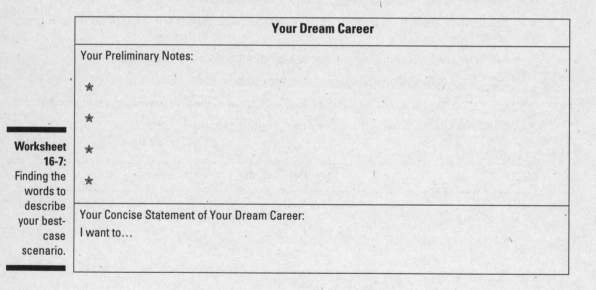

Worksheet 16-7: Finding the words to describe your best-case scenario.

Your Dream Career
Your Preliminary Notes: ☆   ☆   ☆   ☆
Your Concise Statement of Your Dream Career: I want to…

After you have your sentence, write it in the lower portion of Worksheet 16-7. Then try it out by saying the sentence to a couple of friends. Notice how they react. Do they get it? Use the questions they raise to tighten or clarify your statement.

With this sentence in your head, you can punch the internal play button whenever anyone asks what you're doing these days or what you're looking for. Imagine how helpful it is to be able to clearly articulate your goal to your network of professional associates, your informational interview contacts, and prospective employers, customers, or schools. After a while, you may find yourself emphasizing different aspects of your sentence depending on whom you're talking with. Then you know you've fully integrated what you want. You're on a roll!

As you move into implementing your goal in Chapters 18 and 19, your one-sentence-that-says-it-all helps you assess whether opportunities are in alignment with your mission. Having this rudder within you helps you steer clear of opportunities that take you off focus and turns you toward opportunities that take you closer to your dream career.

If you're torn between two different career directions, create a sentence for each one. As you talk about your interests with contacts, you may find more opportunities associated with one of your ideas, you may discover that your skills are better suited to one option, or you may find a way to weave the two ideas together after all. Don't be concerned that you have two ideas at this point. Just proceed along both tracks at once.

If this process of coming up with a concise statement is difficult and you identified some conflicts in Worksheet 16-6, spend time with Chapter 17 to find creative solutions to alleviate the conflicts before you try to come up with your statement.

If you find that writing this one sentence about your goal is difficult but you aren't overwhelmed by any specific conflicts, proceed to Chapter 18 to identify your next step and create a personalized action plan for yourself.

Chapter 17

Reconciling Differences between Your Life and Your Dream Career

While searching for your dream career, you may discover that a couple elements you want in your work and need in your life appear to be diametrically opposed. In fact, you may have made this discovery if you worked through Chapter 16.

At first you may feel stumped. The ideas you've come up with initially don't seem feasible or practical. Although you may be tempted to give up at this point, keep in mind that you can probably find a host of creative solutions for any conflicts you see. You just need to know how to find them.

In this chapter, you discover a brainstorming process that gets you beyond the details of your situation that aren't working and helps you focus your attention on the aspects of your situation that are deeply important to you.

To guide you through each step of this process, you find the brainstorming that John, a scientist from New Mexico, did as he wrestled with a key issue in his life. Although John's situation may be different than yours, use his example to see how to approach your dilemma in a new way.

Focusing on the Pieces That Appear to Clash

Before you begin trying to find a creative way to resolve the clash between your life and your dream career, think about how to describe the key issues of your situation as concisely and clearly as you can.

In Figure 17-1, you can read how John describes his dilemma. Notice that he defines his situation as he sees it, laying out the cause that leads to an untenable effect for him.

John's Dilemma

John's Preliminary Notes:

   ✴ I hate coming home all stressed out from driving.

   ✴ The best jobs in my field are in a city one hour away — longer in rush hour traffic.

   ✴ Driving stresses me out.

   ✴ I love working in my industry.

John's Concise Statement of His Dilemma:

To work in the industry of my choice, my commute may be a stress-filled, three-hour round trip, which means I'm going to arrive home exhausted and unable to enjoy my kids.

Figure 17-1:
John's description of what's not working about his future work picture.

In Worksheet 17-1, describe the clash you feel. Be as specific as you can be about what doesn't work for you about your picture. Begin by making notes in the top portion of the worksheet, and then, as your ideas crystallize, create a sentence or two that clearly describes your dilemma.

If you face a couple dilemmas, make several copies of the worksheets in this chapter. Rather than trying to work on all your dilemmas at once, I recommend focusing your attention on one dilemma at a time. Who knows? Finding a solution to one of your dilemmas may open up new opportunities to help address the other clashes.

Your Dilemma

Your Preliminary Notes:

   ✴

   ✴

   ✴

   ✴

Your Concise Statement of Your Dilemma:

Worksheet 17-1:
Describing the dilemma you face.

Stepping Back to Focus on the Big Picture

To find new solutions, you need to step away from the specifics of your picture and focus on the overriding truth of what you want. Regardless of the particulars of your dilemma, how do you want to feel when all is said and done? When you discover the essence of what you want, you may well feel a sense of relief as you realize that you've been focusing so much on the details that you've lost track of the big picture. Lifting your point of focus allows you to see other ways to reach the outcome you desire.

After thinking about his clash, John discovered that the essence of his desires was best stated as shown in Figure 17-2.

The Essence of What John Wants

John's Preliminary Notes about What He Wants:

☆ I want to eliminate the stress of my commute.

☆ I want to feel recharged.

☆ I want to enjoy seeing my family when I arrive home at night.

John's Concise Statement of the Essence of What He Wants:

I want to be calm when I walk in the door after work.

Figure 17-2: John's description of the essence of what he wants.

Although John doesn't know exactly how it's going to happen, recognizing and articulating his bottom-line desire — feeling relaxed when he gets home from work — opens John's mind to new solutions.

As you look at your bigger picture, don't worry about how to make it all happen; just stay focused on the essence of what you want to bring about. As you read the description you wrote about your clash in Worksheet 17-1, what is the essence that shines through? If you'd like, you can use the top portion of Worksheet 17-2 to jot down some thoughts and then write the final statement of the essence you'd like in the lower portion.

The Essence of What You Want

Your Preliminary Notes about What You Want:

☆

☆

☆

Your Concise Statement of the Essence of What You Want:

Worksheet 17-2: Describing the essence of what you want.

Having a Brainstorming Blitz

After you have your target essence in mind (see the preceding section), you begin brainstorming a slew of solutions. As in all brainstorming situations, all of your ideas are viable. Take a look at John's brainstormed list in Figure 17-3 before you start your own, using Worksheet 17-3.

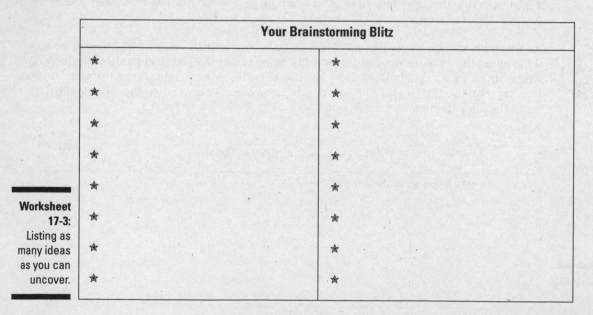

John's Brainstorming Blitz	
☆ Telecommuting	☆ Quit
☆ Working at a satellite office	☆ Commute during off hours
☆ Carpool	☆ Commute by plane
☆ Take the train	☆ Find a way to start a home-based business
☆ Relocation closer to work	☆ Explore another industry closer to home
☆ Find a job closer to home	☆ Hire a driver

Figure 17-3: John's list of ideas.

Boost your creative juices by eliminating any perceived or real constraints on your time, money, and resources. Be outrageous! Elements of outrageous ideas often can become useful when looking for creative solutions. If you've had fantasies about how to handle similar clashes in the past, by all means, include them in your list.

Your Brainstorming Blitz	
☆	☆
☆	☆
☆	☆
☆	☆
☆	☆
☆	☆
☆	☆
☆	☆

Worksheet 17-3: Listing as many ideas as you can uncover.

Don't be discouraged if you don't see a workable solution right off the bat. Although you may be tempted to hope that your answer is sitting among those on your list, you're more likely to realize that your list contains pieces and ideas that you can use in the next section to create a viable solution.

Spotting Creative Solutions

As you review your brainstormed list, notice the elements of your list that are intriguing, give you hope, or give you a new view of your situation. As you get a feel for your list, look for any pieces that you can combine to create the essence you want.

See Figure 17-4 for John's list of possible solutions. At the bottom of the figure, notice that, with the list at hand, John was able to develop a short-term plan and a long-term plan to resolve his dilemma. Now, instead of focusing on what's not working, he can dedicate his energy to putting his solutions into place.

John's Potential Solutions
☆ Telecommute two days a week and carpool the others.
☆ Work at a satellite office three days a week and take the train the other two days.
☆ Investigate career options closer to home to eliminate the commute entirely.
☆ Talk to friends about creating a vanpool.

John's Most Workable Plan	
Short-term plan:	Explore carpool and telecommuting options.
Long-term plan:	Look at career options closer to home.

Figure 17-4: John's list of creative solutions.

As you build your own list of possibilities in Worksheet 17-4, feel free to take a little of this idea and a little of that idea to come up with your possible solutions.

Keep your focus on the solutions that give you the essence you're searching for. If a solution doesn't feel quite right, identify what doesn't work about it. Can you make a change to one element to make the pieces fit together better?

TIP

If you feel blocked, you're probably still too close to the situation and having a hard time letting go of particular methods and outcomes. Ask a few friends to help you explore your ideas. They may see something that you don't because they aren't attached to the details in the same way you are.

After you have a list of possible solutions, step away. Let your ideas sit for a couple of days. Due to the thinking you have done thus far, you may, in the course of living your life, come across a solution that goes a long way toward resolving your clash.

When you return to your list, you may discover a few more angles to think about. Add any additional solutions you've identified into Worksheet 17-4.

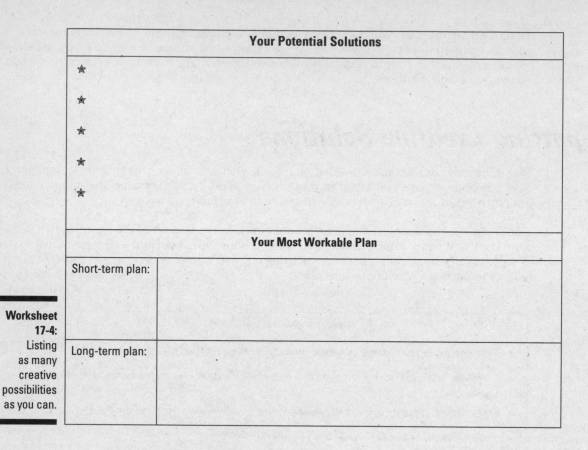

Your Potential Solutions

☆

☆

☆

☆

☆

Your Most Workable Plan

Short-term plan:

Long-term plan:

Now look at your list of possible solutions with an eye toward deciding which one or ones look appealing to you. Look for the ones that are relatively easy to implement in the short term and are likely to be effective. Keep in mind you may need to tweak things a few more times to work out all the kinks in your situation. At the same time, look for any long-term solutions that might be useful to work toward. Record both your short-term and your long-term plans at the bottom of Worksheet 17-4.

If your clash seems insurmountable (no matter which way you look at your situation, you keep coming up with the same unworkable answers), you may be asking yourself the same series of questions again and again — a tactic that ultimately gets you nowhere. Instead, look for a new question you can ask yourself. Search the Internet for an article about the topic, listen to a radio interview on a related topic, or ask a friend a hypothetical question that's related to your dilemma. Take the new information you read or hear and use it as a new filter through which to understand your situation. Perhaps you learn about a new term, a new resource, or a new perspective. Any of these experiences can trigger you to ask yourself a new set of questions about your quandary. With new questions come new answers because they shift your perspective just enough that you see new avenues you never could have seen from your old position. With the right questions, perceived clashes often evaporate into thin air.

Reconciling True Differences

On occasion, you may discover clashes between two desired elements that you can't readily resolve. In these cases, you may be able to do little to get the pieces to fall into place exactly as you would like, in the time frame you desire.

To resolve the conflict, lift your view even higher to look at aspects of the decision you haven't thought to look at before.

As you check out the following strategies to see whether you can find a solution that is at least workable, begin to discern how you can minimize the negative impact the clash has on you and your family while maximizing the aspects of it that are most important to you.

- ✔ **Use a delay tactic:** Postponing what you want until your circumstances change may cause the clash to lose its punch. Perhaps you need to wait until your kids start school, your kids get out of college, or you move.

- ✔ **Revisit your values:** Which option allows you to live closer to your values? Does this clarity help you discern which element of your clash must take priority?

- ✔ **Talk it over with your family:** Consider any way the family can adjust to allow you to meet your needs. Be honest and creative. Don't get defensive. If the words, "Yes, but" come out of your mouth, stop in your tracks to see what idea you're not allowing in.

- ✔ **Take vacation time:** Maybe you can relegate one element of the clash to your vacation or find enough satisfaction expressing this part of yourself off the job. For example, if you want to build a jewelry-making business but you can't afford to do it full time, you could devote one week's vacation to a jewelry-making blitz each year. If you time it right, you could have pieces to sell to friends for the holidays. Although it's not a full-fledged business, it's enough to keep you engaged in your passion and learning what you need to learn to start a full-time business in the future.

- ✔ **Turn the ideal into a hobby:** Perhaps you can get what you want through a hobby instead of making it part of your daily, full-time work.

As you think about your clash from these angles, notice whether you can combine any of these ideas to create a workable solution. For example, you may focus your energy on a hobby basis until your children leave for college in two years. If you play your cards right, by the time you have the time to devote to pursuing your ideal career, you may have also gained the experience you need to break into the field or saved enough money to start the business you've been dreaming of.

Dealing with What Can't Be Reconciled

If you can't yet see a way to reconcile the conflict you feel, take some time to write out your dilemma and as many of the particulars as possible in Worksheet 17-5.

Time may change your life circumstances in ways you can't predict today. Instead of turning away from your idea entirely, keep your radar up and notice any shifts in your world that allow for movement toward your dream. I realize this may sound rather far-fetched to you in this moment, but over the years, I've seen people create their dream career within a couple years of telling me it would never work.

In each case, something shifted, and they noticed a new possibility opening up. As you live your life, pay attention to the following:

- ✔ Something changing within you, whether it's your interests, values, priorities, or needs
- ✔ Circumstances changing for your spouse or within your family
- ✔ Something shifting within your community
- ✔ Something happening at an economic level
- ✔ Changes occurring in the realm of technology

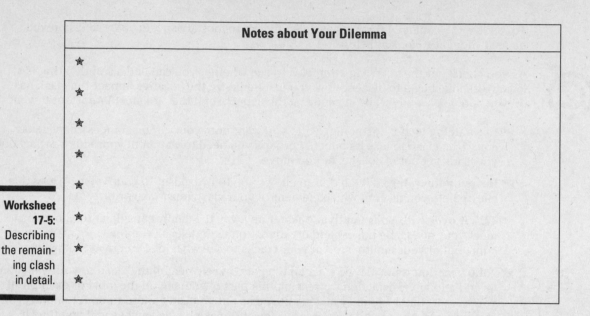

Notes about Your Dilemma
★
★
★
★
★
★
★
★

Worksheet 17-5: Describing the remaining clash in detail.

As long as you're passionate about your idea, claim your passion and stop banging your head against a closed door. Accept that you can't take the step you'd like to at the moment and be willing to wait for a while, until you experience a shift that reopens the door you now see as closed.

Every three to six months, take a new look at Worksheets 17-1 through 17-5 to notice whether anything's changed in your vision of your dream career or your needs.

If you can pursue even one piece of your passion, put your energy there and trust that when the time is right you'll find a way to move in the direction you desire. Sometimes taking a couple steps down the path changes your view significantly. At this point you can't know how things will unfold as you step forward. All you can do is take the steps that most closely align with your vision of your dream career. Stay alert for new clues and be agile if opportunities arise that point in new directions.

Chapter 18

Moving Ever Closer to Your Immediate Goal

In This Chapter

▶ Doing more research

▶ Finding ways to sample the work you want

▶ Exploring your options for more training and experience

▶ Preparing to get a new job or start your own business

▶ Creating your own action plan

Suppose that you've reached the point where you have some idea of where you're headed with your next career. (If you've been doing the worksheets in the earlier chapters in this book, you're probably clearer about possible directions than if you haven't done the previous chapters.) Depending on your situation, your career idea may be a bit sketchy, crystal clear, or somewhere in between. This chapter helps you chart your next steps regardless of whether you're narrowing your options, searching for opportunities to test your idea, looking for ways to increase your training and experience, or preparing to launch your job search or business.

Begin by reading through each path described in the chapter to identify where you are in the process and where you ultimately want to be. Use the appropriate section to guide you in defining and mastering your immediate goal. Achieving a certain degree of comfort in your current path is essential before you move on to the next path.

If you aren't sure about or comfortable with the results you're getting in your current path, don't leap ahead to the next path, thinking that action will fix things. For example, rushing to test-drive a career when you haven't done the research to be sure that the career fits your life is the equivalent of spinning your wheels. You make the best impression and get the best results when you step into a test-drive, job search, or school setting with confidence that you're comfortable with your target goal. No matter what your intentions are, rushing forward to the next path isn't going to resolve your discomfort. Instead use the recommendations included in each path to take the steps necessary to feel comfortable moving on to the next path.

After you have your next steps mapped out and in progress, use Chapter 19 to create your overall plan to go back to school, get a job, or start your own business.

Path One: Expanding Your Research

Your main objective at this point is to confirm that your target career is a good fit for you. If you feel uncertain about your proposed direction, if some part of your picture has you worried, or if you're intrigued by a different career that caught your eye during your research, continue your exploration.

There's no way to rush this verification process, so please don't attempt to. If you must get out of the job you're in, think about finding an interim job that takes you out of the bad situation but doesn't lull you into thinking it's the end of your journey. After you get settled in your new job, reactivate your exploration to clarify your ultimate career picture.

No matter what your reason for continuing your exploration, your next step is to revisit Chapters 14 and 15 to deepen your understanding of your target career. Then use the information you find to refine your picture in Chapter 16.

If your research on your top two careers isn't working out the way you thought it might, revisit your top ten career ideas to see whether anything new pops forward. If it does, switch gears to explore your new idea. If a new idea isn't immediately obvious, use the following list to trace your path back to where things became unclear.

- ✔ Because nothing in your Top Ten list is ringing your chimes, take another step back to look at your lists of passions and interests in Worksheets 7-7 (Chapter 7) and 8-5 (Chapter 8). Reacquaint yourself with your lists and update them as needed. Confirm that every item on the list aligns with your true interests. Remember that each item is a building block for your new career, so it must be solid for your career to withstand the test of time. If you significantly rebuild your lists of favorite passions and interests, you may want to do a few more brainstorming rounds in Chapter 10 to see what new career ideas surface.

- ✔ If you second guess the items you put on your lists of passions and interests, take some time to review the activities in Chapters 7 and 8 to rebuild your list. If, in the process, you realize that you aren't sure what you truly enjoy, revisit Chapter 2 for some ideas on how to connect with your interests.

- ✔ If you find yourself flitting from one possible career to another, wondering at each turn whether "this" is the one, stop and take a deep breath. Find a quiet place and review the last worksheet in each chapter to reconnect with your personal style, your lifestyle needs, your work environment preferences, and your passions and interests. Reading the lists in the same sitting allows you to integrate your ideal picture. With this information fresh in your mind, review your top ten career ideas to refocus your attention on the careers that are the best fit for you.

- ✔ If you came up with your career idea without working through any of the worksheets in this book and you're finding that the idea isn't quite working out, take the time to work through the chapters in order, so you can build your dream career layer by layer. By having a clear picture of your needs and desires, you have a much better chance of finding your dream career.

You don't have to be 100 percent sure about your career idea before you move to Path Two to test it out. In fact, you can't possibly know the status of this career in absolute terms. What you do need to know is that you're attracted to the career, there are no immediate red flags, and you're interested in knowing more about it. Keep in mind that some of your answers can't unfold until you move forward and test the waters.

Path Two: Taking a Test-Drive

If you have a pretty good idea what you want to do next but wish you knew for sure, your best next step is to find a way to test-drive your career.

Most people wouldn't think of buying a car without taking it for a spin first, so why should it be different with a career? Although trying out the exact job you're thinking about may be impossible, with some ingenuity, you can find an opportunity that's a close facsimile. The key is to find a way to use the skills, perform the tasks, and interact with people as you would in the real job. Check out Chapter 20 for some ideas about how to test-drive your career ideas.

Even if your test-drive gives you a part-time venue, in a smaller company or a different environment, with a minimal salary, you can still gain a number of insights from the opportunity.

✔ You get to experience how you feel while doing the work. It's one thing to think about and talk about a profession but quite another to take a sample bite!

✔ You can discern whether it's worth investing the time, energy, and resources required to get the training and experience you need to enter the field full time.

✔ You begin building your network.

✔ You get some face-to-face time with your cohorts in the profession. Pay attention to your interactions and how comfortable you feel. One key clue is whether you get their sense of humor or are turned off by it.

Due to the limits inherent in a test-drive, you may not feel as if a test-drive gives you a complete picture of the profession. However, if you evaluate your experience, keeping the limited scope of your test-drive in mind, you'll probably be able to come to several conclusions, including whether you feel good doing the work or whether you feel uncomfortable, frustrated, or bored in the field. If the jury is still out, you may need a second test-drive with clearer parameters or a better understanding of the role you'd play if you took this job for real.

In each case, you want to combine what you know from your research with what you gain from your test-drive experience to decide how to proceed. If you're intrigued with the career, move on to Path Three. If you aren't sure whether the career is right for you, try another test-drive or swing back to Path One to find a more suitable niche.

Path Three: Assessing Your Need for More Training

After you're comfortable with your career goal, it's time to look for ways to gain the knowledge and skills you need to succeed in your new career. Review the career profiles and informational interview notes you collected in the course of your research. (See Chapters 14 and 15 for tips on gathering this information.) Pay particular attention to the education requirements and the discussion of any traits and skills you need to succeed in your target career. If you have any questions about what's required, check with your contacts.

After you know what skills are essential, compare your education and the experience you already have with what's needed. Identify any hot spots you must target. Use the following questions to focus your thoughts:

- ✔ Do you need to update your knowledge in a certain area?

- ✔ Is there a particular skill you must add to your repertoire?

- ✔ Do you need to work toward a certificate or license?

- ✔ Do you need to get a specific degree?

- ✔ Do you have any options in the amount of training you need, or does one standard hold for everyone in the field?

- ✔ Does making a slight change to your career goal impact the education requirements in any way?

If the thought of going to school makes your skin crawl or your stomach sink, don't give up just yet! Depending on your situation, a class or two may put you in a great position to move forward. If you do need more education or training, keep in mind that a number of new educational formats, such as online training or training by teleclasses (classes by phone), expand your options far beyond the traditional classroom setting.

Before you decide the best way to get the training you need, take some time to assess your own learning style in Worksheet 18-1. Use the questions and prompts in the worksheet to guide you in thinking about your learning style. Record your thoughts in the right-hand column. Knowing how you learn allows you to make better decisions when it comes to evaluating your various education options.

Even if taking on the challenge of additional training seems impossible right now, keep an open mind until you have more information about your options. Who knows? You may discover something that works surprisingly well.

After you complete Worksheet 18-1, take some time to record any conclusions you come up with in Worksheet 18-2. As you think about your best learning format, blend what you know about your personal learning style with what you know about your lifestyle realities.

To make your training as productive and successful as possible, choose the educational options that feel good to you. For example,

- ✔ If writing isn't your forte, don't take on a master's program with a thesis requirement.

- ✔ If you don't learn well on your own, don't talk yourself into believing that a self-paced course is going to be different.

- ✔ If you hate pure silence, don't think that you can suddenly force yourself to go to the library on a regular basis to study.

Learning is hard enough without adding the extra burden of force to the equation. Think about your natural tendencies and leverage off those, so you can put your energy into learning and studying rather than fighting the learning format.

If part of your path includes a formal degree, look at Chapter 19 to discover how to locate the best program to meet your needs and how to submit your application.

Your Education Options	
Elements to Consider	Your Thoughts
When in the past have you learned with ease? In school, was there a particular kind of project or assignment that you enjoyed most? On your first few jobs, what helped you become proficient at your work? When you want to increase your knowledge about something on your own, how do you approach the topic?	
What is your primary learning style? *Are you a visual learner? Do you learn best by reading about a topic, looking at illustrations or pictures, or taking notes? *Are you a kinesthetic learner? Do you learn best by doing a task, using trial and error, and practicing a new skill? *Are you an auditory learner? Do you learn best by listening to instructions, attending a lecture, or hearing someone describe what you need to do?	
What form of education is most likely to blend with your life? *Full-time school *One course a semester *Evening or weekend classes *Self-paced classes in a school setting *Internet courses on your own schedule *An internship or apprenticeship *On-the-job training *Mentoring from a successful individual in your field	
Where do you think, concentrate, and study most effectively? At home, at a public library, in a café, outside, at your office, or at school.	
Where are you likely to learn best? *At a school with a live instructor *Observing an instructor via video *At home via telephone *From home by Internet *Through a written correspondence course *By video *On the job	

Worksheet 18-1: Assessing what works for you when it comes to training.

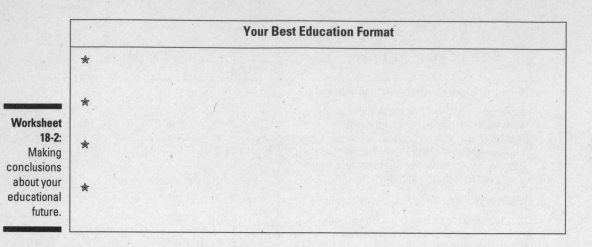

Worksheet 18-2: Making conclusions about your educational future.

Path Four: Gaining Work Experience

After you have the knowledge you need, you're ready to gain some experience in your field. Although you may be able to use an entry-level job in your new field to obtain your real-life experience, you may need to be a bit more creative.

Most companies are interested in hiring those who already have experience. Although this position makes perfect sense from their point of view — low training investment and a high return on what they do invest — it's one of the most frustrating aspects of changing careers. How can you get experience in the new field if companies hire only people with experience?

Your ingenuity and determination come into play here. Start looking for ways to gain experience. At first, you may need to work on a side project or in a volunteer position. Take whatever targeted opportunities come your way. Choose experiences that build your case so that eventually you can apply to your desired job with ample evidence of your experience. Read Chapters 20 and 21 for ideas to get you started as you consider the stepping-stone experiences that will take you where you want to go.

Even if you plan to start your own business, increase your chances of success by getting some experience in the field or at least in a small entrepreneurial company first. Although you're no doubt anxious to get started, you save time, money, and angst in the long run by learning the ropes the easy way — with someone else's money at stake.

If you enter into a working relationship with someone who may ultimately be a competitor, pay close attention to the agreement you sign. You don't want to sign a non-compete clause and limit your ability to start your own business where you choose.

Path Five: Preparing Your Job Search

If you have enough related experience from your past jobs, you may be in a good position to begin preparing for your job search. Please note that starting to prepare is not the same as announcing your intentions to everyone you know. Take some time to get several key pieces in place before you raise the flag to signal that you're off to search for your new job.

Reworking your resume

Of course, just about anyone you talk to about your new career direction is likely to ask for a copy of your resume. Instead of stumbling your way through these conversations, take the time to rework your resume before someone asks for it.

If you're entertaining two similar, but different, career directions, you're embarking on two simultaneous job searches. Create a distinct resume for each one by listing your experiences in a way that highlights the skills that are particularly relevant for each career.

To be effective, your resume must catch people's attention and hold it long enough for them to see that you're a viable candidate for the job. To increase the readability of your resume, make sure that the following crucial information is easy to spot:

- ✔ If you state your objective at the top of your resume, use the title of the job you're applying for in the statement so that your resume is categorized correctly by those reading it. Avoid meaningless, showy phrases about how you want to contribute to the company.

- ✔ Use a format that gives the reader a good sense of what you did in each job you've held. Use paragraphs to describe your responsibilities and then list three or four bullets to illustrate your accomplishments in each job.

- ✔ Make your accomplishments more convincing by weaving quantifiable results, such as creating a 50 percent increase in annual sales, managing a million-dollar project budget, producing a 30 percent cost savings, or managing a team of 20 volunteers, into your resume.

- ✔ If you're changing careers, translate what you accomplished in your old career into the terminology of the new industry. You want the reader to get the gist of your experience without stumbling over unfamiliar terms.

- ✔ In the past, experts recommended limiting your resume to one page. Now, with career changes and shorter job tenures, you may need more than one page to show all your relevant experience. However, your resume should be as concise and easy to scan as possible.

- ✔ If you gained experience in your new area through volunteer work, part-time work, or project work in your job, incorporate the information straight into your resume. If the information doesn't fit into your resume, include a paragraph or two in your cover letter to highlight your experience.

- ✔ Use a carefully crafted cover letter to justify why you are the person for the job.

Producing a polished resume printed on high-quality paper used to be the job applicant's goal, but times have changed. In today's world, you must have a high-quality resume that can be e-mailed, faxed, scanned, posted on the Internet, and handed out in person. Before you start your job search in earnest, test these various delivery methods to verify that your resume comes across as intended.

For additional tips on writing an effective resume, consult *Resumes For Dummies,* by Joyce Lain Kennedy (Wiley).

Reconnecting with your contacts

By this point in your career exploration, you probably have developed an extended network of contacts. (If not, see Chapter 15 for more information on building your list of contacts.) Your list may consist of friends, colleagues, informational interview contacts, and people you have met through professional associations. Although you may have talked to some of them fairly recently, reconnect with them to let them know exactly what kind of employment situation you're looking for.

Be explicit in your request. Ask your contacts to forward your resume if they know of any openings that fit your description or of anybody who may know of openings in your field.

The more clearly you can describe your ideal job, the better your contacts can assist you. When you call your contacts, have a carefully thought-out description of what you're looking for. After your conversation, be prepared to forward your description as part of your cover letter, whether in bullet or paragraph form, to them, along with your resume.

If you don't already have a recruiter or two in your network, ask around to see whether your friends can put you in touch with one. Recruiters are connected; networking is their business! If they don't place people in your area of expertise, they can refer you to someone who does. Recruiters work in several ways under several different titles, including the following:

- **Headhunters:** They place qualified full-time applicants in a range of companies. They often serve a particular industry or profession.

- **Recruiters:** They work within an agency to find temporary or contract employees for a variety of client companies.

- **Staff or on-site recruiters:** They search for applicants to fill the staffing needs for one specific company.

Recruiters find qualified people to fill job openings. They talk with people constantly and are extremely busy professionals. Don't ask them to help you figure out what your next career should be. Don't expect them to be a walking job board either. Inform them of what you want and then continue your search on your own.

Searching for job openings

In addition to tapping your network for openings, do your own footwork to find potential jobs. Start by brainstorming the places that are likely to post jobs in your field. Consider the following ideas:

- Check out the jobs listed by your professional association.

- Visit your local career center to review its lists of openings. Depending on your location, you may be able to find a career center on a local college campus, through a governmental agency, or in a privately run business.

- Check to see whether your alumni organization has any career support services.

- Attend any relevant job fairs in your geographic area.

- Surf Web sites related to your industry or profession for sites that provide job listings.

- Scan the want ads in your Sunday paper.

- Target key companies in your area by visiting their Web sites or their on-site job boards.

Consider posting your resume on a Web-based job board so that recruiters and hiring personnel can find you. Here are some tips on sites to check out if you want to pursue this option:

- At the Monster (www.monster.com) and Yahoo! HotJobs (http://hotjobs.yahoo.com) Web sites, you can search jobs in a wide variety of locations and industries.

- Job-Hunt (www.job-hunt.org) and the Riley Guide (http://rileyguide.com/jobs.html) provide lists of job search sites for various professions, industries, and regions.

- Visit your professional or industry association's job boards.

Companies pay a fee to gain access to many of these job boards, so don't refer a recruiter or contact to your posted resume unless you have verified that they have access to that particular board.

If you put all your eggs in one basket to find your job through an online job board, you may be disappointed in the end. There are estimates that only 10 percent of jobs are filled from online job boards. As in the dark ages before the Internet, it still pays to network, network, network!

If you're currently employed, your employer may use these same job boards to find qualified applicants. Think about the ramifications of your employer finding your resume posted on one of these sites. To avoid this potential problem, you have two options:

✔ Some job boards provide a confidential resume option in which your name and your current company are hidden from view. Interested recruiters can send you a blind e-mail, and then you can decide whether to release your identity to them.

✔ You can post your resume, along with articles or examples from your portfolio, on your personal Web page. Then, when you e-mail potential employers, you can include your Web address in your e-mails. If you send recruiters to your site, think through the personal information you reveal on your Web site. If you decide to keep this site alive after you get a job, you can give the Web address to people who want to know more about you.

Use Worksheet 18-3 to plan for your steps during your job search. Use the right-hand column to make notes about your specific situation. As soon as you have a live job opening in sight, you are no longer preparing for your job search. It's time to switch gears and create your action plan for your job search. Refer to Chapter 19 for details.

Your Job Search Action Plan		
"X" When Complete	Your Task	Specific Notes for Your Situation
	Update your resume.	
	Create a clear description of what you are looking for.	
	Announce your job search intentions to your network contacts.	
	Evaluate whether you want to locate a recruiter to help you with your job search.	
	Explore places that list job openings for your field.	
	Investigate Web-based job boards.	

Worksheet 18-3: Keeping track of the steps of your job search.

Path Six: Refining Your Business Idea

If you've determined that you want to start a business, you have many steps to take before you throw open your doors or launch your Web site. One of the first steps is to start getting clear about the product or service you plan to offer.

Although you're likely to evolve your ideas as you do more research and talk to your prospective clients, make a stab at describing your current business ideas on paper.

Many new businesses mistakenly think that if they offer anything and everything to everybody, they're more likely to be successful. Fortunately, just the opposite is often true. If your offerings are so broad that no one can clearly describe what you do, people don't become customers, and more importantly, they can't refer other people to you.

You need to focus your business so that it provides a particular product or service to a definable target population. Then those who hear about your business know exactly what you do and can send qualified leads your way. For more information about establishing a viable niche, read *Nichecraft: Using Your Specialness to Focus Your Business, Corner Your Market and Make Customers Seek You Out,* by Lynda Falkenstein (Niche Press) or visit her Web site at www.falkenstein.com.

Describe your product or service as clearly and concisely as possible in Worksheet 18-4. Be sure to list the key features your product or service provides as well as the benefits your customers receive. While you're thinking about it, list the characteristics of your target customer as well. All of this information becomes the cornerstone of your marketing as you move forward with your business idea. As you write the description of your products or services, don't be surprised if you notice gaps in your logic or find that you have a difficult time putting it all down on paper. Although neither of these outcomes is likely to dash your hopes of being a successful entrepreneur, you must take the time you need to sort it all out long before you open your doors or launch your site.

As soon as you can articulate your offerings clearly in as few words as possible, you're ready for your next steps.

- ✔ **Talk to potential customers about the products or services you have in mind.** You need to see how they respond. Listen to their questions and comments with both ears. Don't defend your idea. If they don't get it, your clients won't either, so take what you hear to heart and revamp your product or service accordingly. Then try again. After a few rounds of testing, you may find that people are anxious to get their hands on your product or service. After you have their attention, ask them how much they would pay for a product or service such as yours.

- ✔ **Check out your competition.** As you clarify your products and services, keep an eye out for others who offer something similar. When you visit their locations, read their advertisements, scan their Web sites, and review their telephone book listings, notice the key features of their offerings, how they price them, and what audience they target. Use this valuable information to help you refine your niche and decide how to run your business.

If you have a hot new twist on a product or service that no one else has thought of, keep it close to your chest for a while until you're ready to launch your business. Do your research and talk with a lawyer to determine whether a trademark or patent is in order to protect your idea.

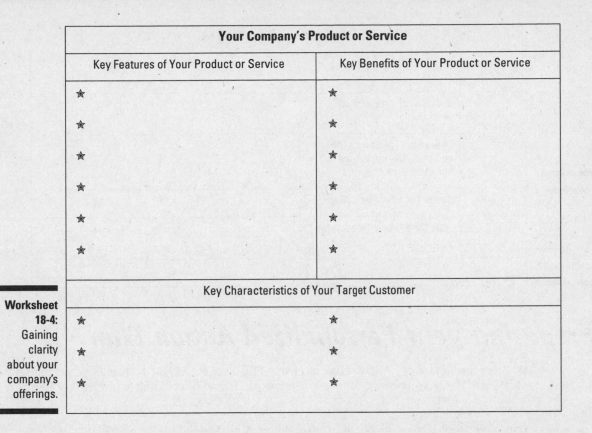

Worksheet 18-4: Gaining clarity about your company's offerings.

✔ **Scout your location options.** To run a successful business, you must choose a location that fits your needs. How are customers likely to interact with your business? Are they likely to contact you in person, by phone, through other companies, or over the Internet? Do you need a retail location, manufacturing space, office space, or an online presence? How do you intend to handle shipping and receiving? Do you need storage for supplies or inventory, a waiting room, or any special equipment?

If you want to work from home, check with your city to determine how it regulates home businesses.

✔ **Think through your financing options.** One of the most important decisions you make in the early stages of your business is how you're going to finance your start-up costs and living expenses while you're building your business. You may decide to finance the venture yourself, look to friends and family members to invest in your business, or apply for a loan. To present a credible explanation of your business to possible investors (including yourself), spend time developing a well-thought-out business plan. Refer to *Business Plans For Dummies*, 2nd Edition, by Paul Tiffany and Steven D. Peterson (Wiley) for the how-to details. Another option, if you aren't in a position to move your business into full gear from the start, is to ease into your business. Turn to Chapter 21 for creative ways to transition into your new business.

Use Worksheet 18-5 to track the steps you take in beginning to plan your business. Look to Chapter 19 for additional steps you can take to launch your business.

Your Business Action Plan		
"X" When Complete	Your Task	Specific Notes for Your Situation
	Define your products or services.	
	Share your ideas with friends and potential customers to enhance your offerings.	
	Check out your competition.	
	Look for the best location for your business.	

Worksheet 18-5: Making progress on your business.

Preparing Your Personalized Action Plan

What's your next step? And the one after that? By creating a clear picture of your next few steps, you focus your energy on moving forward instead of spinning in circles wondering what to do next.

Use Worksheet 18-6 to lay out your plan. Put an X next to anything you feel you've completed. Place a 1 adjacent to your next step and a 2 to indicate the next step after that. Always keep your focus on your current step with an eye on what's next in the pipeline.

After you have a sense of how to focus your attention, use Worksheets 18-7 and 18-8 to specify your actions for your 1 and 2 priority paths. Be as specific as you can and track your progress as you go.

As you complete the tasks associated with your first priority path, take stock to verify that your second goal is still relevant. As that path becomes your top priority, take some time to look into the future to start sketching out your next priority. By keeping an eye to your future goal, you minimize the risk of finishing a task and not knowing where to go next.

If you're ready to begin searching for the right school, your job search is in full swing, or your business idea is ready to go, proceed to Chapter 19 to develop your longer-term plan.

	Your Action Plan	
	If you want to do more research, follow Path One.	Revisit Chapters 14 and 15 to explore your career ideas in more depth. Both online research and informational interviews enable you to gain enough confidence in your idea to move to Path Two.
	If you want to take a test-drive, follow Path Two.	Find a way to try on your job or business idea to verify that it's a good fit for you and your life. When you feel comfortable with your choice, move to Path Three.
	If you want to pursue more training, follow Path Three.	Work through the details in this chapter to discover your best learning style, locate your key learning areas, and find the classes to fulfill your needs. If your path is to include a formal degree or certificate program, review Chapter 19 for additional information about finding and applying to the best programs for you. When your knowledge level is where it needs to be, move to Path Four.
	If you need more experience, follow Path Four.	Explore the ideas in Chapters 20 and 21 to discover ways to gain more experience in your new field. After you have the necessary experience to begin your job search or business launch in earnest, move to Path Five or Path Six.
	If you want to launch your job search, follow Path Five.	Prepare for your job search by using the steps included in this chapter and then move into Chapter 19 to activate your search.
	If you're ready to start your business, follow Path Six.	Begin to get your business ideas and plan together in this chapter and then move to Chapter 19 to map the next steps to take to launch your business.

Worksheet 18-6: Identifying your next two steps.

Your First Priority Path: _____		
"X" When Complete	Your Tasks	Specific Notes for Your Situation

Worksheet 18-7: Laying out your top priorities.

Your Second Priority Path: _____		
"X" When Complete	Your Tasks	Specific Notes for Your Situation

Worksheet 18-8: Clarifying your next priorities.

Chapter 19

Turning Your Dream Career into a Reality

· ·

In This Chapter

▶ Setting up your path to your education

▶ Landing your dream job

▶ Getting your business underway

▶ Deciding the best way to transition into your future

· ·

If you've identified your new career, tested it out, and taken some preliminary steps, now you're ready to get the show on the road.

To bring your dream goal to life, you must focus your attention, energy, and resources on the steps required to achieve success.

If you have any lingering questions or doubts about your goal, swing back through Chapter 18 to identify what's not falling into place. Refining your goals so that you can stand behind it 100 percent is a crucial precursor to your success. Any doubts and questions act like a braking system, keeping you from devoting all you have to your cause. Ever tried to reach a destination with one foot on the gas pedal and one on the brake? Didn't get very far, did you?

This chapter gives you pointers on how to reach your ultimate goal, whether you're applying to your dream school, going for your dream job, or launching your dream business.

The last part of this chapter helps you choreograph your transition from where you are now to where you want to be. In most cases, it's not as easy as flipping a switch and being in the middle of your new life. How your transition unfolds depends on a number of factors and can be, to some extent, orchestrated to fit your needs professionally and personally.

Having a clear, committed focus doesn't mean that you have complete clarity about how each step of your journey will unfold. That kind of omniscience isn't possible. The key is having a strong enough commitment to your goal that you're willing to hang in there when the path isn't clear, to find creative solutions when stumbling blocks appear, and to follow through on your plan until you reach your goal.

Goal One: Heading Back to School

If taking a class here and doing a project there doesn't give you the training you need to enter your new profession, you may need to get a degree or work toward licensure.

Going to school requires a commitment of your time, money, and attention for an extended period. I don't recommend making this decision lightly. Devote the time it takes to research and think through your decision before you take action.

If you haven't been in school in a while, take one course as a test run before you apply to a full degree program. Although this goal isn't insurmountable, knowing how much attending classes, doing your homework, preparing for tests, and doing projects impacts your life and your family gives you an opportunity to make some adjustments before your school workload tests your limits.

Enrolling in school because you don't know what else to do or because someone told you the degree is the ticket to more money is a bad idea. Go to school if and only if the degree enables you to do the work that you want to do.

You may find yourself shying away from your goals because you think that you're too old to go to school. News flash! You will be that much older in several years whether you go to school or not! Wouldn't it be better to have options and feel fulfilled rather than be stuck in a dead-end career going nowhere? People of all ages return to school to fulfill their dreams. Don't let your age become your excuse for passing up your dream of a satisfying career.

Locating potential programs

A vast number of educational programs exist these days. To narrow your initial quest for appropriate programs, answer the following questions:

- ✔ **To achieve your career goal, what level of education do you require?** An undergraduate degree? A certificate? A graduate degree?

- ✔ **What geographic area are you willing to consider?** In addition to the schools in your area, include schools that have extension programs and distance-learning options. Think carefully about your willingness to relocate in case the right program is located out of your area.

- ✔ **How much can you spend on your education?** Don't limit yourself before you do a preliminary exploration of your financial options. In doing a search, you may find solutions you didn't know were available to you. For instance, did you know financial aid is available to nontraditional full-time students at accredited schools? To understand how to apply for scholarships or grants, visit the Free Scholarship Search Web site at www. freschinfo.com/strategy-nontrad.phtml. In addition to valuable how-to information, this site has a database of information about 169,000 scholarships provided by over 2,000 organizations. If you'd rather look at a book, enter the term "scholarships" into any online bookstore search engine to find the latest scholarship compendiums. You can uncover other creative financing solutions by checking with your current employer about educational reimbursement programs or scholarships, talking with your accountant about tax credits for educational expenses, or investigating a home equity loan. Knowledge about your financial options gives you power and hope.

Each school you look at may have a slightly different name for the program you're interested in. Don't limit your search; explore several content areas and departments to make sure that you find all the relevant programs. The following advice may help you find the right program:

- ✔ Talk with your contacts to discover where they were trained and which programs they recommend.

- ✔ Visit the Web sites for the schools in your area and search their online course catalogs and offerings.

✔ Visit `www.collegiate.net/infob.html` on the Web, a collegiate information site, to find links to numerous colleges, universities, community colleges, and specific departments.

✔ Check your local bookstore or library for books describing schools with programs in your field.

✔ Investigate distance-learning options including Phoenix University (`www.phoenix.edu/general/index.html`) and the United States Open University (`www.open-university-online.com`), which are designed specifically for working adults pursuing degrees. *Distance learning* refers to any learning situation in which the instructor and student are not in the same place at the same time. Course work can be delivered through the mail, video, cable television, interactive television, satellite broadcasts, e-mails, message boards, Web sites, chat rooms, computer conferencing, telephone, or some combination of these methods. Distance learning can be used to take an individual class or to earn a degree. You can learn more about distance learning and check out the accreditation status of possible schools at the Distance Education and Training Council Web site at `www.detc.org`. *Distance Learning Online For Dummies,* by Nancy Stevenson (Wiley), is also a valuable resource.

✔ If you don't find just the program you want, consider applying to a school that allows you to design a degree program that fits your interests and needs. Check the school's Web site for links entitled individualized learning, self-designed programs, interdisciplinary studies, and joint degree programs. Although this option isn't available at every school, if you find the idea intriguing, it never hurts to ask.

When you find a program that interests you, print out the relevant pages and request an informational packet from the school.

Choosing the right program for you

Depending on the number of schools you consider, selecting the best program may be a bit overwhelming at first. Between the amount of information you receive and the number of possibilities you are trying on, your mind may spin in all sorts of directions trying to figure out a workable plan of action. Take it one step at a time. Use the following step-by-step process to keep focused and moving forward:

1. **Get an overview of each program.**

   When you have a collection of possible programs in hand, read over the material in detail to get a sense of each program. Pay attention to the program description while taking note of any special features that are particularly relevant to your target career. Keep track of the faculty research interests. This information is important because most faculty members prefer to guide students who have interests similar to their own, so if you expect to do research as part of your degree program, make sure that their research is relevant to your goals. Double-check that the program prepares you for any additional licenses or certifications you may need.

2. **Compare and contrast the various programs.**

   Each school is likely to use a slightly different format to describe its program, so you may want to make a chart for each program to keep the details straight. Determine what you want to know about each program and then fill in the details. Don't be surprised if your chart has some blanks. You can fill in these answers in Step 4.

3. **Get a sense of which programs interest you most.**

   Tune in to your intuition as you study each program. Which programs feel the best to you? Your sense of excitement, or lack thereof, is a clue worth paying attention to. Make note of what about your top picks appeals to you.

4. **Check out the interesting programs.**

   If you're considering a traditional school, visit the school in person if at all possible. Call ahead to make an appointment to meet with a professor or an admissions counselor. Ask to talk with some current students. See whether you can sit in on a class in progress. Be sure to prepare questions ahead of time based on the blanks in your detail sheet. This is a good time to ask about prerequisites and any anticipated faculty changes.

   If you are considering a distance learning format and haven't taken an online course before, take a single course through the school to see what it's like before you commit to an entire program.

5. **Apply to your top choices.**

   Be sure to leave yourself enough time to complete each application with thought and care. For any required recommendations, choose people who have some clout in your target field or a related field. The people you ask should also know you well enough to have knowledge of your talents and abilities, a sense of your ability to complete an education program, and the confidence to affirm your character. Create a packet for each reference that includes a description of what each school wants, including any forms they must fill out, a copy of your professional resume, a list of courses you've taken with them, a list of projects you worked on with them, a list of extracurricular activities that you've participated in (such as professional association memberships, volunteer activities, related course work, and leadership roles), and an explanation of why you're applying to the program. Be sure to thank your references and keep them posted of your progress.

Becoming a student at this point in your life is bound to be a transition. Ease into the lifestyle and increase your chances of success by taking only one or two courses your first term, especially if you plan to work full time while you're in school.

Making time for school

Because your time is at a premium while you're in school, you may need to rearrange some parts of your life in order to make the most of your schooling. Think about the following as you prepare to start your studies:

✔ **Adjusting your priorities:** With school entering the picture, your life may change form. Make a list of your three top priorities. By being clear about your new priorities, you can make decisions in alignment with your current reality.

✔ **Giving friends, family members, and co-workers a heads-up:** Tell the people in your life that you may not be as available as you have been and why. If you take care of this in an upfront manner, you're less likely to offend people who don't understand why you've pulled back or disappeared. Be sure to warn people when midterms and finals roll around.

✔ **Setting aside time to study:** Create a system to stay on top of your schoolwork. Keep up with reading assignments and begin thinking about projects as soon as they're assigned. You're investing too much time, money, and effort to shortchange your learning by cramming before tests and rushing to finish projects.

✔ **Finding new ways to get things done at home and at work:** Simplify wherever possible. For example, if doing your hair takes you a half-hour each morning, get it cut in a way that takes you only five minutes. Eliminate tasks or delegate what you can by finding someone else who can accomplish the task.

You're not alone. You're part of the fastest growing segment of the student population in most colleges. To find out how others are doing it, check out the Association for Non-Traditional Students in Higher Education (www.antshe.org). Your time in school won't last forever. While you're there, focus as much as you can on enjoying the process.

Goal Two: Going for Your Dream Job

After you track down a qualified job lead, you must be ready to act. Following the guidelines in this section gets you off on the right foot.

Preparing a stellar application packet

To have the opportunity to interview for the jobs that interest you, you must have a well conceived set of documents that accurately describe your skills, experience, and interest in the position and attract the attention of the hiring manager. Take the time to create a thorough packet that you can customize for each lead you want to follow up on.

Your first task is to rework your resume, which I discuss in Chapter 18. Next, write a cover letter to demonstrate that you can do the job. Use phrases from the want ad or online listing to strengthen your letter. If you can't get your hands on a written description of the job, talk with your contacts who have a working knowledge of the kind of job you're applying for to make sure that your cover letter is on the mark. For more info, check out *Cover Letters For Dummies*, 2nd Edition, by Joyce Lain Kennedy (Wiley).

Pay close attention to all the details in the packets you send out, whether they go by mail, e-mail, or fax. Remember to proofread everything, verify that your own contact information is accurate and easy to locate, sign your cover letter, and check the overall presentation one last time. If possible, ask a friend or family member to look over each packet before you send it out. A second pair of eyes never hurts.

If appropriate for your profession, prepare a portfolio with samples of your work, such as newsletters you've produced, articles you've written, photographs you've taken, or logos you've designed. Talk with your informational interview contacts to determine whether it's appropriate in your dream career to prepare a portfolio to take to your interviews.

Making the most of your interview

Any interview is a two-way street. Just as your interviewer asks you pointed questions to verify that you're a good fit for the company's culture and the position, you must ask questions to determine whether the company suits you. After you get the call to set up an interview, do the following two kinds of research and create a list of questions to ask during your interview:

✔ **Review what you know you need in a job.** Pay particular attention to work environment issues and your personal lifestyle preferences. Develop questions you can ask to verify that the job can blend well with your life.

✔ **Increase your understanding of the company and the industry.** Check out the company's Web site and read about their products, technology, key players, and history. Check the local press for information about the company and the company's competition. Visit Quintessential Careers (www.quintcareers.com/researching_companies.html) for a variety of links for researching companies and industries.

When you can, conduct your research several days before the interview to give yourself a chance to think about what you read. Then the night before your interview, review the information again so that it's fresh in your mind.

The following list includes additional tips to help you prepare for your interview:

- Be prepared to talk with the recruiter or the in-house interviewer about any specific expectations you have regarding your salary range, benefits, vacation time, and stock options. Be upfront about your needs and listen to the interviewer's comments about the likelihood of fulfilling them. Although you may not get everything you want, you're more likely to create a job that fits your needs if you speak up at this early stage.

- Your first interview may last about an hour, but be prepared to interview with a series of people. If you have time constraints, make that clear when you arrange the interview. Most companies are considerate about time limitations, but sometimes interviews start later or run longer than anticipated. Take this into account when scheduling your time. As you finish your interview, inquire about the next step. The interviewer's answer gives you some idea of when you may hear word.

- Know your resume inside and out because your resume is your interviewer's starting point. Be prepared to talk about specific jobs and particular projects in detail. In your interview, you may be asked questions that require you to explain and defend your experience and how it relates to the job that you're interested in. This is especially true if you're changing careers.

  If certain aspects of your resume make you feel uncomfortable, don't expect to hide them from your interviewer. Find a way to make peace with them. The more confident you feel about your explanations, the less time your interviewer may spend digging into the issue.

  Come up with plausible explanations for the gaps and bumps in your employment history before the interview. Ask yourself the following questions to help you prepare:

  - Were you in school, parenting, caretaking, recovering from an illness, or traveling?
  - Were you laid off, fired, downsized, or right-sized?
  - Did you quit? If so, why?

- Give enough detail about your career history to adequately answer any questions, but don't ever speak about your former employer or manager in a petty, blaming, or vindictive manner. If there was a problem, have a solution or an idea to share with your interviewer to show that you have a proactive attitude about the situation.

- Fidgeting, breaking eye contact, or taking on an apologetic tone of voice while responding to these questions tips your hand. Recruit a friend to help you role-play your answers to a few key questions. Practice until your response rolls off your tongue without hesitation.

Interviewing is like dating. Both parties purposely portray themselves in the best possible light. Look and listen for clues to uncover the whole story. Does what the interviewer says match what you read in the newspaper yesterday or saw on the newsgroup discussion last night?

As you review your interviews, notice any gaps or inconsistencies in what you saw, heard, and sensed in each job. Don't side-step your intuition for any reason. If something doesn't add up, dig deeper to uncover the real story. Although no job is perfect, you want to go into a new career with your eyes open, as aware of the whole story as possible.

In addition to asking questions, keep your eyes and ears open during your visit. You can discover a fair amount about the company culture by observing what happens around you.

Take in as much information as you can by sensing the pace, checking out the décor, noticing how work groups are laid out, and observing interactions among co-workers. Can you imagine yourself working there?

After the interview comes the wait. This wait isn't easy for anybody. While you're waiting, give your interviewer a reason to remember you. Send a note to those you interviewed with to thank them for their time. Reiterate your interest in the position.

Depending on the job market, events at the company, the scheduling of other interviews, and what you were told at the end of your interview, you may get a call immediately, or you may not hear from the interviewer for a week or so.

If you don't hear from the interviewer or your recruiter when you think you should, place a call. Thank the person for the interview, reiterate your interest in the job, and, if the person doesn't have any news, ask when you should follow up again. Listen to what the interviewer or recruiter says. A delay doesn't necessarily mean bad news. The company may have more people to interview, a key decision-maker may be out of town, or the company may have had another job open up unexpectedly, which means the company's interviewing resources are spread over two candidate searches. If time passes and you still haven't heard anything, place another call.

Even as every cell in your body waits for the phone to ring, keep talking with contacts, keep track of any openings that are available, and keep interviewing in case this job offer falls through. Balance your job search activities with stress relievers such as exercising, socializing, and relaxing with a good novel.

Evaluating your options

Now that you feel fairly certain about what you want and need in your work life, don't let the excitement of finding a possible job make you forget everything you've discovered about your needs.

Think about all you know about each job you've interviewed for so far. How well does each job fit your needs? To create an objective comparison, assess how well each position fulfills your personal needs in Worksheet 19-1 and your environmental needs in Worksheet 19-2. Use the following symbols to rate each job on the elements in your list. Be as honest with yourself as possible as you complete this assessment process using the following rating system:

- ✔ **+:** I am likely to have this element in this job.

- ✔ **0:** I may have this element some of the time, but not all of the time.

- ✔ **–:** I'm unlikely to have this element in this job.

- ✔ **?:** I'm not sure that this element is likely to be present in this job.

Sometimes, at first blush, a potential job may appear great, but how does it really compare to your current or most recent job? In the third column of Worksheets 19-1 and 19-2, evaluate your prior job, using the same elements and scoring system. Doing so helps you see whether your new options are a better fit or not. If the new position is a better fit, you're on your way. If it's not, take a moment to evaluate how taking this job improves your situation. Perhaps it gives you valuable experience in a new arena or is closer to home, which cuts your commute. Whatever your rationale, be clear about why you want to take the job.

Identifying What's Compatible and What's in Conflict with Your Personal Needs			
Your Personal Needs	Job 1:_____	Job 2:_____	Your Current/Last Position: _____
Your personality traits			
Your values			
Your definition of success			
Your longings			
Your health			
Your reasons for working			
Your meaning in work			
Your relationship			
Your home			
Your faith			
Your service			
Your hobbies and interests			
Your fun time			
Your location			

Worksheet 19-1: Spotting pluses and minuses of each potential job in regard to your needs.

Identifying What's Compatible and What's in Conflict with Your Work Environment Needs			
Your Work Environment Needs	Job 1:_____	Job 2:_____	Your Current/Last Position: _____
Your work schedule			
Your contract			
Amount of pay			
Pay options			
Your benefits			
Kind of company			
Company size			
Company purpose			
Company reach			
Company location			
Your work area			
The dress code			
Your co-workers			
Other players			
Your manager			

Worksheet 19-2: Determining how each potential job lines up with your work environment needs.

Look at the overall patterns revealed in Worksheets 19-1 and 19-2.

> ✔ Do you see more +'s than –'s for one job than another?
>
> ✔ Are there too many ?'s or 0's in one column for your comfort? Ask your recruiter or other people who work at the company questions to gain the information you need to resolve any crucial unknowns.
>
> ✔ Are any of the –'s deal breakers or trade-offs?

A *deal breaker* is an element of the job that directly conflicts with your needs or those of your family. Taking a job with this kind of clash means that you sacrifice a crucial part of your desired lifestyle. Depending on your lifestyle, deal breakers might be too much travel, too long a commute, or too much required evening or weekend work.

A *trade-off* is something that you can give up or take on in order to have the rest of the job which does suit you. For example, trade-offs may include more client interaction than you would prefer, a more formal dress code than is ideal, or a location that's too far from home to walk to work.

If you come face to face with a deal breaker, share your concerns with your hiring manager or your recruiter, if you're working with one, immediately.

Don't hide your concerns from your recruiter or hiring manager. Be upfront about what you discover. Because bringing up concerns is always uncomfortable, there is no good time to have this conversation. Yet have it, you must. If you're clear enough about your concerns during your interview, mention it then. If your concerns become clear after your interview, place a call to the person you've been working with. You must do your best to share your thoughts before you actually receive an offer.

When you share your perspective, listen to the recruiter's or hiring manager's explanation, but hold firm if you feel the issue can't be resolved. No matter how good the job looks, if a deal breaker lurks in the details, you face a no-win situation. Better to back off now than after you're fully involved in the position or lifestyle. If the job looks like a great opportunity, walking away won't be easy, but then again, trying to work and live in a situation that you know from the get-go won't work can be pure misery.

A trade-off is a different matter. In this situation, only you can determine whether you can live with the consequences of taking a position that includes this particular element. Take some time to brainstorm ways to minimize the impact the trade-off may have on your family and your work life. Check in with your recruiter to see whether anything can be done to align the job more closely with your needs.

Receiving an offer

When hiring managers extend an offer, they expect you to say yes with great enthusiasm. If you feel confused or uneasy at the thought of receiving an offer from one of the companies you interview with, take some time to think through the situation before the offer is presented to you. Is a deal breaker or trade-off bothering you (see the preceding section for more information on deal breakers and trade-offs)? Are you afraid the job isn't a good fit? Talk candidly with your recruiter or hiring manager to get to the bottom of the situation.

Go over the offer in detail. Ask the recruiter or hiring manager to clarify any points that seem unclear. If everyone has communicated clearly, the offer should contain no surprises.

Unfortunately, that's not always the case. If the offer comes in with a lower job title, a lower salary, or fewer benefits than you expected, ask for some time to think over your situation. Return to the section "Evaluating your options" earlier in this chapter to rate the elements of the job with this new information in mind. Even if it's not ideal, is this job still a good opportunity to expand your experience in your target career area?

After you have a full understanding of exactly what the offer includes, give the recruiter or hiring manager your answer:

✔ If the offer isn't what you expected and doesn't give you what you need to survive or thrive, and you've tried to negotiate for what you want with no success, you must say no. As hard as it is to do, walk away, especially if a deal breaker is part of the package. Although this offer didn't work out, keep in touch with the recruiter or hiring manager in case other employment opportunities arise.

✔ If you determine that you feel comfortable with any trade-offs present in the offer, accept the position. If you find that you need help resolving a trade-off, you may decide to make your acceptance of the job contingent on finding solutions together.

✔ If the offer matches what you were told during the interview process, you can take the job with some confidence in the communication channels.

After you accept and sign an offer, you need to give notice at your current company, if you have one.

Although giving two weeks' notice is customary, be prepared to leave sooner in some cases. Some companies with sensitive data may walk you out as soon as you resign, giving you only a moment to pack up your personal items. If you want to have closure with people you worked with, create a list of phone numbers and e-mail addresses and take it home with you before you give notice so that you can let these people know where you went.

If you remain for the full two weeks, continue to participate fully. Finish projects, leave instructions for whoever takes over your active projects, and create closure with those you worked with. Feel free to daydream about your future career to help the time pass. You may also have to field questions from every corner about where you're going next. Depending on the situation, these conversations may be fun because you get to talk about your next adventure, or they can be a bit awkward if you're going to a competitor or doing something that seems like an unusual move to your co-workers. Share as much or as little detail as feels comfortable.

As you leave one company to join another, share your news with all the people in your network. Thank them again for their assistance and give out your new contact information so that they can reach you if they ever need your help.

In the changing world of work, keeping in regular contact with your network makes sense. Although you're employed today, you may not be in the months and years to come. Having a solid, active network can make all the difference in your job search.

Feeling at home in your new career

As you walk in the doors of your new career for the first time, you enter a different world with a new language, new players, and new goals. Keep these tips in mind as you settle into your new profession:

✔ **Stay calm in the midst of change.** Although starting something new can be exciting, you may also feel a bit unsettled or overwhelmed by the differences. Rather than fight these feelings, accept that you don't know, and can't know, all there is to know yet. Breathe and give yourself permission to ease into your new career.

✔ **Manage your expectations of yourself.** Before you can expect yourself to perform at the level you did in your last career, you must give yourself time to get a feel for the ropes. Expecting too much of yourself too soon can sabotage your performance. Have patience with yourself and the process of learning again.

✔ **Listen to the lingo.** Your first mission in a new job is to understand the language. Don't be shy. Inquire about acronyms and phrases you've never heard before. Ask whether the company has a glossary or translation Web page for new employees. Before criticizing yourself, remember that acronyms often crop up so rapidly that even seasoned employees have a hard time keeping track of them.

✔ **Get to know the players.** In your previous career, you probably knew whom to contact for what without even thinking about it. You can reach that point again — it may just take some time. Sometimes the best person to approach isn't the obvious choice. Establish a relationship with a trustworthy co-worker to help you tap into the infrastructure more quickly.

✔ **Put your best foot forward, staying true to yourself.** Obviously, as you start a job in your new career, you want to make a good impression. To accomplish this, you may go out of your way to exceed your managers' expectations. Although you may win points this way, you may also significantly raise the bar of what others expect of you. Don't set up unrealistic patterns of availability or productivity if you don't want to sustain them. Be clear about your boundaries. Where you can, set limits from the start, so that your boss and co-workers know how you work.

Although it's not something you want to think about just now, at some point, you may find this new job isn't as fulfilling as it once was, or that a change in management or the company mission has irreparably changed your job. Take stock of your situation by reading Chapter 1. The more involved you are in the strategic side of managing your career, the fewer surprises you encounter. Check in every three to six months to see how you can enliven your career.

Goal Three: Launching Your Dream Business

If you've done the preliminary planning in Chapter 18, you have a clear concept of your product or service, your location needs, your competition, and your financial funding options. Now it's time to start revving your engines.

One of the best ways to ramp up a successful business is to learn as much as you can about how to run a business. Don't rely on just what you know. Don't rely on just the chapters in this book, because there's no way to do justice to the topic of starting a business in just a few pages. Do more research by reaching out for other references. For instance, you might look at *Entrepreneurship For Dummies*, by Kathleen Allen, or *Starting an Online Business For Dummies*, 4th Edition, by Greg Holden (Wiley).

Creating your business identity

Developing an identity for your business typically involves creating a business name, logo, and tagline or motto that gives your potential clients a clear understanding of what your business offers. As you select your colors, font, logo, paper, and Web site design, make sure that they appeal to your target market. Whether you hire a designer or do the work yourself, create the most professional-looking business identity you can afford.

Because your business focus may change as you gain more understanding of what your clients want, figure in some room for modifications and limit your first print run of any printed materials until you're confident that your text is finalized.

Choosing the name of your business takes careful thought and some research. By law, the name of your business can't compete with the name of a similar kind of business serving the same geographic area. If you expect to have only local clients, verify that your name is available by checking with the county department that assigns fictitious names and the state government office that tracks corporations and trademarks. Use the Small Business Administration Web page at `www.sba.gov/hotlist/businessnames.html` to find the right state office for your research.

If you expect to have a national or international clientele, do adequate research to ensure that the name you want to use is available. Even if you aren't sure you want to establish a trademark, you need to do this research, because if someone else owns the trademark, you have no right to use the name yourself. You can conduct a free initial search, pay for a more complete research report on the availability of your name for a trademark, and apply for your trademark by visiting `www.nameprotect.com` or contacting a trademark lawyer.

You may also want to verify that you can obtain a domain name that works for your business. Although you may want your domain name to match your business name, consider incorporating your key benefit into your domain name. For example, when I started the blog for this book, I chose the domain name, `www.findyourdreamcareer.com`. Not only is this domain name easy to spell, but it also spells out the main benefit of the book and is easy to remember. To investigate whether your preferred domain name is available, visit `www.godaddy.com`.

After you have your domain name, make each page of your Web site count by writing compelling copy, building a well-organized site, and submitting your site to search engines.

Establishing your work space

To be an effective entrepreneur, you must have a space dedicated to your business. If you have a store or office outside your home, carve out a place within the larger area that you can call your own. If you plan to work from home, establish a physical location for your office and set up some ground rules with your family so that they know how to interact with you while you're working.

As you design your space, pay attention to how you like to work. Don't spend big bucks on a formal desk if you prefer to sit in an easy chair or at a worktable with your laptop. Modular furniture can be a good investment because, as you and your business grow, you can rearrange your office to fit your changing needs.

Developing sustainable marketing strategies

To get business to come to you, you must create an effective marketing strategy to get the word out to your prospective clients. For the best results, you must develop a coordinated strategy that you can sustain over time. Check out *Marketing For Dummies* by Alexander Hiam (Wiley) for a variety of ideas.

Marketing is an art. Begin with your best marketing piece, track its successes and failures, and then modify what doesn't work or replace it with something that has a better chance of working.

To be effective, you must feel comfortable enough with your marketing methods that you can make them an integral part of doing business. Having three or four strategies you employ consistently is generally more effective than a scattered approach done intermittently.

Just because your business is booming, don't think you can stop your marketing efforts. You must market continuously, even when your business is thriving.

Feeling at home in your own business

If you've always worked in a corporate situation, becoming an entrepreneur may take some getting used to. For possibly the first time in your life, you can call your own shots, which may feel refreshing and unnerving all at once.

In a corporate setting, a number of people are involved in making things happen. In your own business, you are responsible for everything — from keeping your supplies stocked and handling shipping to negotiating deals and delivering products or services to clients.

You may be absolutely amazed at how long it can take to get what seems like a simple letter drafted, printed, and out the door to the mail box. Just the handling of everyday correspondence, e-mails, and phone calls can consume your entire day.

At some point, you may find it worth the expense to hire someone to help out with certain tasks. Keep the following tips in mind when considering recruiting help from others:

- ✔ Start by making a list of all the tasks that must be done to run your business and provide your product or service to your clients.

- ✔ Group the tasks by functions, such as administration, development, production, marketing, sales, inventory and distribution, and customer follow-up.

- ✔ Identify the tasks that you enjoy doing and are good at.

- ✔ As you look at the remaining tasks, ask yourself whether you are the best person to do a particular task. If you have the skills but lack the desire, you can handle it, but if you lack both the skill and the desire, you're probably better off finding someone to support that aspect of your business. This is especially true if you tend to procrastinate each time you need to handle the task.

- ✔ Go through all the tasks and group the ones you'd rather not handle. As you look at the list, think about who may be able to help you step toward your dream. Do you have a family member who can pitch in or a friend who has some extra time on her hands? Does an independent contractor have the specialty that you need or could you hire an employee to take on particular tasks?.

If you choose to hire employees, you must look at the tax and liability implications of your decision. The Small Business Administration has a Start-Up Kit for New Employers, which outlines the basics. A conversation with your accountant is also in order.

Faced with your growing to-do list, you may feel that you must tackle everything today. The truth is that you shouldn't even try to do that.

As you begin each day or week, identify the tasks that must get done on that particular day. Then focus your attention on accomplishing those tasks and putting out any fires that crop up during the day. If you make a dent in your list, call it a good day. Over time and with experience, you'll find it easier to create a focus for the day and stick with it.

Although you may have strategic decisions looming over you, discipline yourself not to obsess over them, especially if you can't or don't have all the information you need to make the decision. If you get thoughts or ideas about a decision you must make farther down the road, by all means make note of them.

Attempting to make strategic decisions while in the midst of handling your day-to-day business affairs is like mixing oil and water. Set aside a day or weekend to get away from your business environment so that you can clear your head enough to make sound, long-range decisions for your business.

Learning from each experience

You will make mistakes. Expect it and accept it. Whether you lack the experience, use poor judgment, or make a decision based on inadequate assumptions, you may wish you could redo any number of decisions, especially when you first start out.

Take any frustration and embarrassment you have with yourself and move it into a more proactive direction instead. First evaluate the situation. Determine whether you can salvage the situation by having another conversation with the party involved, or if the next decision you make can reverse the damage. If neither scenario is possible, your only option may be to let it go.

Rather than berate yourself, think through how you would handle the situation differently if given the chance. Then the next time you face a similar situation, call upon your experience to guide you to a better decision.

Finding the balance in your new life

When you first start your business, you may find yourself eating, breathing, and sleeping your business. No matter how you look at it, a growing business takes a tremendous amount of dedication and focus.

And yet to succeed, you must keep yourself in tiptop shape. Find ways to eke out enough time and space for yourself, your family, and your friendships. Several strategies may help, including the following:

- ✔ **Combining activities:** If you make friends with other entrepreneurs, you can set up a regular time to problem-solve, brainstorm, or offer support while having lunch or taking a walk.

- ✔ **Creating boundaries:** Designate a certain time of day or day of the week where you step away from your business and your responsibilities. When you take this time off, you must discipline your mind to let go of work, as well.

Ensuring a Smooth Transition into Your Next Career

Regardless of which goal you're going after, several factors impact the pace and intensity of how your journey to your new venture unfolds.

Use Worksheet 19-3 to ascertain the parameters that are likely to influence your transition most. Use the following list of questions to deepen your thinking.

✔ **Your status at your current job:** Do you enjoy your job? Is it critical that you get out of your job immediately? Are you okay hanging out in your current position while you put new pieces into place? Are there any ways your current job limits you in taking the actions you need to take? Can you find any other more creative ways to keep money flowing in while you put your plan into action?

✔ **Your time horizon:** In an ideal world, when would you like to be transitioning into your new venture? From a realistic standpoint, what does your time frame look like? When can you start making your move? Are there milestone dates you can target?

✔ **Your available funds:** How is your financial situation impacting your choices? Do you have the funds you need to invest in yourself? If so, create a budget and stick to it. If not, how can you come up with the funds you need? Do you need a cash-producing job for the short term, do you need to find a loan, or do you need to scale back your initial plans?

✔ **Your current skill level:** Do you have all the training you need? What are the gaps you need to fill? How and when are you going to do this? Review Chapter 18 to think through your best strategy to build the skills you need.

✔ **Your family's needs:** How do your family's needs impact your decisions and actions? Chapter 4 helps you look at this question in more detail. What new systems or support resources can you put in place to free up your time and energy?

✔ **Your location realities:** What's true about your location that impacts the unfolding of your venture? Do you need to restructure your office? Do you need to rent space? Do you need to move?

Factors that Impact Your Transition to Your New Career	
Elements to Consider	Your Thoughts
Your status at your current job	
Your time horizon	
Your available funds	
Your current skill level	
Your family's needs	
Your location realities	

Worksheet 19-3: Assessing what defines how your transition unfolds.

As you clarify where you stand with each issue, focus on each one to see how you can massage it to work with your ultimate plan. If you're really stumped, use the brainstorming activity in Chapter 17 to find creative ways to weave all of your considerations and goals into a workable plan.

Record your best plan in Worksheet 19-4. Revisit your plan periodically to update it as your situation evolves.

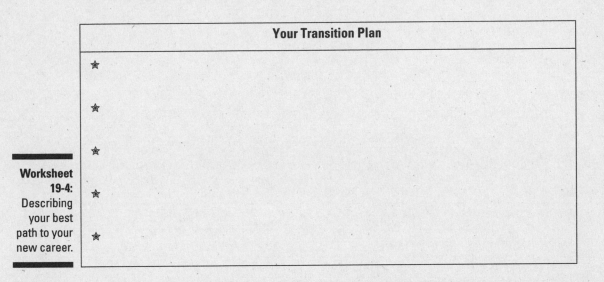

Worksheet 19-4: Describing your best path to your new career.

You can plan the timing and pace of your transition to take your personal factors into account. You have several options to choose from:

- ✔ **Make the leap:** One option, the one most people think of first, is to just take the leap. Jump into school, your new job, or your business, without looking back. This option takes some inner strength to handle the abrupt, potentially risky nature of this path. For a time, you are the trapeze artist who's suspended in midair between bars. If you have a good safety net in place (think money and moral support), this path may work.

- ✔ **Easing out of one and into another.** If you don't have the constitution for an all-at-once jump, you may feel more comfortable easing from one situation to another. With this overlap, you may be quite busy, but you have a chance to resolve any unforeseen problems before you completely let go of the old. This path means you're in transition longer, so your tolerance for being in motion versus your need to feel settled may define how long this in-between plan works for you.

- ✔ **Doubling up for a time:** You may discover that your best course is to keep your current job and go back to school, or keep your current job while you get your business going. This path gives you a bit of security and stability. Although your ultimate intention is to shift out of the old, you feel no sense of urgency to complete the deed.

- ✔ **Creating a composite career:** In this model, you purposely weave your various paths together so that you have multiple streams of income and enjoy multiple ways to express and use your talents. Sometimes the threads of your composite career are similar in that they capitalize on related topics or skills. In other cases, your fabric is woven from several completely unrelated talents, skills, and interests. If this work style appeals to you, the flexible nature of your work is probably a crucial piece of your career puzzle.

Part V
The Part of Tens

The 5th Wave   By Rich Tennant

THOUGH SUCCESSFUL IN HIS FIELD, BOZO THE SURGEON ALWAYS FELT HIS TRUE CALLING LAY OUTSIDE THE OPERATING ROOM.

@RICHTENNANT

In this part . . .

No matter how you look at it, changing careers is quite an experience. To ensure that you make the best possible decisions, review the ten ways to verify that your dream career is right for you. Then when you're ready to put your plan into action, look at the last chapter for creative ways to transition into your new adventure.

## Chapter 20

Ten Ways to Confirm Your Dream Career Won't Be a Nightmare

. . . .

In This Chapter

▶ Getting information from a class, Web sites, or journals

▶ Meeting and observing people in your ideal careers

▶ Finding a way to get hands-on experience

▶ Determining how a new career will affect your lifestyle

. . . .

A career idea has captured your attention. You know something about this potential career from visiting Web sites, doing informational interviews, and reading about the work, but you still don't know whether it's the right career for you. Now is the best time to test the waters to discover all you can about the work you're considering.

In this chapter you find ten ways to experiment with the profession in question to ensure that you fully understand and enjoy the work, the professional community, and the work's impact on you and your life.

Depending on how familiar you are with your idea, your exploration may take a couple weeks to several months. Write down your observations periodically so that you won't have to reconstruct your impressions when the time comes to make a decision to move forward.

Paying Attention to How You Feel

As you try on your new career, using the methods described in this chapter, the most important thing you can do is pay attention to how you feel each step of the way. Your visceral reaction as you step closer to the profession speaks volumes as long as you're willing to listen. Whether it's love or loathing at first sight, these feelings are likely to become even more intense if you actually decide to work in the field.

Always base your conclusions on your reactions to multiple sources of information and on the quality of your source. For instance, don't give as much weight to a disgruntled member of the profession as you would to information you gather from a reputable trade journal.

If you come across information that troubles you, calm yourself down and then do more investigation until you have a full, informed picture of the situation. If you discover conflicting information or information that doesn't fit your needs, don't abandon your dream prematurely. Use Chapters 16 and 17 to find a creative solution that resolves your concern.

Taking a Relevant Class or Two

Early in your exploration, look for a short course that can give you a taste of your potential career. Your goal is not to get fully trained in the field at this point, but to explore whether the field is a good fit for you.

Pick up class schedules for local community colleges, universities with local satellite campuses, and specialty schools in your area or search the Internet for online courses or teleclasses. Look for an introductory course or a course that deepens your knowledge.

As you take the course, notice whether you feel excited by the material or bored. If you're excited, pay special attention to what aspects of the course intrigue you most. If you're bored, is it because the class is too elementary or because the topic isn't as interesting as you thought? Is there a related topic that might be more interesting?

If you run across a full-degree or certification program, make note of it but don't commit to it — even if it looks like a perfect match. Starting a training program before you've confirmed your direction limits your career investigation and your future career choices.

Searching for Online Sources of Information

As you search the Internet for informative Web sites about your target career, keep your eyes open for relevant online newsletters, discussion boards, and blogs that can tell you more about your possible career and profession.

Each of these resources is free and takes just a moment of your time to read. In return, you gain access to hot topics within the field, key events for professionals like yourself, crucial issues that may impact how you work, new techniques and perspectives you can incorporate into your work, and key players in the field.

Bookmark any items that appear relevant. As you become more familiar with the field and refine the direction of your career change, review what you've saved to see what other angles, contacts, and companies may be salient.

If you aren't running across discussion groups and blogs in your exploration of your target career, use these directories to find relevant places to visit:

- ✔ **Yahoo! Groups (http://groups.yahoo.com):** Access a group by using the search function or by scanning the groups under categories that interest you.

- ✔ **Monster.com (http://discussion.monster.com/messageboards/):** This site includes several profession-specific message boards as well as several boards for particular situations such as age issues, diversity at work, contract, and temping.

- ✔ **Wetfeet (www.wetfeet.com/discuss/home.asp):** You find career and industry boards on this site as well as a number of topical boards.

- ✔ **Blogarama (www.blogarama.com):** If you want to find a blog by someone in your target profession, visit this site for a directory of blog categories. The Business/ Professional link lists blogs that comment on particular industries, jobs, and companies. You may also find the search function to be helpful if you can be specific enough about your keywords.

- ✔ **Globe of Blogs (www.globeofblogs.com/?x=topic):** This link takes you to a directory of blog topics. Click on Careers and Occupations for a list of professions and the number of related blogs. Click away until you find the ones that interest you.

Immersing Yourself in Trade Journals

Another valuable source of information comes from trade journals. Ask your professional contacts what they read to stay on top of industry news. Whether online or in print, trade journals offer you a more in-depth look at the profession.

Depending on the publication source, you may gain access to the views of the professional association, an independent journalistic source, or an alliance of vendors. As you read, make a point of identifying the source and the source's place in the industry or profession.

Reading a trade journal gives you a window into the priorities, politics, profession-specific language, and humor associated with the industry or profession. If elements of these areas are counter to your interests, pay attention! Now is the time to become aware of a lack of fit if there is one.

Your reading also gives you a synopsis of current and past events, upcoming special events, and key issues that are impacting the profession. Gaining an accurate understanding of the state of the profession is crucial to your ultimate comfort as you step into the career.

Interacting with People in the Field

As you consider becoming an active member of a profession, find ways to interact with others in the profession. One of the best places to start is to locate a local chapter of a key professional association. Attending these meetings allows you to get a sense of how it feels to be in the company of those in your target profession. You can learn a lot by listening, observing, and interacting with others in the community. In the process, you enrich your understanding of the career, begin building a thriving network, learn from more experienced members, hear about local job leads, and enhance your visibility within the profession.

Some chapters allow you to attend their local meetings as a guest before you become a full-fledged member. To make the most of the meetings, follow these guidelines:

- ✔ **Attend several meetings before you decide whether to stop going.** This advice holds true even if you feel uncomfortable at the meetings at first. (The truth is that almost everyone feels somewhat uncomfortable walking into a room full of strangers.) The only reason to cut this plan short is if the group's purpose is clearly not a good match for you.

- ✔ **Announce yourself.** Tell the person at the door that you're attending for the first time so that he or she can introduce you to people right off the bat.

- ✔ **Think about how to introduce yourself before you walk into the meeting.** Write your introduction down if it helps to have something prepared in front of you.

- ✔ **Introduce yourself to the people sitting around you.** Asking questions about the organization is a good way to start a conversation. If you want to follow up with someone after the meeting, ask for the person's business card. Always bring a supply of your own cards as well. You can create a simple business card at your local office supply store or on your own computer.

- ✔ **Notice who plays key roles during the meeting.** Keep their names and faces in mind for future reference.

The more frequently you attend chapter meetings, the more people you recognize, and the more comfortable you become. Another way to feel at ease is to reconnect with people outside the meeting. Several days after you meet someone, e-mail or call to share a book title, a recent article, or the phone number of a contact you discussed. If you sense that you have a lot in common with someone in the initial conversation, invite the person to join you for lunch or coffee. Although you can't expect every interaction to result in a long-term connection, you never know where a connection will lead you.

Don't let a hot or warm connection drop away out of ambivalence or apathy on your part. Even if you aren't sure there's a match, take a chance and check it out.

Attending a Professional Conference

A professional conference can be a great place to get a sense of a profession while building your skills. As you review conference brochures that come across your desk at work, evaluate how the conference could give you a better understanding of your target career. This opportunity is especially likely if your new career is related to your current position.

If your target career isn't related to your current career, your inbox probably isn't going to deliver the information you need to find a conference that's relevant to your target career. Instead, turn to trade journals, association Web sites, professional discussion groups, or your informational interview contacts to identify possible conferences that meet your needs. Keep your eye out for regional conferences as well as national or international opportunities.

If you see a strong link between the conference and your work and can convince your manager of its value, the company may even foot the bill for some of your expenses. If your company chooses not to fund your trip, or if the conference is something you find on your own, do what you have to do to attend. Take some vacation time, use your frequent-flier miles to get there, stay with a friend, or pay for the conference yourself, if necessary.

As you set up your personal agenda for the conference, read the conference brochure and preconference workshop descriptions carefully for opportunities. Consider the following:

- ✔ If a session addresses a new software package that's essential for people in your target career to use, sit in on that session.

- ✔ If you see a niche or application that you've never heard of before, explore it to see whether it gives you a better understanding of your new career.

- ✔ If a key expert is giving a talk on a topic that has always confused you, attend the session so that you can resolve your confusion before you enter your new field.

Observing Someone on the Job

Watching someone interacting with clients, co-workers, suppliers, and management and doing the tasks you might perform gives you a great opportunity to evaluate how well that potential career fits you and your needs.

Before you ask your contacts if you can shadow them for a couple hours or a day, think through what you hope to gain from the experience. (To discover how to find contacts in careers you're interested in, turn to Chapter 15.) Make a list of what you want to look for during the observation. Build in time at the beginning of the appointment to determine the length of your observation time, whether you can take notes about what you see, and the appropriate time to ask questions — for example, on the spot or during a break.

If watching someone as he works isn't possible, see whether you can meet the person at his workplace for a conversation or for lunch. Seeing the work environment can also give you a feel for how it might be to work in that environment.

Talking to People Outside the Field

To make sure that you get the full picture of your target career, don't limit yourself to talking with only those who do the job you want. Think of others you may interact with on the job. You might gain a unique perspective of your target career by talking with vendors, potential customers, professional colleagues who work at a similar level but hold different jobs, or individuals who report to the position you're targeting.

Use your current contacts to gain access to people in these various roles. No matter whom you end up talking to, each person can help you reach your goal of broadening your understanding of the job.

Getting Hands-On Experience

To get some hands-on experience with your new profession (and strengthen job-relevant skills while you're at it), search for a way to work on a project that's relevant to you. You might consider volunteering to work on a relevant project or committee within a nonprofit, taking a part-time job, getting an internship, or helping a friend with a project. This extra project doesn't necessarily need to be a long-term commitment. Your goal is to see how it feels to engage in this sort of work.

If you have a difficult time finding an appropriate opportunity in your area of interest, visit www.idealist.org, www.onlinevolunteering.org, or www.volunteermatch.org for local, global, and online volunteer opportunities that relate to careers that appeal to you. Or explore internship and short-term options by putting the term "internships" and your chosen field into your search engine. Although some internships are geared toward students or recent graduates, opportunities do exist for others as well.

With some ingenuity, you may even find a way to get some hands-on experience within your current company. After researching your organization to identify experiences that most closely match your target career, build a case for doing a rotation in that department. Be sure to lay out the benefits to the company and the details of how your proposal would work. Have several variations worked out in your mind so that if your employer doesn't buy into your original plan, you can present her with some other attractive options. For example, your manager may flinch at the idea of assigning you to another department for several months, but she may see value in allowing you to do some cross-training in the same department over a couple weeks. As you work in the new department, take advantage of any opportunities to strengthen skills you know you need to succeed in your target career.

Assessing the Impact on Your Lifestyle

A truly fulfilling career gives you professional satisfaction and also allows you to live the life you want. Rather than assuming that your new career and its related lifestyle will work for you and your family, take some time to verify that you're comfortable with the changes.

Whether you're interested in rural living, telecommuting, working part time while parenting, being an entrepreneur, or another lifestyle, you can gain insight about your new life by trying on your new lifestyle for a few days or by spending time with people who are living the life you think you want.

Begin by inventing ways to mimic your desired lifestyle for a few days in your current situation. Even if your efforts aren't completely accurate, you can at least get an idea of how you might respond to living this way over time.

During the days you've set aside for your experiment, live as if you've already made the transition to your new lifestyle or work arrangement. From the moment you wake up in the morning until the time you go to bed, approach your life through this new lens. How might you interact with others? Would you think about different things? Start acting the part you want to play. Although creating a new way to live evolves over time, you can begin to get a sense of whether the change is a good fit for you.

Sometimes the idea of something feels better than the reality. Don't just focus on the rosy parts of the picture. Notice what makes you feel uneasy about this way of living and working. What do you need to explore in more detail as a result of this experience? Be as realistic as you can about determining whether this transition would be a good one for you.

Use the following ideas to start planning your experiment:

- ✔ **If you want your new career to be part-time:** If your job allows, set up a week when you work three out of five days or when you leave early three days in a row. Notice how the time off impacts your life. Project how the decrease in salary might affect you.

- ✔ **If your new career is entrepreneurial:** Think about what your workday would look like as an entrepreneur. Would you work at home? Out on the road? In a small office? At client sites? If you're currently in a job, take a couple of days or a week off and use the time to explore this work style and lifestyle. Even if you use the week to get your business plan in order, you can discover what it feels like to plan your own day and find the self-discipline to do what needs to get done. If you have children, arrange for day care as you would if you were running your own business.

- ✔ **If your new career involves relocating:** Take a couple trips to scope out the new area. If the move means a longer commute, drive the commute several days in a row — during rush hour, of course! — to get a feel for the traffic, travel time, and alternate routes.

Your next step is to find others who are doing what you want to do (Chapter 15 might give you some ideas on finding these people). If you don't know someone you can visit, talk about your desired lifestyle with people you know or meet. Often people pipe up and say, "Oh, Janet's sister is doing the very same thing!" Follow up to see whether you can connect in person. If the potential contact lives too far away to meet in person, set up a conversation by phone or via e-mail.

To make full use of your visit, make your appointment at a time when you can witness the aspects of the lifestyle that concern you the most, which could be the morning shuffle of getting the kids off to school before work, returning home after a long commute, or working at home with toddlers in the house.

Come with a prepared list of questions to ask. Observe the environment and what happens in the home. Notice the interruptions. Get a feel for the flow of activity. Don't get discouraged by what you see. Instead, use what you observe to think through how a potential change might unfold in your home. Get creative to come up with ways to counteract things that may not work smoothly at first.

Chapter 21

Ten Creative Ways to Make the Leap to Your Dream Career

• •

In This Chapter

▶ Making the most of your current income

▶ Creating a way to use a mix of jobs to make your transition

▶ Using your own business to implement the change

▶ Finding ways to return to school

• •

*W*hen all is said and done, the biggest factor in your transition from one career to the next is money. Although you'd love to just quit your current job and dive headlong into your new career, financial realities keep you from acting rashly. The truth is that you need to continue to make a certain amount of money to survive as you make your move.

To transition as gracefully and effectively as possible, think through the best way to choreograph your entry into a new job, your own business, or back to school. In this chapter, you find ten creative ways to move from where you are now to where you want to be.

Some options may be a better fit for your circumstances than others. Feel free to mix and match if you see a way to combine parts of several strategies to meet your needs.

Regardless of the path you take to reach your dream career, keep your focus on the essence of what you want for yourself and your life. Keeping this focus as you implement your plan allows you to discern your best next step each time you face a key decision. When you feel stuck because you can't identify a direct path to your goal, brainstorm possible solutions, using Chapter 17 as your guide.

Using Your Current Income Wisely

If you know that a career change is in your future, be proactive in getting your financial house in order. An honest assessment of your financial situation, while you're still employed if possible, gives you far more options in the long run than assuming you know where you stand.

Before you initiate your move to change careers, make as much progress as you can toward the following four initiatives:

▶ **Increasing your savings:** Sign up for an automatic transfer to your savings account. Create a monthly or weekly savings goal and do everything in your power to reach it.

▶ **Reducing your monthly expenses:** Look at every monthly expense you have. Does the value it provides match what you pay for it? Is it an essential expense? Eliminate bills where you can; downgrade others if possible. Don't focus only on your small expenses; take this opportunity to evaluate your biggest expenses as well to see whether you can find a creative way to restructure them.

✔ **Eliminating, or at least significantly reducing, your debt:** Whether you make payments toward student loans, a car loan, or a credit card balance, your income requirement is likely to decrease rather dramatically as you eliminate each source of debt.

✔ **Practicing living within your means:** When you launch your new career, you don't want to rack up new debts to replace the ones you've just paid off. Instead, you need to get in the habit of living within your means — without the use of plastic. When you begin acting on these initiatives, your *discretionary income,* the money you get to use for whatever you wish, decreases dramatically because most of it is going into savings or to pay down your debt. This doesn't mean you have to stop having fun; it just means you need to become a little more inventive when it comes to planning your social life, vacations, and weekday lunches.

Taking a serious look at these initiatives and following up with the necessary actions is important if you're moving into a target career that's likely to lower your salary in the short term. If you're going back to school or starting a business, these steps are crucial to your long-term success.

Don't worry — this financial situation may not be a life sentence. In addition, gaining control of your financial situation opens up more options than it closes. Imagine knowing with certainty that you could, if you chose to, work part time to care for your children or go back to school for a year. Without having an accurate assessment of your situation, your options are limited by the assumptions, fears, and worst-case scenarios that spin in your head.

Supplementing Your Full-Time Position with Part-Time Work

Taking on a part- time job on top of your regular job can be a viable strategy if you want to do any of the following:

✔ Build your cash reserves

✔ Gain some experience in your new field

✔ Develop a particular skill

✔ Strengthen your network of contacts within a new field

✔ Add new breadth to your resume

If you're going to invest your time and effort in a second job, get some extra bang for your buck by finding a part-time job that's in alignment with your target career in some way. Think about what you want this job to do for you. Do you want to use the job to get a look at your target industry, to strengthen one key skill you need to move forward, or to check out the competition of your target company?

By taking the time to sort through your long-term priorities and goals, you're more likely to benefit from your stint at your part-time job.

Doing Contract Work

Although you may think that your only option is to land a full-time job, your chances of landing a job improve if you open your mind to include the possibility of taking on project or contract work. Although a series of short-term gigs may not fit your ideal picture, having some money coming in while you gain some relevant experience isn't anything to sneeze at.

The world economy has shifted. More and more companies are turning to a project-based philosophy that allows them to hire just the talent they need to complete a particular project. As soon as a project is finished, the company releases those they no longer need.

Although there's always a chance that your contract will be extended or converted to full-time, you can't know that for sure. Given the fluid nature of the economic climate, you may move from contract work to a full-time position, and back to freelance work over the course of a couple years. Living with this level of unfolding security takes a certain level of confidence and trust.

Your best bet is to become comfortable with this fluid reality because it's here to stay. The keys to surviving or — better yet — thriving in this kind of economy are understanding all the skills and talents you bring to the party, being able to articulate the benefits you provide, and having an active, well-connected network that is plugged into what's happening in your industry and your target companies.

Instead of thinking of yourself as an employee, begin thinking of yourself as the head of your own operation. Scan the horizon consistently to know when things are turning and when opportunities are available. Make the most-informed decisions you can about the best ways to promote your talent, both for your own future and for your customers, whether they're employers, clients, or contractors.

One side benefit to this work format is the opportunity to test out a company or an industry sector to see how you like it — before you enter into a long-term, full-time commitment. Another benefit, if you have skills that are sought after, is that you can call the shots to some degree. You can accept jobs that look interesting, turn away jobs that aren't a good fit, and choose to give yourself some time off for travel or study. The latter is obviously far more comfortable if you're confident that more jobs are in the pipeline.

Helping a Friend While Bringing In a Paycheck

Another way to build your skills is to use your talents to help out a friend with a project or a business task. Whether it's helping a friend organize her wedding, market a new product, or do some financial analysis, you have the opportunity to test how it feels to do the work, to identify where you want to get more training, and to have some fun along the way.

Don't accept just any offer, however. Take your time to analyze your situation from a strategic vantage point first. Think through the following steps before you make a proposal.

1. **Reaffirm your long-term career goal.**

2. **Take an inventory of the skills you already possess.**

3. **Decide what skills you want to develop.**

4. **Figure out what your friend's actual needs are.**

   To be a good match, your skills must overlap with your friend's needs to enough of a degree that your friend truly benefits from the alliance.

5. **Decide what you're willing to offer your friend.**

   Based on your skills and the areas you want to develop and your friend's needs, what solution is coming to mind? Do you want to consult on the subject at hand, do a research project, or work with your friend to achieve a goal? Be as specific as possible as you formulate your offering.

6. **Consider your goals in doing this project.**

How do you benefit in the long run?

As you piece together your proposal and plan, remember to do the following:

✔ **Stay focused on the present project.** Don't get seduced into thinking this is the first step to a long-term partnership. That's like planning your wedding during your first date, and you all probably know how well that scenario plays out!

✔ **Specify the exact parameters and deliverables for the proposed project.** Don't promise the moon and don't fall into the trap of saying you can figure something out later. You want to be as clear as possible upfront about what you can and will provide.

✔ **Put your proposal in writing and put both of your signatures on the document.** If your friend balks at such a business-like action, explain that you want to practice each step as if she's a client. Having a written agreement means that you both have something to look back to if your memory of the details differs from your friend's memory.

✔ **Develop an exit plan that you both agree upon.** Completing a project with your integrity intact is just as important as starting on good footing. Think beyond the beginning of the project. How will you both know when the project is finished? How might you want to use the final results to advance your career? Come to agreement about each of these issues before you start working on the project.

With forethought and honesty from both parties, doing a project for a friend is a win-win for everyone involved. If you leap-frog over a step or jump in headfirst, the entire project and the friendship can turn into a lose-lose proposition without much warning.

Adding a Part-Time Business to Your Full-Time Job

Adding a part-time business can give you a leg up when it comes to gaining new skills or launching your ultimate venture. A part-time business on the side allows you to get your feet wet, build your client base, and refine the exact form your business will take while you still pull in a regular paycheck.

Yes, you'll be busy, but it's a good busy — one that fires you up each morning, motivating you to step into your new role with excitement and optimism.

Think about your future goal and the realities of your current job to find a part-time business and business format that blend well. Can you see a few clients or do a few projects at night or on the weekend? Can you build an online business that provides services 24/7 while you work?

After you have a business idea that's a reasonably good match, consider how, when, and where to market your services. The success of your business depends on your ability to make prospective clients aware of your products or services. Look for local networking groups in your area. Ask your friends about local online networking lists that communicate with each other via e-mail. Set up an online marketing strategy. Build your momentum by making marketing a regular part of your week's activities.

Running Your Own Business with a Well-Paying Part-Time Job

Whether you're building up a business that has been part-time or leaving a full-time gig to start a business, it never hurts to have a regular paycheck coming in. With a part-time job that covers your basic expenses, you have a better chance of approaching your business with hope, creativity, and focus.

The minute you don't know where rent or dinner is coming from, your business begins to suffer from your feelings of fear and scarcity. You begin holding back because you don't know which move will create the big results you need to get back on your feet financially. You lose your stomach for experimentation and new marketing schemes. You spend so much time worrying about and scrambling after money to pay the bills that you have no energy to think strategically about your best long-term moves.

A part-time job can provide a number of key benefits besides a stable source of cash. Think through what you want this job to do for you. Do you want a job that gives you the highest pay per hour worked, gives you social interactions to balance out your solo entrepreneur lifestyle, or blends well with the off hours of your business? Think through your priorities to find the job that offers what you need without impinging too much on your business success.

Working part time means that you can devote your key hours to building your business. Your ultimate goal may be to build your business to the point where you no longer need the part-time job, or you may find comfort in knowing that the part-time job offers a dependable level of income that gives you more flexibility with less stress.

Adding a Second Business

If you decide to start two businesses of your own, launching a couple businesses at the same time isn't a good idea. A better approach is to launch them sequentially, especially if one leverages off another or is completely different. This kind of composite career creates multiple streams of income that may allow you to cover seasonal dips in your income or weather the loss of a key customer.

Begin by evaluating the strengths and weaknesses of your current business. Obviously you have a reason for wanting to start another business. Perhaps your goal is to increase your income potential or to build a business that's ultimately a better fit for you.

When you think about the tasks you do and the customers you reach, do you see any overlap or opening for potential? If the businesses are similar, you may be able to increase your offerings and quickly build sales with your existing base of customers. If the businesses are quite different, you probably want to verify that you have two distinct marketing strategies so you don't confuse your customers.

Strengthening Your Position through Consulting

If you decide to use your key strengths in a consulting role as you build toward your dream career, use your consulting gigs to get to know your ultimate target customer. Consciously take projects that allow you to use your talents to get into your target market's world. When you're inside, make good use of the opportunity to observe, ask questions, and get a feel for your target market.

As your knowledge increases and deepens, you have a great opportunity to fine-tune your plan. You might refocus your approach based on new information. You might identify a need that no one is filling, or you might see that your competition in the market is losing its edge or missing the point. The insider perspective gives you the background you need to make a big splash when you open the doors to your business or go after your dream job.

This strategy increases your chances of success because you're building your venture on real-life observations and knowledge rather than assumptions and theory. Knowing what your clients or employer need and are willing to pay for is what takes you to the bank.

Working Full Time While Attending School Part Time

Face it: Returning to school while working full time is no easy feat! You need a fair amount of motivation and stamina to work all day, attend classes at night, and spend time with your studies. Although you must put some aspects of your personal life on hold while you enhance your training, taking on this lifestyle is well worth the effort if you need a degree to go for your dream!

If you truly want to enter your target field, look beyond the short-term costs to see the long-term benefits. In the end, you'll be more fulfilled having trained in your field of choice.

 If you aren't able to take on a degree program at this time, consider some alternatives. Explore your field to see whether there's a related profession that doesn't require the same degree of training. Look at the various training options to see which one best fits your needs and lifestyle. Investigate your company's education benefits as well. Will it fund some of your schooling? Is your company at all flexible if your classes meet during work hours? If so, great! Make the most of your situation. If not, explore other companies in your area to see whether you can create a more supportive, education-friendly situation. It never hurts to explore.

Regardless of what kind of educational program you decide on, take a careful look at your life to see where you can streamline your personal life so your attention is focused on meeting your education goal. Look for committees, volunteer projects, peripheral friendships, and other nonessential commitments to determine whether you'd like to dedicate that time to your studies. Remember you can return to your favorite projects (or new ones) when you finish your program.

Attending School with a Part-Time Job on the Side

Another education option is to attend school full time with a part-time job to cover at least some of your expenses. This option may take some creative financing and require that you change your living situation to lower your rent, but the big benefit of this option is that you get through the education phase more quickly.

Look for funding at Free Scholarship Search (www.freschinfo.com). Perhaps you can find a way to go to school full time and not work at all during certain key semesters. Although this idea may seem far-fetched, do yourself a favor and at least check it out, especially if you're more productive when you devote all your time and energy to a single goal.

Index

Notes

Notes

BUSINESS, CAREERS & PERSONAL FINANCE

0-7645-5307-0

0-7645-5331-3 *†

Also available:

- Accounting For Dummies †
  0-7645-5314-3
- Business Plans Kit For Dummies †
  0-7645-5365-8
- Cover Letters For Dummies
  0-7645-5224-4
- Frugal Living For Dummies
  0-7645-5403-4
- Leadership For Dummies
  0-7645-5176-0
- Managing For Dummies
  0-7645-1771-6

- Marketing For Dummies
  0-7645-5600-2
- Personal Finance For Dummies *
  0-7645-2590-5
- Project Management For Dummies
  0-7645-5283-X
- Resumes For Dummies †
  0-7645-5471-9
- Selling For Dummies
  0-7645-5363-1
- Small Business Kit For Dummies *†
  0-7645-5093-4

HOME & BUSINESS COMPUTER BASICS

0-7645-4074-2

0-7645-3758-X

Also available:

- ACT! 6 For Dummies
  0-7645-2645-6
- iLife '04 All-in-One Desk Reference
  For Dummies
  0-7645-7347-0
- iPAQ For Dummies
  0-7645-6769-1
- Mac OS X Panther Timesaving
  Techniques For Dummies
  0-7645-5812-9
- Macs For Dummies
  0-7645-5656-8
- Microsoft Money 2004 For Dummies
  0-7645-4195-1

- Office 2003 All-in-One Desk Reference
  For Dummies
  0-7645-3883-7
- Outlook 2003 For Dummies
  0-7645-3759-8
- PCs For Dummies
  0-7645-4074-2
- TiVo For Dummies
  0-7645-6923-6
- Upgrading and Fixing PCs For Dummies
  0-7645-1665-5
- Windows XP Timesaving Techniques
  For Dummies
  0-7645-3748-2

FOOD, HOME, GARDEN, HOBBIES, MUSIC & PETS

0-7645-5295-3

0-7645-5232-5

Also available:

- Bass Guitar For Dummies
  0-7645-2487-9
- Diabetes Cookbook For Dummies
  0-7645-5230-9
- Gardening For Dummies *
  0-7645-5130-2
- Guitar For Dummies
  0-7645-5106-X
- Holiday Decorating For Dummies
  0-7645-2570-0
- Home Improvement All-in-One
  For Dummies
  0-7645-5680-0

- Knitting For Dummies
  0-7645-5395-X
- Piano For Dummies
  0-7645-5105-1
- Puppies For Dummies
  0-7645-5255-4
- Scrapbooking For Dummies
  0-7645-7208-3
- Senior Dogs For Dummies
  0-7645-5818-8
- Singing For Dummies
  0-7645-2475-5
- 30-Minute Meals For Dummies
  0-7645-2589-1

INTERNET & DIGITAL MEDIA

0-7645-1664-7

0-7645-6924-4

Also available:

- 2005 Online Shopping Directory
  For Dummies
  0-7645-7495-7
- CD & DVD Recording For Dummies
  0-7645-5956-7
- eBay For Dummies
  0-7645-5654-1
- Fighting Spam For Dummies
  0-7645-5965-6
- Genealogy Online For Dummies
  0-7645-5964-8
- Google For Dummies
  0-7645-4420-9

- Home Recording For Musicians
  For Dummies
  0-7645-1634-5
- The Internet For Dummies
  0-7645-4173-0
- iPod & iTunes For Dummies
  0-7645-7772-7
- Preventing Identity Theft For Dummies
  0-7645-7336-5
- Pro Tools All-in-One Desk Reference
  For Dummies
  0-7645-5714-9
- Roxio Easy Media Creator For Dummies
  0-7645-7131-1

 **WILEY**

SPORTS, FITNESS, PARENTING, RELIGION & SPIRITUALITY

0-7645-5146-9

0-7645-5418-2

Also available:
- Adoption For Dummies
  0-7645-5488-3
- Basketball For Dummies
  0-7645-5248-1
- The Bible For Dummies
  0-7645-5296-1
- Buddhism For Dummies
  0-7645-5359-3
- Catholicism For Dummies
  0-7645-5391-7
- Hockey For Dummies
  0-7645-5228-7

- Judaism For Dummies
  0-7645-5299-6
- Martial Arts For Dummies
  0-7645-5358-5
- Pilates For Dummies
  0-7645-5397-6
- Religion For Dummies
  0-7645-5264-3
- Teaching Kids to Read For Dummies
  0-7645-4043-2
- Weight Training For Dummies
  0-7645-5168-X
- Yoga For Dummies
  0-7645-5117-5

TRAVEL

0-7645-5438-7

0-7645-5453-0

Also available:
- Alaska For Dummies
  0-7645-1761-9
- Arizona For Dummies
  0-7645-6938-4
- Cancún and the Yucatán For Dummies
  0-7645-2437-2
- Cruise Vacations For Dummies
  0-7645-6941-4
- Europe For Dummies
  0-7645-5456-5
- Ireland For Dummies
  0-7645-5455-7

- Las Vegas For Dummies
  0-7645-5448-4
- London For Dummies
  0-7645-4277-X
- New York City For Dummies
  0-7645-6945-7
- Paris For Dummies
  0-7645-5494-8
- RV Vacations For Dummies
  0-7645-5443-3
- Walt Disney World & Orlando For Dummies
  0-7645-6943-0

GRAPHICS, DESIGN & WEB DEVELOPMENT

0-7645-4345-8

0-7645-5589-8

Also available:
- Adobe Acrobat 6 PDF For Dummies
  0-7645-3760-1
- Building a Web Site For Dummies
  0-7645-7144-3
- Dreamweaver MX 2004 For Dummies
  0-7645-4342-3
- FrontPage 2003 For Dummies
  0-7645-3882-9
- HTML 4 For Dummies
  0-7645-1995-6
- Illustrator cs For Dummies
  0-7645-4084-X

- Macromedia Flash MX 2004 For Dummies
  0-7645-4358-X
- Photoshop 7 All-in-One Desk Reference For Dummies
  0-7645-1667-1
- Photoshop cs Timesaving Techniques For Dummies
  0-7645-6782-9
- PHP 5 For Dummies
  0-7645-4166-8
- PowerPoint 2003 For Dummies
  0-7645-3908-6
- QuarkXPress 6 For Dummies
  0-7645-2593-X

NETWORKING, SECURITY, PROGRAMMING & DATABASES

0-7645-6852-3

0-7645-5784-X

Also available:
- A+ Certification For Dummies
  0-7645-4187-0
- Access 2003 All-in-One Desk Reference For Dummies
  0-7645-3988-4
- Beginning Programming For Dummies
  0-7645-4997-9
- C For Dummies
  0-7645-7068-4
- Firewalls For Dummies
  0-7645-4048-3
- Home Networking For Dummies
  0-7645-42796

- Network Security For Dummies
  0-7645-1679-5
- Networking For Dummies
  0-7645-1677-9
- TCP/IP For Dummies
  0-7645-1760-0
- VBA For Dummies
  0-7645-3989-2
- Wireless All In-One Desk Reference For Dummies
  0-7645-7496-5
- Wireless Home Networking For Dummies
  0-7645-3910-8

HEALTH & SELF-HELP

0-7645-6820-5 *†

0-7645-2566-2

Also available:
- Alzheimer's For Dummies
  0-7645-3899-3
- Asthma For Dummies
  0-7645-4233-8
- Controlling Cholesterol For Dummies
  0-7645-5440-9
- Depression For Dummies
  0-7645-3900-0
- Dieting For Dummies
  0-7645-4149-8
- Fertility For Dummies
  0-7645-2549-2
- Fibromyalgia For Dummies
  0-7645-5441-7

- Improving Your Memory For Dummies
  0-7645-5435-2
- Pregnancy For Dummies †
  0-7645-4483-7
- Quitting Smoking For Dummies
  0-7645-2629-4
- Relationships For Dummies
  0-7645-5384-4
- Thyroid For Dummies
  0-7645-5385-2

EDUCATION, HISTORY, REFERENCE & TEST PREPARATION

0-7645-5194-9

0-7645-4186-2

Also available:
- Algebra For Dummies
  0-7645-5325-9
- British History For Dummies
  0-7645-7021-8
- Calculus For Dummies
  0-7645-2498-4
- English Grammar For Dummies
  0-7645-5322-4
- Forensics For Dummies
  0-7645-5580-4
- The GMAT For Dummies
  0-7645-5251-1
- Inglés Para Dummies
  0-7645-5427-1

- Italian For Dummies
  0-7645-5196-5
- Latin For Dummies
  0-7645-5431-X
- Lewis & Clark For Dummies
  0-7645-2545-X
- Research Papers For Dummies
  0-7645-5426-3
- The SAT I For Dummies
  0-7645-7193-1
- Science Fair Projects For Dummies
  0-7645-5460-3
- U.S. History For Dummies
  0-7645-5249-X

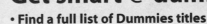

Get smart @ dummies.com®

- **Find a full list of Dummies titles**
- **Look into loads of FREE on-site articles**
- **Sign up for FREE eTips e-mailed to you weekly**
- **See what other products carry the Dummies name**
- **Shop directly from the Dummies bookstore**
- **Enter to win new prizes every month!**

* Separate Canadian edition also available

† Separate U.K. edition also available

Available wherever books are sold. For more information or to order direct: U.S. customers visit www.dummies.com or call 1-877-762-2974.
U.K. customers visit www.wileyeurope.com or call 0800 243407. Canadian customers visit www.wiley.ca or call 1-800-567-4797.